Hall of mirrors

Language & shapes

Even the title

FINDINGS:

1) Traumatized long-distorted; aggrieved victims

2) Coped by affirming self + ethnic identity

3) Healed probably affected → grp. scorned response

Disappointed - lost opportunity → postpond?

Symbolic ~~interpretation~~
↳ deeper
cries out for interpretive voice

attenuated revenge over decades

echoes from fieldwork my own labor over 15 yrs.

Fear of Jasenovac/Ustashi - yes!

BUT NO connection to whats occurred in B'ljina/Srebrenica Zvornik etc - MUSLIMS!

Power of "BIG Lie" → Nazism

NO evidence + close to - comparable

Sense of pre-emptive massacres + cleansing strains credulity p.98 - 4 c's → ?

Irony → German Nazis were Serbs

SERBIAN AUSTRALIANS IN THE SHADOW OF THE BALKAN WAR

"gone native"? apologist

attachment to land 75-76/92

Gadamerian?

rigor — p.51-52   facile-refers to (selective)
p.62   quotes
p.173

symbolic interaction p.47

clinical boundary confusion p.49

— Serbs → Croats → Muslims
my own work—late 70s   "positivist
insularity   ethnogphy"

Relativism run amuck
Facts on the ground — "in" the ground → mass graves
p.46 grotesque   — cardinal rule
↳ Serbs were   ↳ reflexivity p.41
appeared to
ignored   "macro" — view of one's self
1991-1994

— These Serbs → a very
non-repres. subset
Četnici

— pt. of entry — Peak time of stress
interrupted routines (rhythms

suspicion → no intellectual tradition of
learning about "other" → intell.
curiosity
turned inward
nor a tradition in Balkans
of critical discourse / democratic give & take

DAMES

Dansk Center for Migration
og Etniske Studier

**EUROPEAN RESEARCH CENTRE
ON MIGRATION & ETHNIC RELATIONS**

Serbian Australians in the Shadow of the Balkan War

NICHOLAS G. PROCTER
University of South Australia

Ashgate

Aldershot • Burlington USA • Singapore • Sydney

Published by
Ashgate Publishing Ltd
Gower House
Croft Road
Aldershot
Hants GU11 3HR
England

Ashgate Publishing Company
131 Main Street
Burlington
Vermont 05401
USA

Ashgate website: http://www.ashgate.com

British Library Cataloguing in Publication Data
Procter, Nicholas G.
    Serbian Australians in the shadow of the Balkan War. -
    (Research in migration and ethnic relations series)
    1. Serbs - Australia - Ethnic identity 2. Serbs - Australia -
    Psychology 3. Yugoslav War, 1991- - Social aspects -
    Australia 4. War and civilization - Australia
    I. Title
    305.8'91822'094

Library of Congress Catalog Card Number: 00-132606

ISBN 0 7546 1247 3

Printed in Great Britain by
Antony Rowe Ltd, Chippenham, Wiltshire

Contents

Foreword

Events in the Balkans in the 1990s fragmented and recast the lives of the people who lived there. It also had a profound impact upon people living far away who had emotional ties to that region. Nicholas Procter's ethnography, *Serbian Australians in the Shadow of the Balkan War*, is a remarkable study of such a people, as they suffered and struggled through this conflict at a distance, and survived the devastation it brought to their own lives in Australia.

Ethnography has always demanded a level of personal engagement; what is most remarkable about this study is the depth of Procter's involvement with a people who, at the time, were distraught, angry and feeling universally stigmatised. Yet it also demands that the researcher is able to disengage, and in this regard too, Procter is a paragon. In this particular field of conflict it would have been all to easy to unbalance, take sides, but Procter keeps his cool. This is not primarily a political study of ethnic groups at war in the Balkans; nor is it a treatise on international human rights; it is not concerned with right, wrong, fault or blame; it is a study from within, a study which traces the imprints that are made by a distant war on the lives of Serbian Australians, on their mental health, and on their ability to maintain civil society.

There is an affinity between ethnographic fieldwork and nursing, particularly as the latter applies to mental health. Both require the creation of a framework of intimacy and respect within which stories may be told, feelings received, and lives revealed. Nicholas Procter comes from a background in psychiatric nursing which he has fed into this research, both as an intellectual foundation—his work is influenced by Barker, Benner and others—and as a practical activity. He is concerned with human suffering, he listens attentively to those Serbian Australians among whom he worked, and together with them he interprets the cultural meanings that make sense of their suffering. As I read this study, and as their lives unfolded, I wondered whether ethnographic work, sensitively handled, might be nurturing in and of itself.

In its anthropological scholarship, the study engages with George Marcus and his insights into the local-global nexus. Procter gives this ethnographic substance but creates an additional nexus with the inner life of his participants. In extending the scope of his enquiry into the psychological and emotional domain he draws firstly on Giddens to explore the sadness and dislocation of Serbian Australians in a global epoch. Secondly, from Gadamer, comes a rigorous scrutiny of his own presuppositions, a reflexivity that extends into his own emotional reactions and into the heart of the methodology.

With these influences, *Serbian Australians in the Shadow of the Balkan War* is a post-modern text, written in the first-person singular, fiercely reflexive, and always revealing the train of events and interactions that led to the construction of the data. It also conveys the feel of a traditional ethnography, largely through Procter's wonderful capacity for description and eye for detail. Describing an episode of vandalism directed against the Serbian community he observes:

> An angle grinder or hacksaw had been used to decapitate a life size statue of the allied Second world War Serbian General, Draza Mihalovic. Fine mental dust lay at the foot of the statue. The presence of the dust caught my eye as it glistened in the morning sun.

It is this capacity for immersion in the minutiae that enables Procter to delineate emotional turmoil with such precision.

In its genre this book stands alongside Loring Danforth's *The Macedonian Conflict: Ethnic Nationalism in a Transnational World*, and Zlatko Skrbis's *Long Distance Nationalism,* further establishing the preeminence of Australian scholarship in the anthropological study of diaspora communities. In common, these works explore different aspects of long-distance nationalism, but of the three, it is Procter who gives the richest insight into the importance of belonging—belonging to a culture, belonging to a place—as a theme which has crucial implications for the mental health of the community in which he worked. In a country whose indigenous peoples remind immigrants of the value of place and belonging, it is not surprising that they should emerge into the centre of *Serbian Australians in the Shadow of the Balkan War.*

As a study of mental health, this book drives home the point that suffering and wellbeing can only be fully understood in a global context, and its relation to the inner lives of individual people. And it serves to remind us of the cultural resources that communities can draw upon when faced with despair, humiliation, and mistrust. It reminds of the importance of a pride in belonging.

Robert Barrett
Professor of Psychiatry
University of Adelaide

Preface and Acknowledgments

This book examines Serbian Australians living in the shadow of the Balkan war and interprets the way in which their experience has become a health and cultural process of long distance dislocation, suffering and devastation. I began the seminal work for this book as a doctoral student under the guidance of Professors Bob Holton and Tina Koch. At the outset of my studies, I was never completely satisfied that the answers to questions that occupy this book could be found through social science alone. The approach taken generated data through journal writing, interviewing, participant observation, document analysis and the encouragement of people to speak for themselves in their own words about how they felt war in the former Yugoslavia had influenced their feelings, lives and wellbeing. The art and science of nursing soon became a means to inform the many anthropological research interests that I had developed during the course of my journey. It was always easy for me to retain a nursing presence throughout the journey for it provided a depth and means for inquiry and interpretation of the health and wellbeing concerns held by participants. To interpret the situations of Serbian Australians, I brought philosophical hermeneutics of the Hans-Georg Gadamer tradition to my experience of their lives, feelings, attitudes, perspective, history, culture and national identity.

The study reveals that war in the former Yugoslavia has been a distressing life event for people of Serbian descent living thousands of miles from the region. The health effects of long distance suffering and devastation included sleeplessness, irritability, inability to concentrate, feelings of frustration, loneliness, sadness, worry, anxiety, nightmares, intrusive thoughts and bouts of extreme emotional exhaustion. Participants' lives were fragmented and recast as the old verities of the Yugoslav identity were falling apart along ethnic lines. For participants the multitude of potent health and social concerns were helped along by an intimate sense of belonging and re-association with Serbian historical, religious, cultural and national identifications.

Serbian Australians coped with the impact of the Balkan war generating a feeling of valued involvement, reaffirmation, friendship, reassurance and spiritual belonging with what they perceived to be sacred aspects of their identity. My awareness of these issues coincided with being awarded a Postdoctoral Research Fellowship from the University of South Australia, which generously funded a secondment to the Bob Hawke

Prime Ministerial Centre in 1999. The Hawke Institute, the research arm of the Hawke Centre, proved to be a valuable place for me to develop personally and professionally, as well as participate in an extensive research seminar program of relevance to issues that were central to my work. It also provided generous funds for travel to Norway, England and Croatia. During my secondment to the Hawke Institute I was able to undertake new writing of the Serbian Australian story, until it became what it is today. I am tremendously thankful to Professors Alison Mackinnon (Hawke Institute) and Annette Summers (School of Nursing and Midwifery) for supporting me during the Hawke Fellowship.

I am grateful to the University of South Australia Editor Trish McLaine, who skilfully helped me to elaborate the arguments of the book. Jenny Pavlakos and Kate Leeson provided expert technical assistance with copy editing. Other friends and colleagues who patiently sat and listened to me talk over and over about what had influenced my thinking and interpretation include Henry Kristall, Chedo Bodiroga, Peter Radan, Slavko Govidarica, Dunka Kovacevic, Jeff Fuller, Ken Walsh, Michael Clinton, Carol Grech and Grace Davey. I thank them for their support and intellectual exchange.

To the Serbian Australian participants who warmly welcomed me into their homes, ready to reveal their deepest concerns in the belief that they would be taken seriously, I say thank you. This book celebrates the contribution they have made to cultural tolerance and the promotion of a civil society.

My greatest thanks goes to my wife and partner in life Maritza, and my children Alexandra and Georgina. Their love and support inspired and enabled me keep writing. Without their encouragement and understanding, this book would never have eventuated. This book is dedicated to them.

Nicholas Procter
Adelaide

1 On Becoming Involved: An Autobiographical Ethnography

This story shows how the Balkan war between July 1991 and early 1996[1] was, both directly and indirectly, a global catastrophic event. It is my research journey into how the Balkan war impacted upon the lives and experiences of Serbian Australians. While many of us have been loungeroom spectators of the conflict, people with cultural and emotional ties to the region identified completely with the pain and anguish of what they saw night after night on the television screen. Television and newspaper images of the conflict sent shock waves through the world and these have included the most horrific scenes of carnage, incarceration and massacre.[2]

My exploration into the cultural impact and interpretation of mass destruction and the dislocation of people and property in the Balkans, led me to examine historical values associated with ethnicity (Ascherson, 1991; Banac, 1992) and geographical borders (Radan, 1992, 1993; Rothschild 1992). In several instances, such values acted as a divisive force, reflecting in extreme form forced family separations and the practice of ethnic cleansing (Dragadze, 1996).

The Balkan war linked historical, religious and cultural events of the recent and distant past to a murderous mistrust, hatred and a perpetual state of life and death struggle in the present (Ahmed, 1993; Glenny, 1992; Kaplan, 1993; Rosenman and Handelsman, 1992; Vulliamy, 1994). Television and newspaper images of the conflict sent shock waves through the world and these have included vision of incarceration and massacre. In writing my journey I came across stories of young girls with their vocal chords torn because they had been repeatedly raped in the mouth. I was told stories of pregnant women whose stomachs have been ripped open, the unborn child removed and a pig's flesh stuffed into the stomach. I was also told stories of young men and women being stripped naked and chained around the neck like dogs, sodomised repeatedly and kept tied like dogs, fed and urinating and defecating like dogs on all fours (Ahmed, 1993). As Neal Ascherson (1992, p. 25) of *The Independent* newspaper interpreted it:

Sarajevo is burning. A new generation of European families is learning what it means to flee from a home, to lose a father killed or fighting on some unknown front, to travel the roads with bags and bundles and hungry children, to be the prey of armed bands who beat, steal, rape and sometimes kill, to be at best refugees in a foreign land without possessions or hopes. For this generation like that of its parents in the 1940s, the world reveals itself as incomprehensible, unmanageable and meaningless.

During the course of my journey, Serbia proper and the Bosnian Serbs in particular were considered by the United Nations and world community as the main perpetrators of the conflict. In January 1993 an Amnesty International report argued that:

Deliberate and arbitrary killings, torture and ill-treatment continued on a horrifying scale and largely by Bosnian Serb forces. They repeated and extended patterns earlier seen which appear to be aimed at intimidating the civilian populations, most frequently Muslims, into leaving their homes areas or being compliant when forcibly expelled (AI INDEX: EUR 63/03 /93).

At the time of my journey the Bosnian Serb leader president Radovan Karadzic and military commander general Ratko Mladic, had been indicted as war criminals by the Hague War Crimes Tribunal for crimes against humanity. United Nations officials were investigating the disappearance of civilians in the former Yugoslavia. They held both Radovan Karadzic and Ratko Mladic responsible for the execution of up to 8000 adult males and young boys as they tried to escape from the Bosnian Muslim enclave of Srebrenica in July 1995.[3] The disappearance and alleged murder of civilians from the United Nations declared 'safe area', was widely regarded as the worst atrocity Europe has witnessed since the Second World War.

With Serbia and Serbians from the region considered by the European Community, United Nations and almost all the governments of the world as the main perpetrator of the conflict and as an obstacle to peace in the region, this research journey took on a very particular character. That is, it involved research into a group which was, and felt itself to have been, stigmatised internationally. My research journey into the life of Serbian Australians[4] in the shadow of catastrophic world events was for me both a physical and metaphysical one. This was due to the 'shadow' being global in outreach, rather than restricted to the complex and seemingly arcane world of Balkan politics. For the impact of the war has been felt not merely by direct participants, nor by a global television spectator audience. Migrants from the former Yugoslavia now living in many other parts of the world have also been caught up in the events. It demanded that I focus on such a group, namely Serbian Australians, exploring the impact of the Balkan war on their social and emotional lives and experiences.

The approach

There was great emphasis in my journey upon interpreting the participants' perspective without relying on complex statistical measures or methods. By the very nature of the depth and complexity of questions I was asking participants, I was delving into issues of a substantive personal nature. This meant asking participants questions about relationships and friendships with others with family ties to the former Yugoslavia, asking questions about how they had felt when, on the television screen, they saw their country of origin being destroyed, or when contact with relatives in and around fighting was lost; how they had felt when they received news that a relative had been killed.

        This story is best read 'cover to cover' rather than dipped into by use of the index. The subjective situations that make up *Serbian Australians in the Shadow of the Balkan War,* incorporate how my *experience* of researching participants served as data and as a means to shape interpretation. The delving into the deeply personal and sometimes fragile life situations of participants has also influenced the way this journey has been written. My asking questions about how participants' experience of events in the Balkans had impacted on their health and wellbeing, gave the study a deeply personal character. My experience of 'being there' in the social world 'as it happened', gave rise to personal engagement with the study. It is, therefore, a study written in the first person rather than an impersonal third-person prose.

        Through an approach informed by ethnography and philosophical hermeneutics,[5] this study closely examines and interprets the meanings, experiences, ideas, reference points and emotions that Serbian Australians have about life in the shadow of the Balkan war, its impact on their health and wellbeing, and the cultural mechanisms at play as they try to make sense of it. The tradition of philosophical hermeneutics was chosen as the interpretive raft for understanding fieldwork with Serbian Australians.

        Philosophical hermeneutics was particularly valuable in this study to explore how the understandings I generated about Serbian Australians were shaped by social, historical and interactive processes. This approach, which will be elaborated further, involved the interrogation of my own understandings in interaction with others and in terms of the interpretive scrutiny of my own perspective, made up of bias, judgement and a point of view about Serbian Australians. Through this perspective came the framework to draw out implications of the Serbian Australian experience for the health and helping professions.

This was therefore, an autobiographical reflective ethnography in which the prominence of myself as researcher within the research context was interrelated with interpretation of social processes that were simultaneously local and global in their character (Fischer, 1986; Giddens, 1996; Marcus, 1986 and 1995).[6] Importantly, the global in this research journey was 'up close' rather than far removed from what participants see, hear and experience. This means that the information I took into account the complexities that helped shape the meaning participants gave to it.

I came to understand Serbian Australians during the Balkan war following a number of life experiences. I have devoted the next section of this chapter to selectively review these because they helped shape both context and reasons for asking particular research questions. I had relationships with people from the region of more than 10 years standing prior to the conflict, and this in turn led to my presence in the region at the outbreak of hostilities. Given the prominence of the conflict within news media I, just like anyone else, had been exposed to the graphic destruction of the urban and natural surroundings of Bosnia. I believe that these past and ongoing experiences, during research, brought to the study of Serbian Australians a particular framework or horizon for data generation and interpretation that cannot be ignored. I have chosen to work out interpretively the implications of my previous knowledge and experience in the research process.

An autobiographical connection with the former Yugoslavia and Serbian Australians

In 1979 I met and later married (in 1988) a woman with family bonds to the former Yugoslavia. Through my relationship with her I learned to appreciate a host of cultural situations, a new language[7] and developed relationships with Australians of Croatian, Serbian, Macedonian and Yugoslav identity. I went to christenings, weddings, funerals, soccer matches, cultural and religious celebrations, private homes and formed many new friendships. I met Serbians married to Croatians, Macedonians married to Serbians and other units of association that often gave the appearance of one ubiquitous homogenising culture.[8]

What struck me about these experiences was that I was accepted, made to feel very welcome, and yet always understood as an 'outsider'. I never really found any difficulty in making or finding my own way in social processes involving Serbs, however I always knew that I was not and never could be a person of Serbian descent. I asked questions, made conversation and took a genuine interest in all that I saw to be part of this culture. I never sought out information about topics situated in 'Yugoslav' politics, identity or any other similar material.

So seemingly straightforward were my relationships and new friendships with people from former Yugoslavia, that our marriage ceremony in the Serbian Orthodox Church was attended by people of Serbian, Croatian, Macedonian, Slovenian and Muslim identity (among others). Three years after our wedding, in June 1991, we travelled to the Balkans to meet my wife's family and 'take in' the places of her homeland. Within days of our arrival war began in the former Yugoslav states of Slovenia and Croatia.

Heavy fighting had erupted between Slovenian Territorial Defense Forces as a Yugoslav National Army column of about eight tanks tried to smash through blockades sprinkled on the main roads between Croatia and Slovenia. Within hours of Slovenia declaring independence from Yugoslavia, there was widespread military activity in the area bordered by Novo Mesto, the major regional centre Trebnje to its north-west and Krsko to the north-east. The crisis in Slovenia and Croatia soon spread to the neighbouring republic of Bosnia Herzegovina.

The outbreak of war in the former Yugoslavia in 1991 led to my exposure to the dislocation of families, and to the experience of newly defined and hurriedly arranged boundaries for friends, relatives and neighbours living nearby. A column of army tanks had departed westward from Zagreb en-route to Slovenia. On the evening of July 2 1991 I wrote in my diary:

> 1910 hours. I am in Zagreb near Marshal Tito Barracks and worried about my life, my future and my safety. The guns are being used and it looks bad. Fighting and war against people who hate each other that's also going live to TV. From the car we saw fighting on the airport road and this stopped us from getting out. From the window I can see men in blue uniforms shooting at the tanks below. Tanks crashing over cars and barricades and people throwing rocks and not wanting us to survive - should we go forward. On the streets below and all around, there are dozens of loud speakers

broadcasting news ... I hear sirens, loudspeakers and see panic in the city.
We must be very careful and not take any risks.

At about the same time I wrote this entry, fighting had also broken out
between the Slovene Territorial Defence Force and the Jugoslav Peoples
Army about 50 kilometres from Ljubljana. Over the hours and days that
followed the outbreak of civil war in former Yugoslavia, I wanted to write
about my experiences. I wanted to make a written record of my thoughts
surrounding events as they unfolded. However, given the stressful nature
of my experience, the organisation of my thoughts surrounding the topic
was poor due to their fragmentation and lack of coherence.

Being in the former Yugoslavia at the outbreak of war was made
more difficult by rumours of an imminent air raid by Jugoslav National
Army jets.   Such stories and fears caused people to gather up their
possessions and seek comfort from friends and relatives living close by in
the basements of apartment sprinkled throughout the city. The urgency
and uncertainty of the situation being faced by the people forced those
around us to act in an erratic and hasty manner. Cars travelled the short
and narrow streets at high speed only to screech during sharp breaking and
emit pressured sounds of car horns. In conversation, decisions and plans
were being made at one moment only to be changed in light of new, mostly
unconfirmed information.

The initial difficulty I had at the beginning of war in Croatia and
Slovenia was that the war had caused people to speak more quickly. There
was a distinct pressure of speech both on the street, among people in our
apartment building and on the radio and television news as well. Despite a
reasonable working knowledge of Serbo-Croatian I could not keep pace
with what was being said to or around me. The lack of clear information
brought home to me in a most powerful and frightening way that I was
powerless to improve my sense of personal safety. It also caused great
pressure on my wife, who, given her better language skills, was then forced
to undertake a key interpreting role.

With limited understanding of what was happening and almost no
mobility outside my immediate area, I was becoming increasingly
disturbed by this situation and knew that I wanted nothing else other than
to leave the country. We did this, travelling on a Croatian government
train being used to evacuate refugees.

Becoming connected with events in Australia

It took several months for the fears and concerns that I had experienced when in the former Yugoslavia to surface in my conversation with others. The reasons for this were both personal and professional. In practical terms conversations with others about my experiences quickly turned into debates about 'right and wrong' in the Balkans. I had been ill at ease with casting the conflict this way as it inevitably involves accusations and counter accusations of atrocities and events expressed in polarities of 'right and wrong'. More fitting to my professional and personal life as a mental health professional is concern for deeper meaning structures that surround experience and which are involved in the health of others. In particular, the meanings and experiences that reflect the interpretation of the Balkan war in Australia. As Serbian Australians have a social, familial and cultural network that reminds them of the recent and distant past (Kazich, 1989) and, as these two dimensions of time are greatly influenced by the present, I thought it important to take account of the potentially volatile and sometimes violent argument that may serve to preserve and protect a particular point of view.

Within two days of Croatia and Slovenia making the break from the Federal Republic of Yugoslavia, tension among people from the region had intensified in Australia (see, for example Borrell, 1991; *Srpski Glas*, July 19, 1991; *Nova Doba,* September 17, 1991; *Hrvatski Vjesnik*, November 29, 1991). In Adelaide, people of Slovenian descent reported receiving abusive telephone calls from callers purporting to be Yugoslavs, and there were warnings from Croatian Australians that physical violence between groups could erupt if the harassment continued. Media estimates were made of up to 12,000 Croatian Australians gathering at Sydney's King Thomislav Soccer Stadium to celebrate their independence and denounce Serbian President Slobodan Milosovic. In Melbourne, almost 7000 Croatian and Slovenian Australians massed in the city square, whereas in Adelaide about 600 gathered at the Croatian Ethnic School at Brompton to be addressed by politicians representing both major political parties who spoke in support of the breakaway states.

Conflict in the former Yugoslavia was also making headline news around the globe. When I arrived back in Australia in August 1991, I was confronted with a barrage of media comment about the conflict. What this war did have in common with other recent conflicts around the globe was an immediacy of communication (Dowmunt, 1993). Throughout the world people could see the suffering of others. It was impossible to get by without witnessing the conflict unfold on the television screen. The entire world watched as dozens of civilians were being killed, made homeless and torn apart from their families. Ugly scenes of mass destruction of entire villages and towns and dislocation of people were being beamed into living rooms of the West making the streets and suburbs of the region as familiar to us as our very own. Stories of lifelong friends and neighbours turning enemies overnight made good media copy. Even 'better' was footage of fierce 'hand to hand' fighting. All of this turned other people's misery and suffering into headline news.

Along with the television news of the conflict were the street protests, media releases and other 'activity' of and by the various groups from the former Yugoslavia living in Australia. It was at this point, that I asked myself, 'What is it about the identity of people from former Yugoslavia living in Australia that lends itself to this kind of response?' And, 'What responses could be made by others of a different ethnic identity, in a situation similar to this one?'

These questions also arose out of a commitment to nursing as a practice-based profession comprising the art and science of caring for individual people. In health and helping relationships with individual people there is significant interest in trying to find out about the influences and issues that shape a person's life. Threats to wellbeing arising from connections with warfare are not especially surprising. Nevertheless, what was significant in the Balkan war experience among Serbs around the world was that they were the group seen by most Western nations and commentators as the main perpetrator of the conflict. What Serbian Australians said about their experience of living during the Balkan war and how they interpreted themselves in it, is shaped by recognition of what others feel about the situation, rather than a simple unilateral response to traumatic events.

Gordana: A deepening sadness and loss

Soon after my return from the former Yugoslavia I began to talk more widely with those who might shed further light on the impact that the Balkan war was having on former Yugoslav migrants. Quite soon after my return I received a letter from Gordana.[9] She had indicated her willingness to be interviewed and help with my research in any way. Her letter stated:

I am a 52 year old Australian Serb (until very recently Yugoslav), who arrived in this 'lucky country' at the tender age of 14. My mother and I arrived in Australia in 1954 to join my father with whom we parted ten years earlier in the terrible turmoils of World War 2. There was no safe place in our country for a Serbian Orthodox Minister following the three years of terror from the Ustashe (who slit the throat of every Serb they came across under the rule of the Independent State of Croatia between 1941-44). The end of the war finally came with the triumphant arrival of our 'liberators', Tito's Partisans, and the new era of terror for all those who were not left on their side. So father left with a heavy heart, never to return, but lucky to survive. At the time we left I prayed that I should die rather than leave my country, together with a vast extended family of grandparents, uncles, aunts and cousins, the many wonderful childhood friends and much loved brother, 7 years my senior, unaware that it would take another five years before he is allowed to join us.

I have taken the liberty of sending this letter as I thought it may be of some interest and help with your research concerning the effects and impact of this dreadful civil war and its biased media reporting on hundreds of Serbs similar to myself. I also enclose several articles from very recent Sydney newspapers, which for the first time in the past two years, put some of the sad and devastating Balkan war into perspective. *I ask that you take a few minutes to read them and my letter as I so desperately feel the need to bear my soul, overflowing with grief, to someone who may take the trouble to hear.* (emphasis added, N.P.)

When Yugoslavia came to its fall and destruction, my whole world seemed to have fallen apart as well. I could never imagine that it would bring me such heartache and have such a traumatic impact on me. I truly believed that I was an Australian of Yugoslav origin. I grew up with a mixture of Serbs, Croats - my best friend was a Croatian girl who I still love as I love myself. *But, as the saying goes 'blood is not water' and only through tragedies we return to our roots.* (emphasis added, N.P.)

I am sure that every single member of our community of about 150,000 has been effected in some form, naturally some more than others, but I can assure you that *it has brought me and some of my close family living here enormous pain, as at times I get to the point of breaking. Always a very happy and outgoing person, I have now lost all joy and sense of fun, wishing no company, finding no diversion in friends and outings* (emphasis added, N.P.). The only positive thing to have come out of this whole tragedy for me personally, is that through the pain and suffering I have felt during the past two years, I have written some 20-30 poems, naturally mostly connected with my Country of birth.[10] This ability would have surely been hidden forever if this tragedy never occurred, but I would gladly return this talent (if I had talent at all) for the peace and happiness of my people and my beloved 'former' Yugoslavia.

[11]PLEASE DO NOT DO TO THE SERBS WHAT THE ALLIES WITH CHURCHILL DID TO YUGOSLAVIA IN 1945! DO NOT TAKE SIDES IN THIS FILTHY WAR! READ UP ON SOME HISTORICAL FACTS! LISTEN TO THE SERBIAN SIDE OF THE STORY AS WELL WITHOUT YOUR BIASED COMMENTS! IT IS A CIVIL WAR AND ALL THREE ARE GUILTY OF THE WRONGS DONE TO THE INNOCENT CIVILIANS WHO SUFFER ENDLESSLY IN THIS NIGHTMARE. SERBS ARE ALSO BEING KILLED! THEY ALSO HAVE MOTHERS AND SONS. SERBS ALSO HAVE AND CAN PRODUCE WITNESSES OF THE MOST HORRIBLE ATROCITIES DONE TO THEIR FAMILIES IN THE LAST AND, INDEED THE PRESENT WAR IN CROATIA FROM MY VERY OWN SMALL CIRCLE OF FRIENDS AND RELATIONS IN THIS CITY.

I feel that not only have I lost my country, I have lost all my many relations as well, with no will nor desire to write to them for I am lost for words of wisdom to sooth (sic) their pain brought by the dreadful consequences of their Civil War. But the most horrifying pain of all, which goes right to the very core of my soul, is the pain of having lost my new country as well. I suddenly feel alone, displaced, not belonging anywhere at all, un-protected from the winds blowing in my direction with no shelter at all. (emphasis added, N.P.)

Gordana's letter was an extremely valuable document. It so clearly conveyed how her personal interpretation of war in former Yugoslavia was mediated by a historical consciousness of events in the recent and distant past. Gordana's voice in telling her story and my use of italics to emphasise particular aspects of it, indicates the methodology of philosophical hermeneutics at work. That is, Gordana's voice in telling her story was given its own integrity, yet it was mediated through my own interpretive interests. This is reflected in my use of italics to emphasise particular aspects of the story for my own interpretive purposes.

The contacts that I established through my relationship with Gordana and those she referred me to, were crucial to the future and ongoing viability of the research process (Clandinin and Connelly, 1994). Gordana's telling of her situation was, in a sense, a pilot process which influenced how I later networked, established and approached interviews with Serbian Australians. My interpretation of Gordana's letter was a starting point for my research journey.

Gordana's letter indicated that the experience of changing identity from Yugoslav to Serbian Australian, was very much a public one. From Gordana's writings I believe that images of homeland destruction and dislocation reflected more than isolated life events taking shape in far away places. Increased mass media, literacy and advanced information technology facilitated Serbian Australians to both *see and feel* the impact of events from their homeland.

One central argument throughout my study, is that international events create and perpetuate an intimacy between subject and observer that present the globe as single social space (Robertson, 1990 and 1992). There was, as Featherstone (1993) argues, a social world no longer bounded by the nation state. A world where information and cultural images flow across borders, as much as capital, time and technology. This means that no-one is outside the information and cultural images that are more or less throughout the world. In this sense the Balkan war is, in a global epoch, not simply an 'out there' phenomenon in some far away European country with unpronounceable place names. It was for Gordana and many others an 'in here' matter, which deeply affected the most intimate aspect of people's lives (Giddens, 1996, p. 51).

The conflict in the former Yugoslavia had, in an epoch of globalisation, become particularly relevant to Gordana by contributing to an understanding of how her identity and interpretation of it had been and continued to be made. George Marcus (1994) speaks to this issue as a methodological one, in his call for the study of social life in the context of the impact of global forces. The goal of contemporary ethnography is to reveal the dimensions and scope of multiple situations. Marcus (1994, p. 566-7) states that ethnography in today's world must be:

> in the form of juxtapositions of seemingly incomprehensible phenomena that might have conventionally appeared worlds apart... *the global collapsed into and made an integral part of parallel, related local situations, rather than being something monolithic and external to them.* [An] ethnography that confronts the remarkable space/time compression that defines the conditions of peoples and culture globally. (emphasis added, N.P.)

An important issue which arises out of Marcus's engaging idea that local situations are intimately influenced by the global condition - that is, for instance, the Balkan war and the majority world view of Serbia and Serbians as the chief perpetrators of the war - caused me to make interpretation of conditions and process surrounding the actual 'doing' of fieldwork. Robertson (1995), in his discussion of globalisation - the idea that the world in which we live has involved and increasingly involves the creation of processes in the larger world which shape the social life and, in turn, the world as a whole - also informed my understanding of people like Gordana. In order to enter into Gordana's home I took into consideration my own analysis and interpretation of the Balkan war in the contemporary world, inclusive of issues geographical and historical significance considered crucial to her. This means that my interpretation of events in Europe were processes which largely shaped the way I generated trust with participants, learnt a new language and performed numerous cultural and religious rituals with Serbian Australians that in turn enabled me to make significant linkages, as a fifth generation Australian health researcher, in interpreting the participants' perspective. This approach, informed by Robertson, Marcus and others, which will be elaborated further in this study, involved simultaneous incorporation of locality and events in the larger world.

Gordana's letter also speaks of her bonding and belonging to the people and places of the past to the 'point of breaking'. This suggests that, as in the present research, individual health and wellbeing is concerned with physical conditions caused not only by local circumstances. Health, in the context of this research, is inextricably linked to the effects of long distance grief and devastation. The idea being advanced here is that health and wellbeing in Gordana's world are interdependent upon events thousands of kilometres away as well as the actions of others at a local level. Could this mean that health must be seen as a phenomenon influenced by powerful elements of identity, belonging, bonding and a historical consciousness that transcend the nations and communities where people live? Is there a 'hurtful' relationship between Balkans violence and events in Australia? In Gordana's situation this meant telling her story through writing and poetry to help heal the loss of a homeland.

The focus of the research journey

This journey originated out of my doctoral study which explored how war in the former Yugoslavia disrupted the life and health of people living in Australia who identify as Serbian, and how this group have responded to dislocation. It does so through an extensive ethnography, and the methodology for this emerged during the early stage of fieldwork.

Whether or not Serbian Australians had migrated from Serbia proper, Bosnia, disputed regions of Croatia, or had never actually set foot in the Balkans, they felt a strong need to talk about their situation. Emotional stress, anger, feelings of frustration, violence and revenge towards other nationalities and groups from the former Yugoslavia living in Australia were talked over as situations which have been framed by both local and international processes. As 'local and global hurts', these situations were influenced by a powerful and ever present international media, national and cultural identity, and as seen through the lives of people like Gordana, deep feelings of long distance loss, loneliness and devastation.

The importance of these situations shows that conditions both near and far influence the process of health. It was my contention early-on in my journey that the Balkan war had for many Serbian Australians cracked open a multitude of potent health and lifestyle concerns that were in part helped along by an intimate examination and re-examination of their perceived cultural and historical roots. To better understand health as a local and global process that operates during difficult and sensitive times, it had been necessary for me to explore and interpret from participants *what their experience of being a Serbian Australian ultimately stands for and what was sacred about it.* It was through this research and the ensuing analysis that I seek an interpretation of health as a social and cultural process.

In outlining more clearly my position regarding health as process, it is helpful to review sections of Gordana's letter that speak of the agony of her life in Australia in the shadow of global events:

> .... I ask that you take a few minutes to read my letter as I so desperately feel the need to bear (sic) my soul, overflowing with grief, to someone who may take the trouble to hear. When Yugoslavia came to its fall and destruction, my whole world seemed to have fallen apart as well. I could never imagine that it would bring me such heartache and have such a traumatic impact on me. ....It [the war] has brought me and some of my close family living here enormous pain, as at times I get to the point of breaking. Always a very happy and outgoing person, I have now lost all joy and sense of fun, wishing no company, finding no diversion in friends and outings. ....But the most horrifying pain of all, which goes right to the very core of my soul, is the pain of having lost my new country as well. I suddenly feel alone, displaced, not belonging anywhere at all, unprotected from the winds blowing in my direction with no shelter at all.

The most striking feature here was the collapse of Gordana's social and emotional world. The suggestion is that her health and wellbeing is now in far more perilous and critical circumstances than it was before the war. For Gordana, health as process was subject to the double implosion of her sadness and pain felt when Yugoslavia fell into war and the breakdown of relationships and friendships in Australia.

In addition to the contemporary global-national-local focus, there was also a historical dimension, ever-present and reflected in Gordana's reference to the Second World War. For many Serbian Australians there is a symbolic past that lives very much in their present situation. This past that can be traced to recent and distant events in the Balkans that are memorialised through a variety of cultural and religious means. Mark Thompson (1992, p. 198) in *A Paper House: The Ending of Yugoslavia*, recounts a chance meeting with a group of Serbian men in Croatia at the outbreak of the conflict:

> You would think that these young (men) had lost at the battle of Kosovo in 1389, rebelled with Karadjordje in 1804, beaten the Austrians in 1914, risen against the Axis in 1941, been terrorised in Kosovo in the 1980s. In Serbs speech the people are conjured as one person, who is also Serbia; every generation becomes one generation, which is Serbia too.

The Battle of Kosovo in 1389 and, as seen through Gordana's perspective the racial and religious massacres between 1941 and 1945 in the Jasenovic concentration camp complex are, important reference points for Serbians that inform what they think, feel and believed during the course of my journey. As also seen with the Croatian and Macedonian diaspora elsewhere in Europe and around the world, (Dogan, 1993; Danforth, 1995; Kolnar-Panov, 1996) events such as these may be seen as elements that transcend nations and communities where people live. For the Serbian Australians who participated in this study, the renewal of historical events has inspired poems, ballads and memories of heroic sacrifice as well as aspects of Serbian national identity that are inextricably linked to health experiences of today. Recovery of this symbolic tradition, is argued in this study, to be of great significance for the recovery of health and wellbeing among Serbian Australians.

In trying to gain access to, and in interpretation of, the kind of human suffering experienced by Serbian Australians, I operated in a range of fieldwork settings. I have conducted interviews in parked cars, hotel basements, people's homes, over the telephone, in restaurants, people's workplaces, in my university office, at the soccer, in cemeteries, on street corners, in church halls, in the aftermath of death threats, street violence, killings and drive-by shootings, bomb threats, Molotov Cocktail blasts, graffiti attacks and decapitation of statues.[12] I approached interviewing with a view to learning as much as possible about the aspects of the

Serbian Australian experience that were most important to the people interviewed at that particular moment. This activity drew on my experience of interpersonal relationships and personal trauma, developed during more than a decade of working as a mental health nurse.

Chapter review

This study therefore, through its timing and nature, emphasised that ethnographic research was not restricted to studies of 'exotic otherness'. Each chapter examines the local, national and international dimensions of the Serbian Australian experience through a series of interpretive moves. In so doing, the study offers a juxtaposition of my first discipline - mental health nursing - with the social sciences.

In chapter two, *Generating Interpretive Information from Ethnographic Fieldwork*, I describe how I generated data from ethnographic fieldwork in the context of global-local conditions. This chapter describes how I networked, established and approached interviews, how I interpreted nods, inflections and how I made up my mind to withdraw from situations that were 'unsafe'. I examine how far such commitments and assumptions influenced the research process in positive as well as negative ways.

By describing my interaction with participants during the Balkan war I outline both the mechanisms for data generation as well as the substantive issues that arose in interaction with Serbian Australians. Foremost among these was the emotional connection they felt between events in the Balkans and their lives in Australia.

In chapter three, *On Interpretation During the Journey*, I explain how my interpretation of Serbian Australians is interpretive, interpersonal and mediated by a historical consciousness for both participants and myself. The interpretation of data was guided by the fundamental belief that nothing speaks for itself in the social world (Denzin, 1994). This means that the world is never directly knowable, and there exists no mono-logic, time-honoured way by which to present it. From this approach I argue that through explicit and detailed explanation of how I arrived at particular interpretations, a credible account of the Serbian Australian experience can be made.

In the drive for understanding I pay particular attention to the presuppositions I hold to make meaning of data generated. My world view - beliefs and ideas - were used to constitute a pre-understanding (prejudice) of the experience of participants. As a researcher and interpreter this means that both myself and participants are self interpreting, and I chose to respect this as a means of data interpretation. Interpretations from ethnographic fieldwork were generated without the use of 'bracketing' so that the unit of treatment and analysis of data was through what the hermeneutic philosopher Hans-George Gadamer (1975, p. 306-7) calls the 'fusion of horizons'. My understanding of Serbian Australian situations through data generation was the result of open interpretation and re-interpretation between my horizon of prejudice and experience in fieldwork and the horizon of participants.

Chapter four, *'We Serbs are Obsessed with Maps': The Experience of Boundaries*, explores the pre-occupation with boundaries in the former Yugoslavia and Australia. Consistent with earlier themes, this chapter draws attention to the interpersonal, interpretive aspects of being Serbian Australian and the way in which individuals impose meanings in the process of boundary construction and maintenance. Before turning to issues of belonging as a vital mental health concept (chapter 5), several background considerations concerning the way people construct relationships with others have been considered.

As previously mentioned, to do this research I needed to cross many boundaries - enter homes, generate trust, learn a new language and perform numerous cultural and religious rituals with Serbian Australians that enabled me to gain access to participants. The fascinating issue for me at this point of the study was that the more I learnt about all that is perceived to be Serbian by participants, the more conscious I became of the boundaries I needed to cross to interpret their interpretation, as well as personal and social boundaries held by participants that I should avoid crossing.

Chapter five is titled *Towards a New Blood and Belonging* and extends the issues raised in chapter four. In the focus of 'We Serbs are Obsessed with Maps: The Experience of Boundaries', I spoke of how crossing boundaries is part of the process of being and believing as a Serbian as much as being a researcher who is trying to find out about Serbians. In chapter five I am concerned with issues of bonding, belonging, national and cultural identity. The idea here is that health as process can no longer be seen as a localised phenomena - it must be seen as something that transcends the national settings within which people live. This means that war in the former Yugoslavia has brought individuals to experience a range of distressing life events including feelings of frustration, nightmares, intrusive distressing thoughts, and bouts of extreme emotional exhaustion. Coping with these problems of living was in part helped along by an intimate re-examination and re-connection with Serbian cultural, religious and cultural identifications. Exploration of these ideas in this chapter take notions of health and healing beyond the specific care of physical conditions bound up with local circumstances, to consider the effect of long distance grief and devastation. These associations imply mental health and wellbeing through positive self concept and a sense of belonging.

To explicate these associations, the chapter includes a fieldwork description of a funeral service in Adelaide for a man who had left Serbia in 1963 at age 17 to travel to Australia. He had never returned to his homeland, and died in Sydney at age 50. During the funeral there were mobile telephone links between Sydney and Serbia to report on the progress of the funeral procession. What was most remarkable was that when the coffin containing the deceased arrived at the church, a telephone call was immediately made to his parents at a church in Serbia. There, a simultaneous service was ready to commence. After the service, the coffin was taken to a local cemetery. When the coffin was lifted over his grave, a second telephone call was made to a cemetery in Serbia where the family of the deceased had re-convened to commence another memorial service.

The coalescence of the issues raised in chapter five is an example of the global linked to the local. It suggests that what it means to be a Serbian Australian - a certain individual - and what is perceived to be sacred about it is a feature of life involving the simultaneity of what is happening in Australia and the Balkans. Mental health issues, and a sense of belonging to the former Yugoslavia, for participants is linked to national and cultural identity, relationships with others, and social life that affirms people and their purpose.

Chapter six is on *The Experience of Long Distance Devastation: Globalisation of Worry* and its construction initially influenced by death threats against people attending two Serbian Churches in South Australia. The interpretation here is that local Serbians were emotionally hurt by the continued accusation about their ethnic and religious identity. This local hurt manifested itself on talkback radio, letters to newspaper editors, graffiti attacks as well as other more serious violations including worrying death threats against Serbians, church bombings, decapitation of Serbian statues and other incidents. Inclusion of such events meant that the study needed to go beyond cultural description of past actions to focus on current actions of an open-ended kind. The focus was on *what people actually do or feel during heightened frustration, anger, hurt, worry and emotional distress as these feelings relate to events both local and global.* This not only meant participant observation in events as they happened, but also heightened problematic interactions between researcher and participant.

My attention in chapter six then turns to the impact upon participants of the relationship between violence in the Balkans and violence in Australia. Emotional distress, like that experienced by Gordana, is felt when community halls, statues, significant (living) people and, local and global events as objects with heavily loaded subjective capability are destroyed. Each object has the potential to be significantly more prominent than other objects depending upon the situation of the individual, and international events. Religious icons, for example, have the potential for dense and rich symbolism full of healing, sacrament and contemplation that bring about spiritual and emotional expression. My formulation of 'local and global hurts' centres upon how people try to cope with their mental suffering. This, in turn depends upon how people understand and engage in their Serbian national and cultural history. As a result of the activity of reconceptualising the Serbian national and cultural history, health and community interventions began to evolve.

Chapter seven, titled *From Trauma to Re-Affirmation: Health and Community for Serbian Australians,* is dedicated to understanding and interpreting what participants did for themselves and others to cope with the frustration and distress of war and events in Australia. As life became more difficult in Australia and as participants tried to deal with this, many sought out friendship, reassurance and a deliberate reconnection with their historical and cultural traditions. This contributes to an understanding of how participants avoided physical clashes, property damage, and violent acts involving other communities from former Yugoslavia who also live in Australia. In an interesting paradox, this chapter reveals that the objects and structures that participants used in order to feel and deal better with the situation, were also the subjects of abuse and destruction.

In chapter eight, *Conclusion,* I draw the main themes discussed in the previous chapters with a view to exploring the implications of the argument of this study. This chapter begins with an exploration of substantive issues emerging from the study and concludes with discussion of methodological and autobiographical concerns.

Conclusion

This introduction proceeded from the presumption that the Balkan war was a tragedy not only for its people but for the world community. My

experience of the Balkan war led me to try and understand how the
experience of people living in Australia, in the shadow of the conflict, was
made up of how they perceived the conflict and their national and cultural
'selves'. My experience as a mental health nurse led me to consider what
life is like for people who see themselves under attack. Consideration of
this view led to Serbian Australians becoming the focus of the study and
also gave rise to questions about health.

My questioning of the Serbian Australians' experience was
dramatised by Gordana's situation. The letter presented by Gordana posed
particularly difficult problems of loneliness, identity, belonging, historical
consciousness and impending health crisis. The time and trouble she took
to write about her experiences complements the large volume of interview,
participant observation and other fieldwork information gathered during
the course of my journey with study participants.

Chapter 2 is devoted to how I generated this text. In it I emphasise
that the modes of interconnection between data generation and the
development of a global-local understanding, as a substantive position, are
largely formed through my interaction with participants.

Notes

1   For the purpose of the present research the ending of the war in former Yugoslavia
was reached at about the time when the Dayton Peace Accord was signed by the
presidents of Serbia, Bosnia, Croatia and the United States at a Paris conference on
December 12-13 1995. The Dayton Accord required that special operations and
armed civilian groups be disbanded within 45 days of the signing. Notwithstanding
this, there continued to be sporadic armed exchanges between the warring factions,
and lives lost due to undetected landmines and snipers.

2   On 27 May 1992 a barrage of mortars killed twenty and injured 160 in an attack on
a bread queue which had formed in the street *Vase Miskina* in the Sarajevo city
square. Television and newspaper pictures showed dismembered bodies of the dead
and injured. A few weeks later there was another massacre involving a queue of
civilians waiting to take money out of a bank. On this occasion writes Ed Vulliamy
(1994, p. 82), 'the dead were victims of one of the many 'ceasefires', people
misplacing their faith by daring to come out of hiding'. Twenty-one were killed
(including some children) and over 130 injured.

3   The working definition of Serbian Australian is adapted from Radmanovic (1990)
and taken to mean a person of Serbian ethnic origin, not just those born and/or
having lived in the geographical Serbia, now living in Australia. This person may
not be obviously Serbian in appearance nor use the Serbian language regularly but
her/his identification as a Serbian is accepted and respected by others of Serbian
descent.

4   Both the Nuremberg and Tokyo war crimes tribunals set up after World War II
established clear principles about the criminal liability of State military and civilian
leaders (Fox, 1993). While not personally implementing ethnic cleansing, rapes or

massacres, it is alleged that these prominent figures did have in place a chain of command leading to their implementation. In the first full international war crimes trial since Nuremberg conducted in May 1997, Dusan Tadic a former police reservist, was convicted on 11 counts of crimes against humanity. He was found guilty of beating and torturing Muslim inmates in Serbian detention camps of north west Bosnia, including Omarska in the summer of 1992.

5   Philosophical hermeneutics emphasises the importance of language in interpretation and the way it is used to give and receive communications through time. My use of Gadamer's (1975) work, which is the focus of chapter 3, was not to propose a particular methodology of interpretation but to describe what was occurring in understanding.

6   Giddens (1996, p. 123) calls for sociology and anthropology in particular to 'concentrate on common areas of interest transforming local and global forms of social life'. As globalisation develops pace there is a 'resurgence of ethnicity, the seeming revival of tribalism in one form or another, and the continuing importance of religion and ritual - among other things, that the social sciences must claim a method to deal with' (pp. 123-4).

7   Between February and December 1988 I successfully completed the Serbian language studies course (code SRB 102) from Macquarie University, New South Wales, as an external student.

8   Australian census data reveals something of the dispersion of Serbians in South Australia. With respect of language spoken at home for persons aged 5 years or more, 1991 census data reveals that 790 males and 722 females (total 1512 persons) reported speaking Serbian and 1, 613 males and 1, 569 females (total 3, 1820) reported speaking Yugoslav or Serbo-Croatian. These figures in total represent 0.1 percent and 0.2 percent of South Australia's population respectively.

9   Here, as throughout the study, all names have been changed to protect the identity of participants. To fully ensure that the identity of participants and their families is not revealed I have also either left out or changed the names of places and community groups that could even remotely compromise their identity.

10   I had wanted to include some of Gordana's poems in this study to help illustrate her torment and eventual coping. But my doing this would have compromised her identity.

11   Capitalisation on this page is identical to the format presented on the original letter.

12   In September 1991 in Cabramatta Sydney 15 year old Sasha Dacic was shot dead outside a social club. In 1993 the New South Wales Court of Criminal Appeal reduced the sentence of the Serbian man found guilty of his murder to 15 years on the grounds that neurological damage from alcohol abuse was found to have diminished his culpability.

2 Generating Interpretation from Ethnographic Fieldwork

(T)he explicit treatment of bifocality in ethnographic accounts is becoming more explicit and openly transgressive of the us-them distanced worlds in which it was previously constructed... the identity of the anthropologist and his world, by whatever complex chain of connection and association, is likely to be profoundly related to that of any particular world he is studying (Marcus, 1995, p. 117).

Introduction

In the previous chapter I suggested that the particular meanings and interpretations Serbian Australians brought to the Balkan war and the ethnic groups involved in it, could only be understood through the historical relationships they hold with the homeland and my interaction with individuals along the way. This chapter describes and explains the techniques used to generate data in this context. Beginning with a description of property damage and death threats against Serbians in Adelaide, this chapter establishes a qualitative research position that is critical of positivist ethnography and supportive of the idea that the researcher is an integral part of the data generation process. This approach gives rise to an explanation of how my presence in the field was an active and sometimes problematic element in the process of data generation.

Consideration of these issues will set the scene for the *next* chapter, where I am concerned with the interpretation of ethnographic materials.

The dynamic and interactive nature of fieldwork: early morning property damage and death threats

The following section was recorded in my journal at the scene of early morning property damage and graffiti (death threats) against people attending two Serbian churches in South Australia.[1]

I have just learned from the radio that there were overnight graffiti and vandal attacks on two Serbian Orthodox Churches in the Adelaide suburbs of Hindmarsh and Kilkenny.[2] The regular Sunday church services (Sluzba[3]) have been cancelled as priests and worshippers were 'too upset' to participate. The attacks reputedly took place around 2.30 am and the Serbs say it is possible that Croatians in town for a soccer grand final are responsible. The report also said that the Serbs fear that younger members of their community may retaliate if the culprits are not caught and they want the Australian Government to intervene.

As soon as I learned of the attacks from the local media I grabbed my camera, notebook and pen, jumped into my car and headed across town to see the damage and to speak with people at the scene. Before I left the house I changed my clothes from a bright coloured T-shirt and shorts to dark blue coloured trousers and shirt. I thought it a good idea to 'look respectable' by wearing clothes that I believed reflected the feeling of the occasion. To me, the wearing of dark clothes was an attempt to empathise with the anticipated sombre perhaps angry mood of people coming to terms with the attacks on their churches. I also thought that it would help avoid any obvious 'standing out' in the crowd.

When I arrived at the scene I realised that most of those present knew me and the work I was doing. Knowing most of those present and speaking in Serbian helped me gain access to the area and to view the damage.

The vandalism was much worse than had been reported on the radio. An angle grinder or hacksaw had been used to decapitate a life size statue of the allied Second World War Serbian General, Draza Mihalovic.[4] Fine metal dust lay at the foot of the statue. The presence of the dust caught my eye as it glistened in the morning sun. Nearby I saw smashed church windows, two doors that appeared to have been kicked in, a large black swastika[5] and the word 'scum' sprawled across the church foundation stone. Slogans, crosses and other symbols relating to the current war in the former Yugoslavia were daubed on walls inside and outside the churches. The spray painted graffiti was easily readable from a distance of several hundred metres away. It read 'USTASA MERTERVE SVE SRBI' (Ustasha To Kill All Serbs, translation, N.P.), and 'SMRT SRBIMA ZA DOM SPREMNI U' (Death to Serbs for this House [Church] We are Ready To Get, N.P.).

On the wall of a nearby property were the following words in English 'CROATIA LIVES 1941-45'. The slogans reawakened memories of those I'd seen in towns and villages during the current war in former Yugoslavia prior to ethnic cleansing.[6] This in turn invoked genocidal images of an utterly ruthless encounter by a former neighbour turned aggressor.[7]

Next, I moved in closer towards the groups of people gathered around. Many were expressing anger at what they had seen. Some were visibly shaken. One Serbian Australian woman pointed to the swastika saying 'Od toga mi ce srce cijepa' (That breaks my heart, N.P.). She immediately began speaking of the Jasenovac concentration camp where during the Second World War (1941-44 in particular) up to 600, 000 Serb civilians (and others) were massacred.[8] She told me that the killers of innocent people in her homeland - the Ustasha[9] - were the same sort of people responsible for today's attack. As she spoke I sensed the build up of anger and frustration inside her and her simultaneous attempts to control it. She grew increasingly angry as the conversation between us continued. Once I had been told of the connections between today and Europe fifty years ago, she went no further. She drew the conversation to a close by saying, in English 'OK, I have said enough about this now. I've had enough of this'.

Elsewhere there were people standing around looking at the damage. Some were crying, others engaged in deep conversation with listeners huddled by their side. One man shouted 'We should get them!' He banged his fist into the palm of his other hand repeating the call. Younger Serbs spoke of wanting to respond with retaliatory violence despite not knowing the individual identity of the attackers. The young men were convinced that those responsible should be 'dealt with'.

Adjacent to the Kilkenny church was a well groomed man being interviewed by a television news crew. Footage of his interview later appeared on the evening news bulletin. The young man, a spokesperson for the Serbian community told the media news crew that:

'The congregation is just outraged, shocked, stressed and dismayed. There is no doubt in our minds that the people responsible are Croatian Nazis and these Croatian Nazis come as part of a component of 2000 Croatian supporters who came to Adelaide, invaded Adelaide, to support their Croatian football team in today's final'.

With all of this happening around me, I began to feel uneasy about my presence at the churches. I paused, withdrawing slightly from the expressions of upset and anger in an effort to 'ground' myself. That is, I withdrew myself from the scene to reflect upon my role as both participant and observer in the trauma. I asked myself, 'Am I influencing the research process by encouraging the rationalisations and experiences of others?' Do I want participants to disclose information that would not normally be probed for in the course of today's events?

Thinking these questions through had become a feature of my ethnographic fieldwork with Serbian Australians over the course of my journey. On this particular day, I saw myself as part of the construction of the situation by Serbian Australians, as much as participant in the generation of data. By dressing for the occasion (in dark colours), speaking the correct language (Serbian), I was self consciously making moves to connect with events of the day and the participants' experience of them.

My withdrawal from fieldwork, albeit temporary, meant a break away from being an alert percipient ethnographer of the immediate environment and the people in it. At this point I took the opportunity to make some brief notes about my experiences and observations. Concentrating on my notes meant that I was less alert and much less concerned with the happenings around me.

What immediately followed was a frightening and ugly incident.

After making brief notes I stood outside the church attempting to photograph the anti Serbian slogans. Unknown to me, an elderly Serbian gentleman dressed in a brown suit and tie had begun to lunge forward toward the right hand side of my body. He moved to confront me face to face, his body very close to mine, hands on hips breathing brandy fumes. In a pressured voice he shouted in English 'Hey! What do you think you are doing? Who are you? Why are you photographing the church? He was very angry. His body was only centimetres from mine and I watched his face turn from white to red. I could sense the build up of energy inside him. I felt very frightened and extremely remorseful that my presence in the field had contributed to his distress. All of these issues made me think carefully about the nature, timing and degree of my response to him.

As I proceeded to answer I tried to avoid words that might agitate him. I knew that whatever I said or did could cause him to increase his aggression. I responded in a quiet, flat tone, 'Today is a very sad day for the Serbian people in Adelaide. I feel sorry that this has happened'. He didn't seem to hear me. Instead, he removed his right hand from his hip and formed a tight fist to which there seemed to be only one possible climax. His fist seemed to tighten during the strained conversation (in Serbian) that continued between us. I tried to answer his questions but was interrupted by further questions and accusations that I 'was from the media'.

What struck me most about this man was the rage in his eyes. His pupils were fixed on my camera and me. His eyes told me, in a most powerful and silent way to be 'very careful'. At this instruction I took a step backwards and thought about the highly tense situation I was in. I thought that the level of his response to me was dependent upon two critical issues: what I was doing right now and what I would do next. In summary, I did not want to say or do anything that could bring on full scale verbal or physical attack. I knew that this man could be made more furious by what I said or did and I needed to provide answers to his questions in such a way as to avoid making him angrier.

With these thoughts, and the likelihood of violence, I moved away from him to my right side, keeping a close eye on his clenched fist as well as the general way in which he moved his body. I also kept note of the way he moved his eyes and the way I looked at them. I did this intuitively believing that I could calculate his anger by the look in his eyes. At the same time I was trying very hard not to 'challenge' him. I did not want to look at him in the face - with an 'alleged' fixing of my eyes on him in defiance of his wishes - as I thought such action might provoke him.

I took a step down so that his height on the steps outside the church was greater than mine. I did this believing that a gentle decrease in the level of my presence may help ease the situation. I wanted to appease him by appearing less of a personal threat. I also wanted to appear relaxed before putting across an explanation of what I was doing.

My lowering of height turned out to be quite strategic. He appeared more relaxed when the height of my body became less than his. I believe this move helped me to diffuse a potentially violent situation that could have quickly deteriorated into something 'out of control'. What had started out as a delicate gesture of passive retreat with the intent to avoid conflict, turned into a context for conversation between us about the emotional hurt and frustration felt about the present war in the Balkans, media portrayal of the war and today's attack on the church.

After explaining myself and what I was trying to do, it became possible for me to take photographs. The elderly gentleman was satisfied with what I was doing and retreated.

And as soon as I had finished taking photos of the church I drove around the immediate area to see if there was any more graffiti like I'd seen on the church. For several kilometres I saw numerous U shaped symbols with a crucifix inserted equidistant between its upright extremities daubed on interior and exterior building walls. These buildings included local shops and businesses that appeared to be un-connected with the Serbian Orthodox church but were still the victim of indiscriminate attacks. I ended the day sitting in my car in the suburb of Hindmarsh writing and reflecting on today's events.

While the research context and fieldwork interactions described above may seem extreme and dangerous, they nevertheless serve to illustrate a distinctive characteristic of my involvements throughout my ethnographic journey in at least three aspects.

Firstly, throughout my journey with Serbian Australians it was not possible to entertain an idealised aim of objective reality in cultural description by adopting Spradley's (1979, p. 34) call for 'a particular stance toward people, trying to understand the world from their point of view, (and) *wanting* to understand the world from their point of view ...*to walk in their shoes, feel things as they feel them*'. (emphasis added N.P.) Understandably, I was perceived by the elderly man at the scene of the graffiti attack to be something of an intruder, and certainly (I think) as an outsider, almost to the extent that I had in some way collaborated with others to cause the damage to the church. Data generation judgements, therefore, were strongly influenced by a constellation of interpersonal and practical considerations.

Secondly, it can be reasoned from the above that it was not my intention to put participants into gender, age, or occupational categories to organise their experience. This is because as the above fieldwork event illustrates, it would bring about an artificial structure not applicable or relevant to this study context (Hammersley and Atkinson, 1990). Rather, the intention of this study was to remain open to the influence of multi-media and acknowledge and work closely with the beliefs generated by participants in response to it. This means that data generation with participants was a constellation of the television and news media, my presence in the field and spontaneous manoeuvres characteristic of qualitative inquiry.

Thirdly, the problem with artificial situations and categories is the assumption that they are both possible and desirable, while at the same time subordinating the interests of participants to the interests of the researcher. This has the potential to force the researcher into the role of 'gatekeeper', thereby constructing Serbian Australians as research 'objects'. Such intentions on my part contrasts sharply with an 'us-and-them' understanding by the so-called 'intellectual and detached other'.

Instead, as will be elaborated in the sections that follow and in the next chapter in particular, it has been important in this research to engage two complementary processes. They are *firstly,* to allow for autobiographical and professional connections between myself and participants to proceed as part of the research process (Charmaz and

Mitchell, 1996) and *secondly,* when transforming these interactions into the written record, to work towards emphasising the shifting and sometimes volatile contexts, meanings and issues encountered in the real world, rather than allowing these issues to be subordinate to certain prescriptive or ideological guidelines of conventional ethnography (Polier and Roseberry, 1989). In addition to this was the view that there is much in this study that speaks to the way that participants *may* to a varying extent, have complex political, historical and social experiences that require careful ethical and methodological consideration. Because this historical and political consciousness is so powerful and penetrating in people's lives, extreme caution, like that taken at the scene of property damage in Adelaide, is necessary to avoid any emotional or physical harm being done to participants. While conventional research ethics centres on issues of informed consent – 'consent that has been received from participants after they have been carefully and truthfully informed about the research' (Fontana and Frey, 1994, p. 372), participant observation at the scene of property damage and death threats represents a different research setting in which ethical issues must as it were be developed and resolved situationally. The principle adopted was that the data gathering exercise through participant observation should be as much as possible subordinate to the commitment to do no physical or emotional harm to others.

My interaction with participants caused me to use affirmations that spoke to the immediacy of fieldwork (eg. nods of the head, brief verbal cues and sentences that described recent television news reports of the Balkan war and hostilities in Australia) as well as appreciation through careful listening of their perspective of events in Serbian history. This technique allowed me to begin to develop and solidify rapport with participants as well as to establish effective communications patterns (Janesick, 1994).

Clearly, fieldwork in this study was not simply a process of unmediated grasping of objective localised facts. Interaction with participants was, as Goffman (1987) reminds us, an act of subjection of the body and personality as well as the social situation at play in the lives of participants. What I said, thought and felt when generating interpretive text was interdependent on interactions between myself and participants. This means that I subjected myself to the lives and beliefs of others as a social, interactive process (Goffman, 1989). Through effective networking, asking questions, seeking out people to talk to, disclosing information about myself and the work that I was trying to do, listening to casual conversations and taking field notes I was able to get involved in people's lives as these lives were involved in and consumed by the Balkan war. These involvements gave rise to data generation through absorbing, witnessing, interacting, collaborating and participating in the lives and beliefs of Serbian Australians.

My approach was aligned to what Denzin (1994) described as offering local, personal and political dimensions to interpretation of events through additional consideration of the relationship between fieldwork and the textual reconstruction. Within this approach to text development was what Clifford (1986) termed the transparency of its (textual) construction. That is, a look inside the ethnographer's tent: the private space for thought and interpretation during and after fieldwork.

I saw interpretation, both in participant observation and in interviewing as an intersubjective social process[10] and my argument for this was based upon three key issues. *Firstly*, it must be said that this data generation approach encouraged an understanding of others and their context as interpreted experience. I understood that the actions, gestures and moves that participants made were culturally and socially significant and must be interpreted as such. This research accessed the Serbian Australian experience through participants' use of songs, dance, costume and ceremony. Observation and interpretation of Serbian Australians through ethnographic fieldwork was grounded in the belief that such understanding was more than the mere inventory of cultural artefacts. It was also the subject of my interpretation.

Secondly, there is a paradox in that, with the proliferation and diversity of professional knowledge, the number of anthropological studies increases, while globalisation reduces the number of tribal peoples - the subject of classic ethnography (Marcus, 1995). With this in mind, the present study persisted in the context of dispersed groups which defy the way ethnography was first framed and designed (Marcus, 1995). Elsewhere, Robertson (1992) tells us that we live in a current phase of rapid globalisation that gives rise to individuals and groups searching for the meaning of the world as a whole. This means that the idea of what is culture, must take into account elements that embrace every facet of human life both near and afar. The once dominant idealised ethnography of localised human civilisations whereby the ethnographer tried to maintain the fiction of being detached and impartial has been challenged and largely superseded as culture, politics and history in the people's lives has become intertwined and brought to the foreground (Rosaldo, 1993). My journey therefore unfolded in a world which Robertson (1992) and

Marcus (1986), in particular, suggest is made up of larger systems and events externally impinging on and abounding little worlds.[11] As will be elaborated further in this and chapters to come these substantive formulations of a global-local framework for social science encouraged and informed my journey to include local insights that simultaneously contextualise globally impacting events and issues.

A selective application of relevant nursing concepts

While not primarily a nursing study, the techniques I used during fieldwork - interviewing, participant observation and networking - drew on experience gained through my professional life as a mental health nurse. In mental health nursing practice, I relate to people who are distressed or disturbed, whether or not their predicament is capable of formal psychiatric classification. Central to the practice of mental health nursing is the capacity to engage others who are in mental distress. In particular, this often means drawing out and interpreting information from distressed people through observation of their actions, carefully listening to what they say during interview, and building trust and helping relationships (Ritter, 1989; Arthur, Dowling and Sharkey, 1992; Barker, 1997).

The practice of mental health nursing is highly charged by the interpersonal, emotional, dynamic and largely unpredictable processes of human experience. The linkages between nursing and fieldwork are illustrated by the incident at the two churches. Issues of self preservation, and my wanting to do no physical or emotional harm to participants, are reflected in the moves I made. I did this through trying to avoid standing at the top of the stairs, standing in a non-threatening way (feet apart to maintain balance, hands by my side, fingers slightly curled, not in pockets or on hips), refraining from raising my hands, pointing, or making sudden movements, and attempting to identify and acknowledge the feelings of the elderly Serbian, as indicated in my answer. Such moves embody interactive skills considered essential in nursing when managing grief and loss (Cowles and Rogers, 1991; Arthur, Dowling and Sharkey, 1992), suicidal behaviour (Gibbs, 1990), and physical violence (Ritter, 1989). They involve actions, words and self disclosures deliberately chosen to reduce the chance of violence by not threatening the angry person. My moves were also designed to 'avoid irritating the (participant), thus giving the impression of being passive, non-threatening and disarming' (Ritter, 1989, pp. 93-94).

It is important to point out that the above skills are not limited to interpretation. Rather, they are, to a varying extent, as much management skills used to provide and 'manage' nursing care for people experiencing emotional distress and agitation. Nevertheless, throughout my journey I drew from the skills outlined above to interpret the mental distress of people. This means that my background in nursing enabled me, in part, to relate to participants, as I interpreted their experience of overnight property damage at their place of worship; the observations I made of people and the relationships I generated in the field were informed by those made in nursing practice (Christensen, 1996).

I am, of course, using the practice of nursing in a very different sense - a sense much closer to Benner's (1994a, 1994b) use. The prominent nurse theorist Patricia Benner points out that nurses do much more than care for the sick, or deal with pathophysiology and underlying disease. Nurses are also concerned with normality and abnormality, and 'the lived social and skilled body in understanding and promoting health and development and in caring for the sick and dying' (Benner, 1994a, p. xvii). Like nursing, fieldwork with Serbian Australians depended upon my ability to talk to and be in close contact with people in delicate situations. Despite differences underlying each activity, the practice of nursing, through its appreciation of qualitative depth in and respect for the situations of others, is congruent with ethnographic research techniques. The important point being made here is that my interpretation of participants emerges from the assumption that effective relationships with others are based on inter-subjectivity and inter-dependence. Both the self and the other are thus bound together in terms of interpretive understandings of the situation, though there is no guarantee at all that understandings will be shared.

Alongside the practice of fieldwork was careful consideration for the wellbeing of participants. Here, once again, I drew from the multitude of interpersonal and social skills employed as a nurse. For example, experience in knowing when to talk or not talk, probe further, or withdraw from participants altogether were also utilised (Martyres, 1995). While spoken language is often considered essential in the conduct of qualitative research, there is also in the present study, a means to understanding the Serbian Australian experience through the emotional experience of silence. I considered silence as an opportunity for generating some awareness of the personal and emotional qualities at the heart of research that deals with participant sensitive topics such as mental distress and emotional exhaustion (Davies, 1993).

Whether as nurse or ethnographer, the act of *doing fieldwork* with participants demanded careful thought about the nature and quality of interaction. The catalyst for my interaction included inter-ethnic violence in Australia, the memory of past events in the Balkans, how I was perceived by participants and the powerful nature of historic symbols, slogans and events in former Yugoslavia and Australia. All of these issues persisted in the ever present shadow of war. I have organised the remainder of this chapter according to these themes and will endeavour to address issues relating to them within the techniques of participant observation, interviewing, and document analysis.

Generating data: a simultaneous interpretive process

Research activity with Serbian Australians involved a series of simultaneous processes built around generating trust and networking with participants. There was no set structure or formula concerning the way I generated data from participants.[12]   Networking, like interpretation of research materials, was an art that I learned by 'thoughtful doing'.

My Serbian language skills proved valuable when trying to establish contact with Serbian Orthodox Priests, church officials and people holding leadership positions within the Church. The act of speaking about my research and informing people of what I wanted to do was undertaken at the same time as establishing contact with new participants. My trying to communicate my reasons for research to participants was also an opportunity to see how what I was saying was being received by them.

The organisational groups I networked with included the Serbian Orthodox Church, the Serbian National Federation of Australia and Serbian Soccer Clubs. My involvements included attending appointments and meetings with participants; listening to casual conversations at religious celebrations, sporting events, cultural celebrations; interviewing; taking field notes; making reflective journal entries; analysing data; writing rough drafts of ideas and interpretations as 'works in progress'; and finally writing up my interpretation of words, phrases, sentences and, most of all, the meanings Serbian Australians gave their situation.

Several Serbian Australians such as religious or political leaders acted as gatekeepers whereby they 'exerted considerable control over key resources and avenues of opportunity' (Hammersley and Atkinson, 1990, p. 65). Gatekeepers from the Serbian National Federation for example, sought to encourage certain lines of inquiry in the research, and they did this while not overtly attempting to block me in any way. One evening I was called to meet three Federation members to be 'checked out':

> SM telephoned to say that he and RM and RK want to meet me tomorrow evening to talk over dinner about the research. The meeting had been called at a northern suburbs restaurant and the idea was that I would tell them what I wanted to do in the present research. So I went to the meeting believing that they would help me.

> I was the first to arrive at the restaurant as the other three were late. When they finally entered the room the tone of their entry was most unfriendly. They made no eye contact with me, nor offered any smile as they walked towards where I was seated. There was a distinct absence of warmth or friendliness about them. Once seated there continued to be no smiles or introductions (I only knew SM).

> After ordering drinks I felt as if they started work on me, asking me a range of questions for up to one hour. They wanted details about my parents' birthplace, my father's occupation and cultural background, brother's occupations, details about my wife's family, a chronology of my occupation as well as how long I had lived in my own home. Each question was punctuated by 'Now Nicholas, how about you tell us why you really want to know about the Serbs, What's the real reason for you wanting to do the research?'[13]

> Towards the end of dinner I was told that the only way to understand the experience of Serbians in Australia is to consider the impact of Serbian history and culture, over hundreds of years prior to and during today's conflict, and this information was to be integrated with the present.

> After dinner, the mood and tone of the evening seemed to be more relaxed. We left the restaurant about 11.30 p.m. and travelled about a kilometre away to a small cafe for coffee and more wine. Our moving from to the cafe had the distinct feel that I was to remain with the group until they had 'finished with me'. I also felt that I needed to remain with the group until I sensed that they were satisfied with what I was trying to do. Put another way, I wanted to stay until I could see myself getting some sense of their trust.

> By about 3.00 am the next morning it was time to leave. I was mentally exhausted and felt that my efforts to inform these men of my work had been successful.

In an interesting paradox, the meticulous and sometimes sceptical appraisal of me and this study by particular members of the Serbian National Federation of Australia turned out to be a source of guidance for actually 'doing' data generation. Of great import and concern to those present that evening was the argument that no survey of Serbian Australians was credible until I had 'connected today's events in Europe with events in Kosovo 600 years ago and the racial and religious massacres against Serbs, Jews and Gipsies during the second world war'. The point of this kind of 'guidance' was to show at a local level that the conflict has its roots in an ever present past. It also suggested that my attempts at trying to understand the Serbian point of view and how this might intersect with the problems of living for participants, could contribute to resolving some of the dilemmas I had faced at the scene of damage against church property and death threats against worshippers.

The trouble with not wanting this kind of collaboration was, of course, that whatever I did to try to avoid it occurring, the more intense and focussed it became. I feared that my withdrawal from Serbian Australian attempts to get me to work a particular approach to inquiry could put at risk any future collaboration with the group. To manage this issue and ensure ongoing relations I chose to work out my concerns interpretively. That is, I chose to view the actions of the Serbs as part of the world I was researching and to let this be representative of itself as a means and source of data (Johannsen, 1992). Working out my interaction and involvement with participants provided the seminal material for theoretical discussion in later chapters.

From early meetings with Serbian Australians, participant observation and interviewing experiences seemed likely to deepen my view of the history of the region and people. Exploring the meanings and actions of participants, no matter how transparent or selfish they might appear, encouraged a more subtle analysis of possible underlying motivations and concerns.

This process also involved a range of fieldwork settings across Australia. Parked cars, churches, church halls, Serbian cafés, the private homes of participants, during telephone conversations, as a spectator at sports grounds, cemeteries, in the lounge room of my home and by fax and E mail. On one occasion, I had negotiated an interview with a leading Serbian Australian figure and to my surprise, the interview was in the basement of an inner-city hotel, in the presence of three men (who were not introduced to me) leaning up against an adjacent wall. The interview began with an interview of me. Questions in both Serbian and English were punched at me:

> Why do you want this information about us, our people?
> Who are you working for?
> What is your ethnic background?
> Where were your parents born?

In response, as Fischer (1986, p. 217) describes, I saw this as a 'dialectical, two directional (ethnographic) journey examining the realities of both sides of cultural difference so that (we) can mutually question each other'. By interview's end, I was completely 'smoked out' (all four - interviewee and 'escorts' were smoking in a small unventilated room) and at the expense of my personal comfort, had penetrated what I later considered an 'inner sanctum' group of Australian Serbians.

I thought it a mistake to see these questions as forms of intimidation, leading to withdrawal from the field. Instead, these questions constituted an excellent opportunity for data generation and interpretation. Viewed this way, fieldwork with Serbian Australians in the shadow of the Balkan war was undertaken with a view to learning about their experience and the people who are 'living it'. As Fontana and Frey (1994, p. 374) put it, 'We must remember to treat them (participants) as people, and they will uncover their lives to us. As long as researchers treat participants as unimportant, faceless individuals, the answers we will get will be commensurable with the questions we ask and the way we ask them. The idea being advanced here is for a move away from any attempt at deceitful use of strategies or tricks to elicit material. Moreover, it was prudent to remind myself that the asking of questions by participants about what I was doing and why (despite very detailed information handouts and discussion sheets written in English and Serbian) was in the context of a serious bloody conflict in former Yugoslavia. As discussed elsewhere in this study, my journey came face to face with Balkan war whereby I found myself in the same room as those participating in it.

Generating data through media and other documents

Outside the Serbian press, little is said or written about Serbian migrations to Australia, settlement experiences, family life or response to the Balkan war. Throughout the period of fieldwork, I gathered up documents and media information and grouped this into three broad categories: (1) documents and films made by Serbian individuals and organisations, including the ethnic press and Serbian Australian Television; (2) published books, newspaper accounts and government records of Serbian Australians; and (3) unpublished papers, theses and other collected works such as church newsletters and memorandums to parish members. During the gathering of this information I asked: *Could it be that words, religious symbols, national symbols and cultural gestures all act as reference points for the expression of the experience between homeland and local situations? Are they a means through which to interpret the relationships between local and worldly situations as described by Serbian Australians?*

The construction of data was built around the idea that as ethnographer, I was part of the interviewees' existence as much as the research questions I sought to answer. This means that fieldwork information was not only a reflection of Serbian Australians, it was also a reflection of my response to Balkan war, relationships with participants, relationships with the way homeland is being reported, and the way I interpret this information.

Generating data through participant observation

Hammersley and Atkinson (1990, p. 8-9) argue that participant observation in ethnography is essential 'even when the researcher is researching a familiar group or setting'. Participant observation, they continue, is a means to take in 'only what can be understood in its natural context with explanations provided as it happens'. In generating data there was a temptation to try and observe everything and a fear that when withdrawing from the field something would be missed. To overcome this concern, I endeavoured to conclude periods of observation with a series of processed notes and reflections 'a sort of internal dialogue, or thinking aloud, questioning what I know and how much data has been acquired so that further lines of inquiry could be examined' (Hammersley and Atkinson, 1990, p.164). Through these activities, participant observation served as shorthand for continuous documentation of events, occurrences and gestures, the meaning which was often situated in wider contexts.[14]

The nature and timing of my participant observation experiences allowed for movement between the human qualities of the participants and the larger order of world events in global as much as local situations. Viewed this way, Serbian Australians and my observation of them was neither static nor atemporal.   Serbian Australians did not 'hold still for their portraits' (Clifford, 1986, p.10), and my attempts to make them do so would have involved over simplification and exclusion of what was really happening.

To illustrate the application of participant observation in this research, I will detail two fieldwork situations.   The following examples are chosen because they constitute behaviours, customs, and symbols that are deemed to retain and perpetuate authentic Serbian traditions:

> In 1994 I was invited by a Serbian Australian family to act as a support person at the grave site during the burial of a family member.   Several factors brought about my involvement in the day; for instance, the family members with whom I had most contact were similar in age to me.   As I got to know and understand them better, I found that they trusted me and believed in the work that I was trying to do.   I thought their trust in me was, in part helped along by my willingness to take the time and trouble to listen carefully to their situation and experience.   I also spent much time with this family (and others known to them) explaining the risks and benefits of my research to them so as to help them decide about their level of involvement. From this start, my involvement also helped me to develop a working relationship and this, in turn, helped me to get involved in what was going on at every opportunity.

> My role at the funeral that day was, in effect, penetrating both the family and the traditions surrounding a Serbian Orthodox burial.   At the church I took photographs of the funeral ceremony.   This meant that I had to move around quite a lot, inside and outside the church, as well as keep close to the cortege as the coffin was transported from the funeral parlour to the church, and finally to the graveyard.   I was also expected to take photographs of mourners as they kissed the body of the deceased lying in an open coffin.

> Taking photographs at a Serbian funeral also meant much more.   It gave me a position of responsibility and level of commitment to the group beyond that normally expected in the research process.

> At the cemetery I set up portable card tables, helped provide liquid refreshments (brandy, soft drinks, and beer) and supervised food distribution for mourners adjacent to the burial site.   (It is tradition within the Serbian Orthodox religion to eat and drink at the graveyard soon after the coffin is lowered into the ground).

> All these tasks gave me a high profile on the day and this profile led to some unexpected opportunities for fieldwork.

Moving around at the church and cemetery exposed me to all those present. Every now and again I would tune in to the casual conversations of people at the graveyard. During the service and immediately afterwards it was also possible to engage people attending the funeral as they spoke not only of the deceased, but also of the Balkan war, political and military solutions to fighting, and their life in Australia during the conflict. I found that casual conversation with participants provided a rich source of data. What struck me most was the feeling that I was being talked to as a person who belonged 'within' rather than 'outside' the group.

My sense of involvement through language leads me to the next fieldwork example:

> During 1993 I attended a fundraising picnic for Serbian victims of war in former Yugoslavia. On this occasion I spoke both English and Serbian with the people I was with. So convincing was my use of the Serbian language, I was confronted by a Serbian male (whose identity was not known to me) for speaking in English language. He told me that I should be ashamed to speak English at a Serbian function. Believing that I was a Serb, he told me to 'stop speaking English and begin speaking Serbian – immediately'! (trans, N.P.)

> When I asked why it was important for me not to speak English, I was told that my speaking in Serbian would 'keep the Serbian tradition and custom alive' (trans, N.P.). I later explained that English was my first language and during the conversation that remained between us, was able to speak briefly about the present research.

The above events highlight concerns crucial to accessing and researching the study setting. Fontana and Frey (1994, p. 367) describe the decision of how to present oneself as 'very important because after one's presentational self is 'case' it leaves a profound impression on the respondents and has great influence on the success or failure of the study'. With such crucial weight being given to what are clearly situations that few non-Serbs could participate in, I was usually very careful to avoid over-representing myself in the social and cultural life of participants.

Interviewing for data generation

A combination of snowball sampling and direct approaches to people of Serbian descent was the means for involvement of fieldwork participants.

Interviews were conducted in either English or Serbian (often both) and the choice of language was left to the discretion of participants. Whenever possible, each interview was recorded on micro-cassette and later transcribed *in toto*. While non-directive interviewing was a means to encourage participants to talk at length, in their own terms, about their life as a Serbian Australian during Balkan war, it was also, as already demonstrated, subject to the ever present influence of the interaction between myself and the interviewees. In the research process, the very nature of my presence formed part of the social relationship at work during interview. Nonetheless, I believe the interviews worked well, to the extent that participants appeared able to find an active voice in the research for reasons that I hope are apparent from the anecdotes described.

The similarities between participant observation and interviewing during my journey were that each required the use of advanced interpersonal skills and perceptive abilities. As for my participant observation experiences, the reporting and analysis of interview data was not without its problems. There was a break with the monophonic style of textual construction that was punctuated by strategic testimonies or stories (Clifford, 1983). This means that the ethnographic method undertaken included several voices of people and their situations that, like the world they exist in, were both complex and varied.[15] Within the strategies of networking and observation in this and other chapters, there was, as Max van Manen (1990, p. 69) articulates, the need to 'assume contact as close as possible whilst retaining hermeneutic alertness to situations to accommodate constant withdrawal and reflection on the potential meanings of certain situations'. This required a certain reflectivity and personal honesty whereby as interviewer I was both participant and observer at the same time.

Clearly, interviewing Serbian Australians was not just a matter of being social and interactive. There were, as I have already mentioned, some interesting moments that constituted the process of generating interpretive materials from ethnographic fieldwork. Much methodological and strategic detail was needed to ask questions, seek out 'permission' from gatekeepers and key informants and take careful note of linkages between international and national issues and concerns. Careful inquiry into the Serbian Australian experience meant that the international and local dimensions of events, such as death threats and property damage, were 'processes that must be understood from the point of view of the actor, a realisation that raises problems of interpretation and presents opportunities for innovation in writing' (Marcus, 1986, p. 166). While a threat may have taken place in South Australia, there appeared to be considerable links between it and the war in former Yugoslavia.

But there were also some interesting differences between participant observation and interviewing. In interviewing, it was not possible to proceed without the exchange of smiles, and information that demystifies what I was trying to do. Interviewing was helped by referral from past interviewees and their associates who provided information about the sorts of questions being asked and the length of time needed to undertake the interview. Introductions then followed, and this in turn invoked questions from interviewees similar to those described earlier in this chapter (eg. my ethnic origin). Sometimes careful and considered, at other times spontaneous, the use of verbal and non verbal cues were a means to follow the trail of thought and language used by the participants.

When I sat and listened to participants, watching them speak and pause between sentences, I juxtaposed a variety of means toward continuous and simultaneous data generation. I did this by encouraging participants to tell their story in whatever way they could. When listening to participants it was not uncommon for me to sit with my eyes closed, concentrating (through visualisation and conscious effort) on what the participants were saying; feeling and gesturing my way during our conversation together. I refer to these moments throughout the remainder of this study as *ethnographic drama*, to describe the unspoken, yet relevant, gestures of communication between myself and researcher. Silences, pauses, facial grimacing, and changes in posture, hand gestures and eye movement were all of significance during my journey with Serbian Australians.

The strategy for interviewing outlined above was not always readily achievable. To illustrate this point I would like to discuss a fieldwork experience whereby the immediacy between research questions and the impact of Balkan war on Serbian Australians were closely interlinked:

> I arrived at a participant's house for interview as planned. I was taken to the house by someone who was known to the family who lived there, and introduced as someone who was 'OK' and, sympathetic to the Serbian people. Those present during interview included the participant's son, mother, uncle and brother in law.
>
> As soon as I arrived I was made to feel very welcome with warm greetings and a freshly brewed cup of thick black coffee. I felt very relaxed in this house and thought that things would go well.

Not long into our meeting the conversation moved to mass killings, the disappearance of civilians and ethnic cleansing in the former Yugoslavia. I was told by the interviewee that most of the 'cleansing' was wrongly attributed to the Serbs by a powerful media who had taken sides with the Bosnian Muslims. The conversation about the media portrayal of ethnic cleansing continued for several minutes when, unexpectedly, one participant arose from their chair rushing to the front door where a .22 calibre rifle was leaning in an upright position against a wall. Within seconds, this person had left the house and was standing at the front of the house with rifle in hand pointing forwards - shooting. All those around the table sat in stunned silence. A family member with fixed motionless eyes told me in a monotone stern voice that he was 'going to shoot us all ... (name) is mad you know'.

I froze in my chair. I was no longer relaxed yet alert to believing that this was somehow true. I did not know what to do at that time. It was too fast and bizarre an event to put into a context of any sort other than one of fear. Internally I was feeling anxious. I could feel my heart rate beat faster and I felt that I wanted to leave. This progressed into a feeling of nausea. I believed that I was going to die.

It turned out that the participant had seen a number of galahs[16] swoop over his vegetable patch and that blank shots were being fired. It also turned out that my being told that we were going to be shot was a joke. Nevertheless, I still found it difficult to relax because, when the participant returned to the room, there was no hint from those present that the behaviour with the gun was strange or unusual. After an uncomfortable silence of approximately 2 minutes, I was told, 'you people think that we Serbs are all crazy. That's what the [world] media say about us all the time. That is what Clinton wants the world to think too. And the belief in our own hatred is just something the media want us to believe about ourselves'.

I immediately asked, why was that so, to be told that media manipulation of hatred was so much a part of this war. I was uneasy about this situation and thought it time to leave the field.

The purpose of spelling out the above anecdote is to demonstrate the nature of interpretive methodology as adaptive to the changing nature of the field.[17] Yet what Serbian Australians said they were experiencing was a feeling of stereotyping by world media that readily revealed itself as part of the local situation. The point being made here is that interviews on sensitive topics such as this one were anchored in both unpredictable fieldwork situations and events unfolding thousands of kilometres away from Australia.

To complement my observation and interview experiences, I undertook to keep a reflective journal. Making handwritten reflective journal entries occurred both in the same space as participants and without participants being present. Locations included quiet evenings at home, public and private transport (including water ferry and train travel), my place of paid employment, while watching and listening to the media, and during cultural celebrations. Viewed this way, van Manen (1990, p. 73) posits that writing as a method of inquiry is a means to make sense of fieldwork experiences and interpretations:

> .... making frequent journal records of insights gained, discerning patterns of work in progress, reflecting on previous reflections (and) for making the activities of research the topics of study.

The fieldwork journal was the place to record and reflect on my experiences, including personal feelings and involvements during research and writing. Insightful and intuitive moments were recorded and reflected upon, as was any emotion surrounding my personal comfort, such as anxiety, surprise or shock: anything of analytical and theoretical significance related to the research question and group under scrutiny (Olier, 1981; Patton, 1990). This was because, as suggested above by van Manen, it was not possible for me as researcher to suspend my feelings from the fieldwork. Personal and subjective responses did, like my physical being, enter into the relationships I engaged in during fieldwork.

My written notes and short 'think' papers provided a basis for the chapters in this study. This in turn helped me to reflect upon the fieldwork process and my contribution to the generation and interpretation of data. I found that this approach freed up the vision of hermeneutic ethnography whereby it was possible to situate writing during fieldwork as a 'means of knowing - a method of discovery and analysis' (Richardson, 1994, p. 516). I came to this approach with a view that, as researcher and interpreter, I am collaborator, partner and stakeholder in the literal creation and evaluation of data (Guba and Lincoln, 1989). Moreover, I found the benefits of disciplined writing to be a dynamic and creative means of giving historical meaning to the research process with Serbian Australians. Finally, writing as a method of data generation was an opportunity to explore and interpret the meanings of vast amounts of text and talk by the international community.

Non-directive interviewing, that is, the use of a casual conver-
sational style in asking questions and seeking out clarification from
participants also helped accommodate participant silences. A break in
talking about experiences was an opportunity for me to seek out
clarification, focus on key experiences and allow for breaks in
concentration and pauses in speech as necessary.

Conclusion

This chapter proceeded from the argument that the particular meanings and
interpretations Serbian Australians bring to the Balkan war and ethnic
groups involved in it, can only be understood in the context of the
geopolitics and historical relationships they hold with the homeland.
Embedded in these meanings is an indication of how some Serbian
Australians come to terms with the present. From this argument the idea
emerged whereby to generate data from participants I must inevitably
intersect - both directly and indirectly - with ongoing events in the Balkans
and Australia. These intersections were active elements in the data
generation process. I came to the realisation that the Serbian Australian
world was one in which interpretations of historical events are subject to
lively debate, re-association with history, as well as understandings
generated by the impact of Balkan war.

In the climate of ethnic cleansing, destruction of religious
monuments and death threats in Australia and the former Yugoslavia, such
as Grubisno Polje in Northern Bosnia (Miljkovic, 1995), there were global
impacting forces through which this study of Serbian Australians in local
situations was influenced.

The application of relevant nursing concepts and the critique of
conventional ethnography led me to interpret the interactive and inter-
subjective processes of data generation with participants. This discussion
looked in some detail at the way I interacted with and related to
participants during participant observation and interviewing, and how this
led to the way in which data was generated.

Clearly, my generating data in the shadow of the Balkan war
encouraged many research participants to both *see and feel* the destruction
of a homeland. As significant cultural and national events unfolded
thousands of kilometres away from Australia, those with an emotional
connection with the names, places and burial sites of a family homeland
had their lives suddenly catapulted into situations that fragmented and

recast everyday experience, and health in particular. Through my seeking out, responding to and respecting these situations, at the same time retaining interest in global-local elements of the study, the opportunities for data generation arose. The next chapter examines the framework through which this information was interpreted.

Notes

1   An article on this incident was later published in the September 1998 issue of the Australian and New Zealand Journal of Mental Health Nursing as 'Nursing Practice and Ethnography: A mental health nursing response to threatened violence in ethnographic fieldwork'.

2   Croatian Australians were also the subject of attacks against their ethnic community centres. In Sydney, the King Tomislav Club in Edensor Park has been the subject of frequent vandal attacks and in May 1993 the club employed a night security guard. In, Queensland, Croatian Catholic priest father Nikica Zlatunic found on August 3 1991, several bullet holes in a shield of Croatia's national symbol above the entrance to his church at Inala in Brisbane's west. Shots were also fired at Croatian community centres at Rocklea and Morningside.

3   Among the Serbian Orthodox people the word *Sluzba* (work, service, translation, N. P.) or *Sluzba Bozja* (God's work, or work of God, N. P.) is used to describe the work of God as liturgy (Bulich, 1985, p. 37).

4   In a subsequent interview I was told of a rumour that the decapitated head was later smuggled out of Australia and into Croatia.

5   A symbol adopted by the Nazi Party in Germany prior to and during the Second World War. It is formed by a cross with equal length arms, with all arms continued as far again at right angles clockwise.

6   A euphemism to describe the forced removal and often genocide of an entire ethnic population by another for the purpose of having one homogenous culture, language and religion in a designated region. It involves the purposeful destruction of significant cultural and social markers such as language, place names, burial sites, places of religious worship, cultural artefacts and monuments (Ahmed, 1995). The net effect of ethnic cleansing is the establishment of an unbroken line of racial and cultural purity and continuity thus ending social life that is borne out of a mixed racial and religious community.

7   Hill (1996) writing in the *Phoenix Gazette* describes vandalism and anti-Serbian slogans with linkages to Second World War Yugoslavia being placed on the St Sava Church in that city. Miljkovich (1995) reports on a near identical incident to this one occurring in Adelaide. On July 19 1991 in Grubisno Polje, Northern Bosnia the Serbian Orthodox church had its walls daubed with graffiti that included 'Death to the Serbs' ('Smrt Srbima').

8   The exact number of civilians to perish at Jasenovac has been disputed by several writers and historians. Magas (1993) cites figures substantially less, around 48,000; Paris (1961) around 700, 000 and Glenny (1992) reports the (combined) number of Serbs, Jews, Gipsies and members of the Croatian opposition at about 200, 000. A more recent figure as cited by the Serbian Orthodox Church Holy Synod of Bishops (1995) and made up of Serbian men, women and children is 356, 000. Whatever

the real tragedy of Jasenovac, the symbolic memory of it remains in the foreground of Serbians both inside and outside former Yugoslavia.

9   The original meaning of the word *Ustasa* was a participant in an uprising. In the uprisings against the Turks in the 19th century the word was used by both Serbs and Croats. Later in the 1930s and during the Second World War in particular, the word Ustasa was used to designate a member of the Croatian regime led by Ante Pavelic committed to fascist beliefs that saw political violence and terrorism as the only way to preserve and protect national ideologies and interests. See, for example, Djilas (1991).

10   I use this term with the view that the philosophical hermeneutics of Hans-George Gadamer (to be discussed in the next chapter) speaks to human consciousness and perception as not being subject to the Cartesian subject/object split. I am in the world with and of study participants and it is my involvements with this world that brings me to realise that both participants and I are self-interpreting beings.

11   I use the term *little world* as a shorthand phrase to describe the present locale of Adelaide, South Australia, as the local world in which Serbian Australians live and work, yet still remain part of the larger world, the world in which Balkan conflict is communicated, in a lively way.

12   Compare with Spradley's (1980) arguments that cultural understanding and truth is best elicited through systematic and carefully structured moves and method.

13   Compare with Thompson's (1985) study of the Hell's Angels Motorcycle Gang, where once the ethnographer had established trust within the group he was badly bashed as the research was coming to a close.

14   See Clifford (1983).

15   David Karp (1996) is also concerned with this issue in his ethnography of depressed people living in the United States. He tries to illuminate the lived experiences of depression by encouraging sufferers (participants) to speak about their personal and emotional experience of the illness.

16   A rose-breasted grey backed native Australian bird.

17   It should be made clear that I am not suggesting that Serbian Australians are armed and waiting to harm or kill the keen researcher.

3 On Interpretation During the Journey

Introduction

This chapter explains the way in which I 'made' my interpretations of participants. By giving an explicit and detailed explanation of how I arrived at particular interpretations, I hope to render a more credible account of the Serbian Australian experience. In the drive for understanding, I have paid particular attention to explaining the prejudices I hold in making meaning out of the data generated.

My preparedness to consider the issues surrounding interpretation, while developing knowledge during my fieldwork, integrates selective aspects of Gadamer's (1975) philosophical hermeneutics and contemporary ethnography as activity undertaken in the context of a researcher-participant relationship. This means that I have embraced an interpretation of 'all that is Serbian', and 'all that is the Balkan war' as constituting part of my analysis. In this study, my own self has not been subject to detachment from the field of study. As Denzin (1994) points out, what is brought to the research relationship is implicated in every observation and interpretation. Instead of viewing myself as a contaminating bias, it is far more beneficial to be 'up front' about being present in the text that makes up the remaining chapters of this study. It will be through the detailing of how I made my interpretations that the veracity of my discussion can be critically examined.

Verica and the Sarajevo market place bombing

To illustrate the practice of interpretation of participants, I refer below to an extract of an interview undertaken in English with Verica, a 19 year old Serbian Australian with family in Sarajevo. In this interview Verica (V) begins by telling me (N) of her experience of watching television news, particularly in relation to an incident in which 68 civilians were killed and more than 200 injured when a single mortar round exploded in Sarajevo's main open market. Smashed and broken tables and chairs, a severed head and several limbs ripped from bodies by the bomb scattered the area. First-hand electronic and print media reports of the tragedy included police and rescuers weeping and vomiting amid the carnage as they frantically searched for survivors. The bombing massacre, which made headline news around the globe, was believed to have been perpetrated by Bosnian Serb forces stationed around Sarajevo. Several weeks later however, a UN led investigation revealed that forces other than Serbian were most likely responsible.[1] I have numbered the transcript (1-50) to facilitate discussion in the next section:

1   V: And another thing that is sad is that people lie so much. The
2   first horrible thing about war is that people are killing each other and
3   then lying about the killing. Those incidents about the market
4   bombing in Sarajevo, I mean it was all done by the other side and
5   Serbs are accused for it. You could see the day after the incident the
6   front cover of the Times, it's like the Serbs shot 50 people in Sarajevo,
7   bla, bla, bla, bla, and a few weeks later when they found out later who
8   actually did it, there was nothing in the newspapers, or somewhere
9   just a little paragraph, small at the bottom of the page so no one could
10 read about that. That really upsets me.

11 N: Can you tell me more about why that upsets you?

12 V: Because I can't understand that there are so many people who
13 don't try to find themselves who are the people who begun the war,
14 who are the aggressors, whose land is that. I'm angry because it
15 seems to me that people are not thinking with their brain, just
16 believe what they hear or read in the mass media. And the people
17 are not even trying to understand that it is our land. They can just
18 go to the library, take a history book and read that land is in title of
19 the Serbs since the 6th Century, I mean it's so easy to go to the library
20 and read something, that's what I feel angry about. What we see is
21 an insult to Serbian culture and Serbian history. It really upsets me,
22 it's really sad.

23 N: Can you tell me how all this makes you feel inside?

24 V: When I see this on TV or think about it, I get really sad, it
25 makes me go to the kitchen and pig out. I eat and eat a lot of fat
26 stuff. It's like I have a stone in my heart *(points to her heart)* and it
27 won't move until the world figures out the real truth. Every time
28 the news says something that's not true I feel that there is one
29 pound more on the stone in my heart *(forms a tight fist over the*

30 *heart and presses this against her chest wall, slightly to the left of the*
31 *sternum).* I really feel like crying, I feel like a pressure inside my
32 head, I feel my head is banging and sometimes I can't sleep at night
33 and I have nightmares and it's really upsetting.
34 N: Do you feel OK telling me about your nightmares?

35 V: Yes. Once I dreamt that I am on this ship with all these people,
36 I mean, I didn't know what they are. I just knew that they are
37 against me and I was in a prison on the ship and trying to get out.
38 They are running after me, it's really upsetting. I woke up all in
39 sweat. I was glad I woke up.

40 N: What did you do to try and cope with that situation?

41 V: I try to talk to someone who wouldn't contradict me, I want to
42 tell someone what's happening, the real truth in Yugoslavia. I know
43 that there are now many Serbian families in Yugoslavia, and I feel
44 that it is important for them to survive. If the truth is not heard in
45 the world I think they're all going to die.

46 N: So it sounds to me that although the war is happening 'over
47 there', you feel it very much 'here' *(pointing to my heart)*, and all
48 of these feelings are related to the Serbian history and Serbian lands
49 of the former Yugoslavia.

50 V: Yeah, that's right, bodily I'm here but mentally I'm over there.

This interview reveals a number of moves, through which I went about interpreting this participant's story. In trying to interpret relationships between the media, events in the former Yugoslavia and Australia, and the impact this had on her health, Verica told me of her 'anger' (lines 4-16); her 'sadness' (20-22 and 30-33); and, her 'pigging out on fat stuff' (24-26). All of this took place amid the frustration of her life, as the majority of world opinion was at odds with the Serbian point of view about the war. By drawing attention to these sections of conversation and selecting particular quotes, I can show the interpretive connections I made between the development of health issues and problems of living for Serbian Australians. And it is this linkage between the situations described by participants and my interpretation of them that encapsulates the way this research was made.

In drawing from the interview with Verica, two additional points help explain the approach I took with interpretation. *Firstly* the works of Denzin (1994), a symbolic interactionalist, and Gadamer (1975), a hermeneutic philosopher, were selectively integrated in a framework to create interpretation. This will be explained shortly.

Secondly, as I made my interpretation, I reached an understanding that was largely informed by the health interests brought to the research. This means that, in trying to reach understanding through conversation with Verica, I was applying the pre-supposition that the health and wellbeing of Serbian Australians was under pressure from events unfolding in the Balkans. I brought to interview the belief that Verica's feelings were caught up in her struggle to cope with the war. When I entered into conversation with her, I did so in part as a mental health professional with pre-judgements and personal understandings about the field of study that simultaneously interacted with the present and thus led me to further questions and conversation. My critical interrogation of this situation led me to questions about the human stress and emotional discomfort experienced by participants. It was through this process of interpretation and re-interpretation that I discerned the Serbian Australian experience.

Philosophical hermeneutics

The basis for the framework of interpretation described above was informed by philosophical hermeneutics in the Gadamerian tradition. The hallmark of Gadamer's approach to interpretation is explicated as *philosophical hermeneutics* in his magnum opus *Truth and Method* (1975). Hermeneutics emphasises the importance of language, and the way it is used to give and receive communications throughout time. That is, the activity of making interpretations through language is the very act of human understanding throughout life.

Mendelson (1979) and Healy (1996) suggest that Gadamer's main concern was not to provide or defend a particular methodology of social science, but 'to describe what is occurring in understanding' (Mendelson, 1979, p. 53). However, as Habermas (1994) has pointed out, Gadamer's interpretation of language use must be alert to the possibility of statements reflecting critical and social structures that lie behind subjective taken-for-granted meanings in understanding.

In applying philosophical hermeneutics to help me discern the Serbian Australian experience, I extracted a number of themes from Gadamer's work to help describe how my interpretation of participants was generated. Most notable of these themes - by no means a comprehensive summary of philosophical hermeneutics - were 'effective history' and 'fusion of horizons'. While these themes do not exhaust the ways in which Gadamer's hermeneutics might be applied or deployed in health research, they became an important means by which my study was influenced. As I move through each theme I will endeavour to show, from the segment of interview with Verica, how they guided my interpretation of the Serbian Australian experience.

Effective history

Effective history, writes Gadamer (1975, p. 302), 'arises from what is historically pregiven. It underlies all subjective intentions and actions, and hence both prescribes and limits every possibility for understanding any tradition whatsoever in its historical alterity'. The effective history of this research involves both participants and researcher, as I will explain.

In my interview with Verica, I projected into the interpretation certain judgements, understandings and pre-suppositions both in interaction with her, and stemming from my background as a mental health professional.[2] Because nursing is primarily a practice discipline built on helping others to heal, it is my 'vocation' to 'manage' people's health needs through a 'nurse-patient' interaction. In this instance, the practice of nursing is understood, in a sense, close to Benner's (1994a and 1994b) standpoint. Patricia Benner points out that nurses do much more than care for the sick, or deal with pathophysiology and underlying disease. Nurses are also concerned with normality and abnormality, and the lived social and skilled body, in understanding and promoting health and development in caring for people.

The difficulty with a nursing influence in my own background was that, at times, I found myself wanting to help and support participants in better coping with problems of living brought on by the war. This can be seen during the interview transcript (lines 29-33 in particular). In my interview with Verica, I asked her to 'ventilate' aspects of how news of the Sarajevo market place bombing had impacted on her mental and physical health. In the role of a mental health nurse, I would normally undertake this task anyway, albeit with less concern for references to Serbian history and ethnic ownership of land in Bosnia-Herzegovina than I took in the role of researcher.

Because of the problem of pre-given judgements and pre-suppositions on the part of both participant and researcher, propositions require careful reflection and scrutiny of the historical traditions brought to them. Hence, I had to scrutinize both the interpretations that participants like Verica made, and my own interpretations of what they were saying.

My approach was to interpret what participants said, thought, felt and did in the shadow of the conflict, without being separated from my own effective history as a health professional. I sought not to withhold or suppress my own effective history as self-knowledge in data generation.[3] I tried to avoid the use of cognitive mechanisms to 'block out' the experiences and points of view I brought to or had during interpretation. Rather, the qualities I brought to interpretation were made up of what I saw and experienced prior to and during the research and, therefore, they constituted a key element in what I put to work in interpretation.

In summary, my use of 'effective history' caused me to engage in conscious use of my personal nursing knowledge and practice as well as my understandings developed within and beyond the field.

Fusion of horizons

Gadamer (1975, p. 302) defines the concept of horizon as 'the range of vision that includes everything that can be seen from a particular vantage point'. The implications of horizon when viewed within the notion of prejudice means that 'to have a horizon means not being limited to what is nearby but being able to see beyond it' (p. 302).

Since both researcher and respondent are implicated in prejudice, Gadamer sees the merging of their particular points of view as creating a fusion of ideas. This means that understanding Serbian Australians could be seen as a coming together of my own past experience and historical understandings with the research question and individual under scrutiny. All of this is undertaken so that the unit of treatment and analysis of data is through what Gadamer (1975, p. 306-7) calls 'fusion of horizons (*Horizontverschmelzung*) between past and present that meet in the particular present'.

The mechanism used to interpret these experiences is use of my worldview and historical consciousness (ie: pre-knowledge, beliefs, ideas and attitudes toward Serbian Australians and Balkan conflict) to constitute a pre-understanding or prejudice about the experience of the respondents. A hermeneutically trained historical consciousness means that we remain open to the meaning of another person, text or experience, with an openness that 'always includes our situation the meaning in relation to the whole of our own meanings or ourselves in relation to it' (Gadamer, 1975, p. 268). The problem I had with Gadamer's notion of fusion of horizons in relation to the interview with Verica, was that it could have led me to over-emphasise theoretical rationalisations of the personal journey attached to her experience, at the expense of practical outcomes of understanding the Serbian Australian experience. There was, as Marcus (1994) puts it, a danger of becoming intoxicated with the personal, or the 'narcissistic I'. At the same time, there was risk of engaging in a 'romantic rationalisation' of what Habermas (1994, p. 140) describes as the 'interpretation of social interest situations, horizons of aspiration and [uncomplicated] expectation'. Such a condition of interpretation runs the risk of being blindly uncritical.

In an attempt to address these potential flaws, I returned to the discourse of contemporary ethnography for guidance. Interpretive understanding, Marcus (1995, p. 109) suggests, 'arises not from monologist authority or voice, however self-critical, but from dialogic relationships in the field'. Marcus (1994, p. 509), in an earlier work discusses the means of making research something of a collaborative project. This opens up the possibility of contributing to interpretation by being critical as well as reflexive about the way in which the voices of participants and researcher can blend. The outcome is reflection of my voice as researcher and the incorporation of other voices and influences during simultaneous inquiry of local and global realities. This means that the researcher's role extends beyond the traditional ethnographic function of describing and classifying the 'exotic other'.

Issues of credibility of interpretation

So far in this chapter I have outlined the interpretive strategies of the study. The important issue to be resolved now is what makes the content of this study credible.

Alexander (1995) examined the problem of what constitutes evidence in the social sciences by critically employing Rorty's (1979) attack on objectivity. This challenge, simply put, is that universal knowledge and mechanistic cause-and-effect knowledge in the social sciences does not exist. The important point here in relation to this study, is that the interpretive statements I have made about the situations that both participants and I describe, and the individual perspective we take during interview, are being accounted for. This means that, in stating what participants such as Verica are saying to me, as well as making other

Selectively

observational statements about being Serbian Australian in a global epoch, I am able to bring the empirical data into full view of the reader.

Despite the abundance of detail pertaining to interpretation, it was not possible to generalise my research findings to all Serbian Australians, for the following reasons. *Firstly,* as previously indicated, I did not seek to claim an overall single homogenous horizon by which all Serbian Australians live in their world. *Secondly,* interpretation using philosophical hermeneutics is an open, changing, and dialectical process made more complex by the context of global understandings. This means that the research was time-bound by the life and social conditions that prevailed during the Balkan war.

Philosophical hermeneutics encouraged me to listen, and to tune in to all that caught my ear, my eye, (my senses, really), throughout the journey. My inclusion of statements about the situations Serbian Australians describe, by those who describe them, brings the data under scrutiny in comparison with what I present as personal experiences, expectations and analysis. Once this occurs, it is then possible for others to judge how and why I generated particular interpretations about Serbian Australians and how the veracity of my claims are represented.

Conclusion

In this chapter, I have explained how I interpreted the materials generated during fieldwork, and how I later constructed this interpretation into the chapters that make up this book. While neutrality and objectivity were neither possible nor desirable in this research, my use of philosophical hermeneutics has helped to reveal my underlying intentions leading to interpretation. As a researcher and writer I have discerned information from the words of those interviewed and observed, as well as from my own interpretations shaped by personal narrative, context, cultural and stylistic conventions.

Notes

floating biases

1   The television scenes of civilians cut to pieces by mortar explosions was something that horrified international public opinion and it is for this reason that such atrocities were carried out as staged attacks in the hope of dramatising the strategic needs of individual ethnic groups (Doyle, 1992a and 1992b; Handke, 1997).

2   I also use Gadamer's notion of 'effective history' in chapter 7 to think about the development of practical and theoretical strategies for working in health and helping

relationships with Serbian Australians. While this study is written as a hermeneutic ethnography, I have been able to combine interpretation with my professional nursing background in the context of global events.

3   Compare with Spradley (1980, p. 145) who argues that interviewing and participant observation are best done by 'cutting oneself off from other interests and concerns and allowing oneself to be taken over by the new culture for insights to emerge'.

4 'We Serbs are Obsessed with Maps': The Experience of Boundaries

Just think about the Socceroos. They are multicultural Australian. I'll never forget the time Ned Zelic scored this amazing goal. When he made the run of glory the first guy to kiss him was the Serb from the Australian soccer team. I thought it was great because on the soccer team they are all fighting for the same cause. But if these guys represented Serbia or Croatia, it would be a completely different story (Peter, an 18 year old Serbian Australian).

'Politics killed my marriage' says Slavica Potrebic, a Croat. 'If my husband lives, and if I live, I'll divorce him. There is no chance for reconciliation now. He is Serbian Orthodox and I am Catholic ...I think the army is just Serbian and will kill us all ...Don't go over to the other side [of the river]. The chetniks (Serb Guerrillas) will cut your throat' (Meares, 1991, p. 12).

Introduction

Consistent with other conflicts in Europe taking place at the same time as this one in the Balkans, the warring factions were preoccupied with the shape of borders between lands. For the former Yugoslav republics of Croatia, Slovenia and Bosnia Herzegovina, this meant that cultural and geographical borders and boundaries in the former Yugoslavia were being re-negotiated, roughly along ethnic lines. This chapter examines the impact of this reality on Serbian Australians. It develops the central idea that the Balkan war caused people to re-evaluate how they constructed themselves and others, and examines what all of this did to relations between the individuals concerned.

The fundamental purpose of this chapter is to prepare the way for further discussion of health and cultural issues in the remainder of the study. I do this by interpreting events surrounding newly defined maps and borders such as those in the former Yugoslavia, and aligning them with a similar process operating in Australia. That is, as Croatians,

Muslims and Serbians in the former Yugoslavia, and the governments that controlled them, were carving up land, possessions and families in the Balkans, roughly along ethnic lines, people from the region living in Australia were breaking away from each other and similarly forming new relationships. Through this interpretation, this chapter draws attention to the interpersonal aspects of being Serbian Australian, and the way in which individuals impose meanings and construct social and cultural boundaries that separate them from specific others.

As I have said, throughout this journey I needed to cross many boundaries; enter homes, generate trust, learn a new language and perform numerous cultural and religious rituals with Serbian Australians; these endeavours are reflected in the contents of this chapter. The important point to be drawn from this is that as I needed to encounter and cross intersubjective boundaries in order to explore cultural and racial boundaries, the methodological accounts of my doing so was a means through which to yield findings. This methodological situation is aligned with what Giddens (1996, pp. 75-77) calls a 'double-hermeneutic'; a process where social scientists must inevitably be alert to the transformative effects that their research methods and methodology might have upon what it is they set out to analyse. This will now be explained in relation to the title of this chapter.

The chapter title was formulated after a clandestine meeting with two Serbian Australian men in an inner-city bus shelter cafeteria. The meeting was initiated by one of the men who was wanting demographic material about the suburban dispersal of people from the former Yugoslavia now living in Adelaide. I had a colour map of this material and, in exchange for it, the men assured me that they would do everything they could to help me with my research. In particular, they were willing to inform potential interviewees on my behalf about my work. As soon as I produced the colour maps, one of the men present drew himself as close as possible to the document that lay before him saying 'we Serbs are obsessed with maps'. This classic statement was the interpretive beginning of the formulations that follow in this chapter.

With the methodological processes described in chapter 2 beginning to yield findings, it became possible to experience, even indirectly, something of what it meant to be a Serbian Australian and what was perceived to be sacred about it. The more I learnt about all that was perceived to be sacred by Serbians, the more conscious I became of the social, cultural and personal boundaries I needed to cross as well as boundaries I should not cross. The fascinating issue for me at this point of the research was that the more Serbian Australians allowed and facilitated research into their life, the more I seemed to be simultaneously crossing some and avoiding other boundaries. The transformative effects of a double hermeneutic was the way in which I simultaneously generated and interpreted information from this process. The double hermeneutic was both theoretically interesting and practically significant because it told me something about how people involved in the research were feeling and reacting to myself and others.

Formulation and consideration of these boundary processes sets the scene for the *next* chapter, where I am concerned with issues of bonding, belonging, national and cultural identity. Before examining 'sense of belonging' as an indispensable mental health concept (chapter 5), several background considerations concerning the way I interpreted the people who constructed relationships with others will be considered.

Creating boundaries

In the local context, consideration of boundaries begins with my reflections on two significant issues: my physical access to the Serbian Orthodox churches and community clubs in Adelaide, and my being married to a women with ancestral linkages to the former Yugoslavia. Access to the Serbian community centres, churches and clubs was by personal invitation only. One of the main facilitators of my access was Drago, an 88 year old Serbian Australian who knew me and the work that I was trying to do. His support for the research led him to facilitate new individual contacts that enabled me to forge new networks into the community.

Dragos' help proved vital, as the increasing frequency of vandal attacks and death threats daubed on church and community buildings had caused Serbians to become greatly suspicious of non-Serbians who entered church property. From the individuals who were distressed by the 'Ustashe' raid on their church, for example, I sensed that they felt as if a violent force had resurrected itself from more than fifty years ago to enact destruction and fear in the 1990s. As events in the Balkans moved toward further destruction, the historical connections of a World War 2 Croatian Nazi party had its meaning brought to life in Australia. The upsetting reminders of the Second World War (ie: Swastikas and concentration camp symbols of genocide), evoked memories of that era as well as contemporary events. These symbols signified violence and the destruction of human lives in the past and offered an intense threat to personal safety 'in the present'. Giddens (1996, p. 237-8), in his discussion of ethnic violence in an era of nationalist sentiment, warns that there are a limited number of ways in which potential inter-ethnic clashes can be dealt with or avoided:

> One is through geographical segregation; individuals of conflicting dispositions, or cultures hostile to one another, can of course coexist if they have little or no direct contact. Another, more active, way is through exit. An individual who, or group which, does not get along with another can simply disengage or move away, as might happen in a divorce. ...In a globalising society in which we now live this option becomes drastically reduced. No culture, state or large group can with much success isolate itself from the global cosmopolitan order ...while exit may be possible for some individuals, it is not available for larger social entities.

The church community, as a social group, unable to 'exit' yet angry and untrusting of the wider world following the violent attacks on their church, had sought to protect itself by erecting a three-metre iron fence with sharp spikes around the church and two community halls. This meant that the group had sought to disengage from all social life surrounding it, with the aim of keeping these buildings and the people who worship in them well beyond personal reach.[1] Clearly, this fence and the way it was designed was a physical boundary between Serbians and non-Serbians. In my view, this fence represented the physical manipulation of material conditions that had been altered to reduce further violence against the Serbians. This means that it was the Serbians' intention to try and prevent people from destroying what was sacred to them.

Consideration of boundaries in the research context is extended by the fact that my wife has ancestral linkages to the former Yugoslavia. This was of assistance to the research in two ways. *Firstly*, notwithstanding my wife's non-involvement in the research, this connection enabled me greater access to the community overall than I imagine would have been normally expected by a non-Serbian researcher in my situation. It was then up to myself to become involved in the social lives of participants. *Secondly*, I believed that my wife's being known by some Serbian Australians helped to generate trust with the study participants. This connection helped to generate a belief by participants in the work that I was trying to do.

It was understood by both myself and my wife that throughout the research she would have no contact with the people being interviewed. We discussed this at length and agreed between ourselves that participants would not be interviewed at our home.   Wherever possible, all appointments would be scheduled through my work office and all correspondence relating to the research were despatched from my university. I had, in effect, created certain boundaries and conditions on this research that guided the way it was done as well as defining the context in which data was generated and interpreted.

Despite my wanting to keep clear boundaries between myself and the people involved, the Serbian Australians I interviewed often wanted me to come to their house. Some wanted me to bring my wife along to the next interview, or even for a meal with the entire family. My experience here bears strong similarity to that of Deborah Padgett (1989) who, as a social researcher of Serbian American settlement and employment patterns in the 1980s, interviewed participants at church and in their homes, and was part of an almost constant round of activities and invitations of support and continued social interaction, as a statement of gratitude from Serbians in support of what they believed to be a worthy cause.

But this wanting to see more of me and what I was doing also included wanting to come and see me in my house. I saw this as a reasonable means to 'check me out'. That is, to check out my 'map' of them and the way that I was using certain information generated as part of the research process. By checking out my 'map' this way, gatekeepers could see how participants were being 'used' by me in the research. The knowledge people gained about the way information gleaned from them could be used was something that found its way into conversations with other potential interviewees. So in order to check me out, and the people who were potential interviewees, there was a constant attempt by some to observe me closely.

This process of watching my moves introduced another important issue: Could I be trusted not to do anything that might 'hurt' the Serbians an/or the Serbian culture? As Marija told me during interview:

> Good on you for doing this research. I'd like to see other people taking an interest in our community, in our nationality. The fact that you are married to a woman with family over there is a different thing altogether, because, I mean, the reasons why you got together are your business, you know. But I think that people will start to listen to you and start to hear our point of view through you.

This quotation draws attention to the inter-subjective and inter-pretive aspects of being Serbian Australian and the way individuals create meanings through their construction of boundaries with others. This point will now be pursued in the first instance with respect to the interplay between myself and the Serbian National Federation of Australia.

The mapping of me: on being watched

The effect of the war in violating the personal and geographical space and trust that participants have previously shared with others over the past centuries, is requisite to the conceptual argument of this chapter. The significance of what people have done to others in war zones and in the shadow of the war in Australia, is intricately connected to everyday life issues of participants and the research process. With respect to the latter, this included the process of becoming aroused by and later involved in the lives of Serbian Australians, in such a way that I was able to constantly revise my position as a researcher poised to generate and interpret data. This means that the access to, and withdrawal from, participants was related to the way in which my proximity to them had been constructed. The proximity I had to Serbian Australians was itself relative to the way in which we related to each other.[2]

My introduction to Serbian Australian networks in Adelaide was largely through groups of people previously not known to me. There was, however, one key feature of this network that remained central to the research participants. That was, as will be identified in subsequent chapters, that many of the people I met along the way were associated, to a greater or lesser extent, with the Serbian National Federation of Australia. Certain members of the Federation were active throughout the research process as both facilitators and gatekeepers of my movements. In working with them, I found that they would provide many valuable insights, networks and sources of information, including documents that related to Serbian activity in Australia as well as a range of potential participants.

With such a powerful nationalist group in command in Australia, it was absolutely essential that I become familiar with them in the research. Establishing networks with people from this organisation was useful as I always found them very supportive and interested in the research. Within days of setting off on the research process, several members of the South Australian Branch of the Federation became involved in the work that I was doing.

After a brief introduction to Serbian National Federation members in Sydney, I was networked with members in Adelaide. Ratko spoke to me by telephone of his concern that I may end up labelling participants as 'unstable':

> Well, what do you think of our people? I hope that you won't be saying that they are all on Valium, or something. I'll give you some names, set up some people, who might be OK to handle your asking questions about things.

Three members of Federation were introduced (assigned, really) to me. Despite this I never felt that the Federation wanted to control my work. Instead, they were careful to inform me that my moving about the Serbian community would need to be a delicate and sensitive process. I was also told that there were many Serbian Australians who had been deeply hurt and upset by the treatment they had been given by the Australian government and international media. I believed that the Federation were sensitive to this issue and saw themselves as guardians against any actions by me that may emotionally upset participants. Below is an extract from my fieldwork journal that speaks to this issue:

> It is apparent that some Serbs, the Serbian National Federation in particular, want to control my work for their own interests. And why not? After all, I should be watched carefully. It seems to me that they don't want things to get away from them. It now seems to me that to get access to Serbs I must be really clear about what it is I am doing. It seems to me that I must be prepared to be interviewed by the Federation about who I am and how I am developing this research project. On the one hand this feels very controlling and difficult for me. Yet, if I begin to write about this experience, understand it and work out what it means, what it tells me about this group, then I am well positioned to interpret their point of view. I always feel that they are keeping a close eye on me. They seem very keen to see some examples of my work whenever possible.

By reflecting upon this situation, I was able to draw out the ethnographic process so that I could see what has influenced the course of theoretical and practical aspects of the research journey. With this point of view slowly developing in the research process, I could enter into interview and participant observation activity in a more informed way. The critical issues at play in this situation came several months later. Once again, I wrote in my fieldwork journal:

> I think that there are two issues operating in the relationships I have developed with the Serbian National Federation. I have always felt that

they are keen to see my research progress. People are working hard to help me establish contact and network with participants. At the same time, they are keen to see my map, my construction of this group. The group are very keen to see how I decide the boundary markers between the issues of long distance devastation and sense of belonging in relation to the conflict. That is, the kind of sketch I make of the group. Put another way, there is a map that I am currently drawing, inclusive of boundaries and they want to know what the boundary of my work looks like. They have an obligation to preserve and protect their map of their selves.

As I moved through the research journey I found that there was a trade-like practice or exchange emerging between us. Zorica, a 36 year old participant, 'explained' what was happening:

This is about them [Serbian National Federation] wanting to help you, but only on their terms. They will always have a rope around your legs, they will let you walk as long as they know exactly where you're walking to, and what for. It's not because of you, you have a good reputation, don't let that get damaged. It's because in this conflict they think there are always enemies. You've got to realise that [to them] there is always someone close enough to you, who is able to get you.

On several occasions I would trade information with participants to get closer to the people that fascinated me. The exchange would be in the form of data (eg photographs of property damage). Of particular importance to participants were humanitarian aid documents from the United Nations High Commissioner for Refugees or the International Red Cross.

The important point here was that there was a trade between Serbian Australians regarding what was valued in the researcher-participant exchange. The strategic exchange of information helped our respective situations. Trade had developed between myself and Serbian National Federation in the form of photographs of property damage and census data information about others from the former Yugoslavia living in Australia. On one particular evening I did not return home after a dinner meeting with people involved in the research until after 4.00 am. I recall this dinner very well as afterwards I offered to help pay for it. I was told in a forceful way, 'No way! It's a Serbian custom you know. We must pay for the meal'. It was shortly before 3.00 am that I was finally awarded the names of seven potential interviewees.

When I received these names I knew from this moment onwards that the success of the research was dependent upon not only getting access to the participants but, more importantly, *how I situated myself in Serbian Australian territory.* That is, like a foreigner walking into a land inhabited by another ethnic group, it was up to me to work out from the reactions of others how and where I should tread. It was my responsibility to work out the borderlands that I must cross. Before I could get freely down to data generation, it was my responsibility to get relationships worked out with all concerned.

I decided that the most appropriate way possible to do this was to remind participants that I wanted to remain involved in all discussions about access and consultation with various groups. I told participants that I wanted to contribute something positive to the way Serbian Australian life in the shadow of the conflict had been interpreted. I was also wanting to move the process of finding people who would be willing to speak with me according to the participants' timetable rather than my own. Zorica saw this as a means to generate an indirect form of control, at the same time warning of a potential breakdown in the work I was doing:

> I think that what you've got [from them] is an indirect form of control. Superficially, it's all nice, but if you did them wrong, said something bad about them, *if you crossed the line, they would react quickly and strongly. It's a fine line. You would not get a second chance.* (emphasis added, N.P.)

At this point it became clear that the 'fine line' I was walking was an unavoidable aspect of the research process. As part of the decision to interpret this process, I accompanied a group of study participants to the Serbian soccer ground. At the soccer ground I was told by Zorica what she and others believed to be my place in this small piece of Serbian society: 'Try to be a person who was going to listen to us without judging us as right or wrong, good or evil'. In the next section I describe how the sport of soccer became an important reference point for interpreting the situations of participants.

Soccer boundaries

At the time I interviewed Peter, whose words open this chapter, the Australian soccer team (Socceroos) had been playing very well on the international football circuit. The Australians had won a series of games against teams from Asia and North Africa. Peter (aged 18) described the

Socceroos football team as 'the greatest team in the world', because there were so many ethnically different guys playing for one nation:

> If we put the ethnic identity of some players aside, for the sake of the team, then it's no problem. But if you get them into different team colours then that's a problem. You [Nicholas] should start to get into it [soccer], look at the [ethnic] names of the players if you want to know what I am talking about.

Peter continued to make his point about player names with ancestral links to former Yugoslavia by telling me that before the war he had never thought of individual players in terms of their ethnicity. Now the situation was different. Linkages had been made between the ethnic identity of Socceroo players and the warring factions in former Yugoslavia.

Before my interview with Peter, I had not been all that interested in soccer. Australian Rules Football had dominated in my household as a child growing up. With this kind of upbringing I had tended to view soccer as sport with British origins, originating in the period after Australia's large scale, post second world war immigration program.[3] But after hearing the words Peter spoke, and the way his point of view was framed and informed by both his love of the game and events in the Balkans, encouraged me to think more broadly about this aspect of the Serbian Australian experience; in particular, how Serbian Australians caught up in the war were somehow able to 'put to one side' their feelings and sentiment towards others in relation to ethnic difference. And so it was at this point that I began to consider the 'ethnic identity' of people who were part of the soccer team. Peter continued to tell me about talking to Croatian people at high school:

> At my high school I had a couple of Croatian guys that I used to talk to and we'd be speaking like 'Yugoslav' language together, Serbo-Croatian, or whatever. One time the Croatian guy offered to buy me a drink after a school soccer game when I scored a goal; it was similar to what I saw with the Ned Zelic thing. But I didn't want the drink because of the groups that I was moving in. If I was not with the others I probably would have had a drink. The other thing was that we had these Australians come up to us in the schoolyard and telling us off, they said to us, 'Oh hang on a minute, you guys shouldn't even be hanging out with each other, you know'.

This quote represents two important dimensions in social relationships between Serbian Australians and others with ancestral linkages to the region.   *Firstly,* this is a graphic example of a relationship that is conditional on not being developed beyond that of a soccer acquaintance. This was demonstrated by the Croatian guy having almost befriended Peter through membership to the school soccer team. As with the example of the Australian national team, it seemed as if Peter's acceptance of certain players was despite the bad feelings he had toward the nations that he believed they 'truly belonged to'. Nations that he knew 'deep inside were trying to destroy the historical and national identity of his parents' homeland'.

Secondly, as I have said, at the time of my journey, the prevailing world view was that Serbia and Serbians were the aggressors in this war, and *every* Serbian Australian known to me was deeply upset by this. For Croatian Australians (and others) the electronic and print media were perceived as an authoritative means to bring Serbians to account for this aggression. Elsewhere, nightly news stories of war from the region were being used to substantiate their claims. Despite a growing condemnation of Serbians by others from the former Yugoslavia living in Australia, the analysis by Peter shows that for the sake of a successful soccer team it was important to put all of this to one side.

This situation is similar to ethnographic research by Trlin and Tolic (1997) with New Zealanders' of Croatian origin, undertaken at about the same time as the present study. The New Zealand research revealed that some individuals and families reported instances of avoidance behaviour among old friends or relatives, through inter-marriage of Dalmatian and Yugoslav identity. In making this point, one participant in the Trlin and Tolic (1995, p. 237) study reported:

> You might see them in the street or [at] funerals or anywhere. A lot of them might say something when you talk to them but you can see them trying to walk away from it. They don't even want to talk.

In this situation there was a general rule of not discussing politics. For some Croatian New Zealanders, this may mean crossing the street to avoid a meeting, sidelong glances to avoid eye contact, the snub of a turned back or perhaps even refusing to shake hands. In this situation, there was a need to develop a strategic non-confrontational style of communication that in itself would be manifest situationally.

Aligned with the New Zealand situation was an uneasiness between groups in Australia. Peter, for example, was keen to build a partition around certain issues and feelings associated with his ethnic origin. It was at this time that his church was desecrated (chapter 2), his friend was bashed by a gang of Croatian youths and his sister verbally abused and spat on at a local soccer match. To my mind, this situation (and others elsewhere in this chapter) called for extensive interpretation and consideration of the issues and ambiguities inherent in it. Moreover, as I moved in interview with Peter, I came to the realisation that in certain situations, limitations and boundaries[4] arising from ethnic identity may be overlooked. While on the one hand it was a great moment in Australian soccer to see two players with ancestral links to ethnic groups currently at war come together as one united team with one common goal (to win the game), there were other situations described by Serbian Australians, including Peter, where it was essential they keep a good distance from others with ethnic links to the Balkans. And it was this interpretation that I took along with me when I went to interview Marija and Djordje in their home the following day.

Negotiating boundaries and borders of difference in Australia

I arrived at Marija and Djordje's house as arranged to be greeted by table full of food and drink. Slivovica, burek (meat pastry), gibanica (cheese pastry), kolac (cake), kiflica (biscuit made from walnuts and almonds), hleba (bread) and a range of fermented meats and vegetables had covered all of the available table space. The conversation got down to what it meant to be Serbian and, more importantly, how this meaning gave rise to a particular set of values and beliefs that set the Serb apart from any other person from the Balkans. Marija and Djordje had wanted to 'set the scene' for me to understand their point of view about what is different about the Serbs, 'what it is that actually sets them apart from anyone else', by setting the table this way. In their opinion, 'the best and only way to find out what its like to be a Serb is to eat some Serbian food with some Serbs'. After the meal Djordje would then take me to the soccer ground where teams with ethnic connections with the former Yugoslavia were playing.

At the soccer ground I saw a strong police presence. I sensed that the police had positioned themselves around the ground in an attempt to prevent the two groups from mixing with each other. The reason for this was that when teams identified as having their origins in ethnic groups also caught up in the conflict in the former Yugoslavia, there was an expectation of heightened tensions as participants from both groups would, at the very least, shout obscenities at each other. Giddens (1996, p. 237-8) in his discussion of ethnic violence following the collapse of the former Soviet Union, the former Yugoslavia and breakdown of values between groups and their religions posits that;

> There are only limited ways that clashes can be dealt with. One is by geographical segregation; individuals of conflicting dispositions, or cultures hostile to one another, can of course coexist if they have little or no direct contact. ...Violence ...often stems from clashes of interest, and jousting for power; hence there are quite strictly material conditions which [must] be altered to contest or reduce it.

The material conditions present at the soccer ground - police on horse back, police cars and wagons at the ready to transport people away from the scene - corresponded with the need to deal with potential clash of cultural interests that day. There were at least a dozen police in uniform and what I thought to be another 3-4 out of uniform mingling with the crowd. Another two police officers were on horseback.[5] With this in mind my fieldwork that day was greatly helped by my being with Djordje. He would get me into conversation with groups of Serbian youth by explaining to them that I was doing research. This also meant that my identity was not mistaken for a member of the police.

At that particular moment I sensed that I had made it over the boundary line (albeit an invisible one, yet certainly palpable all the same) that separated the Serbians from the non-Serbians present that day. I was physically and linguistically there as part of the group. Below are my participant observation notes from my fieldwork journal:

> There are plenty of hand and voice gestures. The Serbians stuck together, in a pack, with little movement from each other. I was in this pack of youth, trying to listen to what was being said by them. Close enough to maintain conversation in a low voice. They gave me a sense of controlled expression. Solid Serbian cohesion and community and their need to keep enough distance from those they perceive to be provoking them. A sense of distance that prevented physical clashes with others.

The above notes from my fieldwork journal serve to illustrate that by gathering as a group of Serbs, participants were afforded the opportunity to affiliate with people angered by others from the former Yugoslavia also present that day. This anger was expressed in words only, 'Hey! Ustashe! Get off our land! Fuck Off Ustashe!' There were also references to ongoing events in the Balkans, 'Nasa zemljia svaki zemljia',

('Our land, [all] always our land', translation, N.P.) and references to the disputed regions of Croatia, 'Krainija, Nasa ljudi, nasa zivot! ('Krainija, our people [are] our life', trans. N.P.). To my mind, the angry sentiment about the Croatian presence on Serbian lands in the former Yugoslavia and Australia was represented by the sentiments of the youth with whom I spent that day. This means that the impact of events in the larger world - conflict over the ownership of land in the Balkans - was palpable in the streets and suburbs in at least one Australian city. The way this was managed was through verbal abuse and creating a safe distance - some 200 metres apart from each other - at the soccer ground. This means that the space of the soccer field and the threat of intervention by police helped prevent physical clashes between groups hostile to each other.

The use of strategies to avoid clashes between Serbian Australians and others was not limited to the soccer ground. In cafes, nightclubs, and leisure centres across Australia, a form of social interaction participants had evolved in relation to the war. Australian journalist Robyn Hill (1993, p. 36-8) writing in *The Bulletin* magazine, quotes Suzie Kolasinac, an 18-year-old Serbian University student who tells of mistrust and tension between groups that was not always conveyed using words:

> 'Where I live in Marylands, it's so weird,' she says. 'I just know when a person is Croatian and they know I'm Serbian. I will look at them and they will look at me and we just know. I don't do anything [but] I am worried they might do something to me when my back is turned – it's just this thing in my head. Even when I was in primary school there was this Croatian girl who used to go to school with me and my two other Serbian friends. Nowadays on the street we see each other all the time but we just don't know each other any more'.

To avoid contact with other groups from the region, Serbian Australians would simply not go to the places where they knew that others from the former Yugoslavia were likely to be present.

Becoming connected with boundaries in both the local and global worlds

As Giddens (1996) and Smith (1992, 1995, 1996a, 1996b) point out, in the contemporary world, ethnic and religious pasts are being uprooted and old cultural traditions updated and recast into a highly emotive and sensitive force. The changes now transforming local and global social life include 'the resurgence of ethnicity and the seeming revival of 'tribalism' (and) the continuing importance of religion and ritual' (Giddens, 1996, p. 123-4). Along with the re-birth of nationalism, and group antagonisms thought to have been long buried, there was a proliferation of suffering and bloodshed for newly defined borderlands and boundaries (Smith, 1996b). Bernd Hamm (1992, p. 14), in thinking through the challenges facing the social sciences in interpreting and understanding the 'new Europe', posited that European society can only flourish and develop if it effectively shows compassion and acceptance of a tolerant multicultural society.[6] From his point of view a peaceful Europe requires 'active support for different cultural heritages, a public opinion which positively esteems every foreign element as enriching [and] a political system which preserves cultural roots, problem solving strategies, languages and religions'.

Since conflict began in the former Yugoslavia there had been repeated disputes, breakdowns and cease fire violations as historical geographical, religious, linguistic and racial boundaries and borders could not be peacefully negotiated and agreed upon. Giddens (1996, p. 63) points out that cultural clashes on a global scale can either 'breed further violence, or generate [meaningful] dialogue'. In instances of dialogue, where there is 'recognition of the authenticity of the other, whose views and ideas one is prepared to listen to and debate as a mutual process' (Giddens, 1996, p. 63), this is only possible where segregation and disengagement from each other is not an option. This was particularly the case in ethnically mixed regions of Croatia and Bosnia-Herzegovina (for example, Mostar, Vukovar and Sarajevo) where the level of inter-ethnic relations was an everyday aspect of the personal life of those living there. Even if it appeared that 'all was OK' in the aftermath of negotiations between groups, it was often the case that negotiations ended in fighting. Long before the ink on the papers used to ratify agreements between parties had time to dry, heated disputes and hostile exchanges - inclusive of weapons fire was well underway.[7] Such breakdowns, stoppages and hostilities were not helping to bring a peaceful solution to the difficulties being faced. Nor had they helped people develop trust between each other. Rather, these breakdowns led to increased feelings of hostility and separation marked by differences between individuals and groups along ethnic and racial lines (Smith, 1981, 1990).

With the preceding discussion in mind, I now consider Slavica Potrebic whose voice also appeared at the beginning of this chapter. Slavica had abandoned her Serbian husband as she fled her besieged home, the mixed Croatian town of *Sunja* South of Zagreb, for *Kratecko,* a small farming village four miles away. She was one of 1000 refugees who fled that day. For many years she had once lived in an ethnically mixed town but now the war was responsible for destroying marriages like this one. Hers was a situation where friendships and marriages between individuals had been strained and broken up along ethnic and religious lines. That is, as matters moved inexorably to a head in Slavica's marriage, so too did events in the Balkans change the nature of relationships and friendships between Croatian and Serbian Australians.[8]

While it was outside the scope of the research to chronicle military and civilian campaigns within the former Yugoslavia in order to see how they may or may not have directly impacted upon friendships and relationships in Australia, it was, wherever possible, important to interpret events and issues in relation to Balkans military activity and the situations described by Australian participants. Aligned with the breakdown of personal boundaries and relationships in the former Yugoslavia there were frequent references to past conflicts and battles, these had, in turn, been brought to bear on events of the present.

Mapping Australian relationships in the shadow of the war

The straining and sometimes breakdown of relationships between people of Croatian and Serbian descent was not limited to the borders of former Yugoslavia. As previously indicated, in Australia there have been reports of violent clashes and random attacks against individuals and groups with links to the regions at war.[9] Zlatko Skrbis (1995) in an ethnographic study of Croatian and Slovenian nationalism in Australia during the early stages of the Balkan war tells that 'labelling oneself as a Yugoslav could be treated by Croatians as a direct provocation'. Skrbis quotes several Croatian participants who would never marry a Serbian Australian, nor be associated with a person who ascribes as Serbian or Yugoslav. The main issue as Skrbis saw it was that such individuals wanted no involvement with others who, they believed, opposed the formation of the Croatian State. To illustrate this, one of Skrbis's (1995, p. 330) participants recounts her father's outburst of violence when he suspected her of being in the company of someone who he identified as Yugoslav:

> We were at a party just last week and my father was in the crowd of people and there was an unfamiliar face. He was the only one with an unfamiliar face and my father noticed the way he was speaking about politics. He

mentioned something like 'moja Jugoslavija' ('my Yugoslavia', translation by Skrbis) and my dad threw something against him-hot tempered.

At that point, a relative of the young girl speaking in the above extract physically intervened between the two to prevent an escalation of the violence.[10]

In the United Kingdom (Cohen, 1991) and the United States (Stone, 1992) the evidence suggests that solid friendships and marriages between Serbians and Croatians had broken down.   As war in the former Yugoslavia became worse, so too did relations between Serbians and Croatians in Australia.   Within the breakdown of longstanding friendships there was a feeling of sadness, as Javorka, a 44 year old participant, explained:

> Since I came to Australia I have had some friends who are Croatian.   We have always been friends, close friends, but now it's all suddenly different. I guess we are still friends, but we just 'keep it up', like keeping up appearances. *It's just a completely abstract friendship if you like.* We call each other up very occasionally to keep up appearances, we don't talk about the situation in Yugoslavia at all. *It's just so hurtful that suddenly we should be fighting for all the same nation.* (emphasis added, N. P.)

What had always been friendship with a Croatian Australian and her family for this participant turned into a sort of 'hurtful' breakdown in communications brought about by events in the Balkans. The 'keeping up of appearances' as an abstract friendship implies is that there was an emptiness in these relationships, brought about by 'the situation in Yugoslavia'. The chief cause of the breakdown was the continuation of war and the constant unravelling of a peaceful solution by both sides accusing each other of broken promises.   What people once had in common with each - their *geographical* belonging along citizenship lines - had become obsolete, as 'south-eastern Europe had become split along ancient lines separating Catholic from Orthodox, Rome from Byzantium ...neighbour from neighbour' (Ascherson, 1991, p. 25).[11]

The straining of friendships with others in Australia was not restricted to adult relationships.   It was occurring across the lifespan. Slavenka talks of the 'rules' she put on her relationship with a Croatian girl in the same year 11 class at a Sydney high school:

> I talk to a Croatian girl at school and she was going out with a Serbian boy. We always got along pretty well, I would give her some of my school work

and she would give me some of her school work. We were always sharing, we were good friends. But eventually on one particular time when we were having a chat, she brought up the situation over there and I told her, 'If you want to stay friends, if you want to stay around me, don't mention this again, because you will be accusing us of doing certain things, you will have your point of view. Neither of us will be in "the right" and in the end we will just end up accusing each other of all sorts of things'.

The important point being made here was that there were limits and boundaries being placed on people from the former Yugoslavia who were struggling to re-negotiate new relationships in the shadow of Balkan war. In Australia the nature of responses and experiences of people in the former Yugoslavia were, as Robertson and Chirico (1985) put it, deeply conditioned by the instabilities and tensions present in the larger and local world.

The breakdown of relationships in health care

While the experience of war is one where the 'motherland is being pulled to bits', and hastily re-configured, the breakdown of relationships along ethnic lines was not restricted to informal friendships and marriages. Two Serbian speaking medical doctors, in general practices some 30 kilometres apart in the suburbs of Sydney, spoke of a dramatic decrease in non-Serbian patients, some of whom had been consulting them for over twenty years prior to the conflict. Dr Zdravlije explained that, prior to the conflict over 80 percent of his patient load was of Yugoslav origin:

> [B]ut since the war started almost all of the non-Serbs have left me. I'd say it was a good 30 percent of them have gone. Many of them were long term patients and none of them came and said goodbye. I don't know what is the reason, whether it's personal or if it was a plan within the Croatian community. What could be behind this decision? I certainly know for sure that I saved lives at least three or four of them and they are not coming. I have done a lot of good things to the others so they don't have any medical reason to not come to see me.
>
> I am surprised, because my attitude toward my patients is just as doctor towards a patient. Not on the basis of nationality. With the Croatians that are still coming to see me, I try as often as I can to tell them that the things that are happening in former Yugoslavia are not going to effect my relationship toward them in any sense and that I am going to be their doctor

and if they are willing to accept me they can decide whether they want to continue so come to see me or not.

On the explanation of why there had been a dramatic decrease in non-Serbian patients, Dr. Lekar, the second Serbian Australian general medical practitioner, was more forward in his explanation:

> The first thing that comes to my mind when I think about how this war has effected me, is that Croatians are no longer coming into my surgery. Almost all of them have abandoned me because of the situation where special interest groups in the Croatian community are telling them 'do not go to butchers ...do not trust them with your life, look what they do to us, they are killing us in Yugoslavia'. Some of these patients have been coming to see me for more than 20 years. I know that they like me a great deal. They are being told by their Church and Club that they are not to come and see me. Instead they are being told to hate me because I'm Serb. ...they told me that I give them a good service, but they say 'hey listen, you know I would be branded in my own community if I come to see you, so I don't want to cause any problem for me and my family so I have to leave here'. I think they left me and my practice to be loyal to the Croatian state and Catholicism. It's a pathological hatred in this war, and its not only to do with ethnics, but it's to do with religion one as well.

The physical act of 'breaking off' therapeutic relationships between doctor and patient was itself subject to various means. Some patients simply stopped attending scheduled appointments, without any apology or follow up for their absence. Through Giddens's (1996, p. 238) notion of 'exit', people 'simply disengaged or moved away as might happen in a divorce'. Some others telephoned the doctor, explaining the reasons for their decision. Here the hope might have been to engage in some sort of dialogue about a personal life decision to help make their 'exit' a little easier. A small group wrote to the doctor telling their story and asking for his sympathy and understanding.

In other instances the termination of clinical relationships marked by belonging to cultures hostile to each other was attempted but not successful. One patient, for example, with chronic respiratory illness had not been seen in the practice for several months. Rather than continuing to see a Serbian doctor, she consulted three other doctors and two hospital casualty departments for emergency treatment of acute respiratory distress. On one of these occasions she nearly died. As Dr. Lekar continued to explain:

She felt that no-one could understand or treat both her and her illness. We've had many struggles together, to get her drugs right for her. She came back to see me, out of desperation, for ongoing medical help. She didn't want to come, she was under a lot of pressure not to come and see me. I can help her ...I speak her language ...I just eyeballed her and knew straight away what treatment she needed. She was very ill and I gave it [treatment] without hesitation.

The difficulty here for the person referred to above was in finding a solution between her health needs and the 'pressure' on her not to be seen by a Serbian medical practitioner. In effect, there was a conflict between ongoing treatment and care for a life threatening chronic respiratory illness by a medical practitioner with more than twenty years experience of the condition, who through a network of ethnically based associations, had been identified as 'the enemy'. The 'new' group of which she now felt a member had left an unambiguous message that her associations must remain ethnically homogeneus. That is, there was an explicit expectation that clear boundaries were to be drawn between her and the doctor. The dilemma being faced was to decide between her health and the conditions of her cultural network.

Notwithstanding some cases of compulsory medical psychiatric and nursing treatments under statutory regulations,[12] it is important to stress that no health worker, irrespective of their professional discipline has automatic 'right' to the unquestioned treatment of any individual. Nevertheless, the seriousness of the situation outlined above cannot be overstated. Within the dilemma being faced was the tension between having a treating doctor who knows and understands her condition, inclusive of a full medical and pharmacological history, and the risk of treatment from professionals who do not fully understand her clinical background. As Kanitsaki (1993, p. 123) points out, when there was a change in health practitioner from one that was culturally compatible to one that was incompatible, there was 'potential for a serious and complex conflict situation significantly affecting the quality and therapeutic effectiveness of care [that is] detrimental to the patient's health and wellbeing'. Viewed this way, it was a choice between the Serbian doctor, a clinician that spoke her language or beginning new relationships with other doctors.

In addition to situations where treatment was urgently needed, this patient, like several others who had abandoned the Serbian medical practices of Drs Zdravlje and Lekar had, by virtue of being unable to speak English, had less access to mainstream health services and was therefore at a greater risk of increased suffering, morbidity and perhaps mortality when compared with their Australian born counterparts (National Health Strategy, Issues Paper No. 6). Continuation of the therapeutic relationship with the Serbian doctor would, as Fuller (1996) points out, help her maintain links with mainstream health care and thus optimum respiratory functioning and the stability of her medical condition. The point being made here is that when both health worker and client have a common ethnicity or cultural background, the client is likely to be more comfortable with a worker who can work to accommodate certain cultural and language needs. In this case, a Croatian speaking Serbian doctor with cultural awareness acceptable to the patient, could understand the patient's cultural as well as medical background, and the important part they played in ongoing treatment.

For another patient attending Dr Lekar's practice, the threat of rejection from his national group was more pressing. By maintaining the therapeutic relationship this patient jeopardised another set of established and long-standing relationships with others of Muslim descent who were also bound up in a set of helping relationships of a different kind. This patient came to see his doctor, handing him a sticker. The sticker read: *Serbia is Guilty of Genocide and Destruction in Croatia and Bosnia Herzegovina. STOP THE WAR STOP SERBIA!* 'See, I can't come to you anymore', he screamed. 'You are a Serb and look what you are doing to our people. Why are you killing us, why do you want to destroy us'? The appalling atrocities of the war and the way they were being reported by the media made sense to the reader of this sticker. At that moment, this man who had been a patient for more than 17 years left the practice and never returned. I was handed the original sticker he had brought to the surgery that day. On my way home from fieldwork on the same day I saw another two stickers, one stuck on a traffic walk light and the other on the side of a building.

Digging up the dead: A historical consciousness mapping the self and other

There was a historical consciousness among the Serbian Australians I interviewed that can be traced back to events of the recent and distant past. As we saw above and in previous chapters, the mass genocide of Serbs by the Croatian Ustashe regime during World War 2 remains relevant to the social and mental life of today. It was a 'chapter in their history that Serbs believed could never be repeated', wrote Ilia Glisic, the President of the Serbian National Federation of Australia, in the *Sydney Morning Herald*, on July 11 1994. Gordana summed up her consciousness of this past-operating-in-the-present conflict with the following sentiments:

> We've been let down before. We were practically exterminated between 41 and 43 in the independent state of Croatia. Now they have the same principles, same uniforms. I don't know one family from the Serb held region of Croatia where I was born that did not have family members who were killed. I've got a book written by a French historian containing war documentation that tells what the local Croats did to Serbs during the Second world war. They used to rip a pregnant mother open and get the baby out and display it on a table.

Nenad, in his attempt to explain his experience of the Balkan war, stressed the need for a simultaneous understanding of the Serbs through history:

> I am very willing to take you, anyone back to Bosnia with me. To go back there and establish contact with the Serbian leaders in Bosnia, intellectuals, people in charge so they can speak for themselves. That's the only way you can understand the Serbian people. Because there is no way that I can discuss what is happening in Yugoslavia now without fully understanding the history of Serbians and of Yugoslavia for that matter. If [you] really took the time, researched and looked into it [the history] what has happened now will be understood.

As emphasised previously, a theme throughout the Balkan war has been that maps, borders and land were something to be disputed. Many of the disputed regions of the former Yugoslavia were the subject of fierce battles. Within this complex set of historical and contemporary arrangements came the Dayton Peace Accord. Within days of the accord being signed the *Guardian Weekly* correspondent Julian Borger (1996, p. 4) describes how Serbians living around Sarajevo began to exhume their dead: 'Like an episode from some mystical Balkan epic', writes Borger, 'the Serb dead are emerging from their graves and forsaking Sarajevo rather than suffer Muslim rule'. Sitting in my home, I saw television footage of an elderly Serbian woman in tears clutching a shopping bag and a shovel. Her head was tilted slightly to her left and her face was grimacing. She looked very pained as she stood over the fresh grave of her son. Serb civilians had come to the cemetery to dig up their dead and take away the bodies to the new lands that, under the Dayton accord, would be under Serbian government control.

Verica, whom I introduced in the previous chapter, told me of her sentiments about this during interview:

> This digging must happen. This land may be under Muslim control, but it will never be Muslim land. We have an attachment to our land like the Australian Aborigines have to this land. It will only ever be Serbian land. It will always be known as our land ...we will get this land back one day, but until we do we must take our people with us. If my father was buried there, I would go in and get him out as well. The enemy will not look after him. No way!

Through my conversation with Verica, I was told that there was a much deeper link between Serbians and land, and this was in the minds of relatives who were digging up their dead sons, fathers, and daughters. The excavation of the dead was an act motivated by a deep-rooted attachment to their ancestral land and the fear that the people they were leaving behind, should they do so, would have their resting place desecrated.

The purpose of exploring the implications in Australia of excavation of Serbian burial sites is to highlight the idea that, for this group of people, there was an intimate attachment to the land that itself contained issues of individual bonding and belonging (a concept to be examined at greater depth in the next chapter). In trying to explicate this deep-rooted connection between land and ethnic identity, Nenad explained that anything *belonging* (his emphasis) to the Serbians in Australia was 'sacred'. In his conversation with me he spoke of the graves in Sarajevo as being 'as sacred as the graves of Serbians in Australia or even as sacred as a Serbian social meeting hall'. Nenad continued:

> This is something unique to all of us. Before the war had started, we had our own hall - it was not a Serb hall though. It was like a Yugoslav hall. It was a Yugoslav hall and club. At that time it was fine for us because 95% of us there were all Serbs and with their occasional Muslim that rocks up and that was it, that was fine, and then when all this broke out and people were dividing away. People were working out their territory. Today we know more about how these people have massacred us over the centuries. It's best for us to stick together.

Consideration of the issues presented so far in this analysis illuminate a range of issues concerned with events occurring in the past for

Serbians in the Balkans and Australia. In an article that was first printed in Russian in the Moscow daily newspaper, *Nezavisimaya Gazeta,* the President of the Federal Republic of Yugoslavia Dobrica Cosic described the international community as trying to resolve the Bosnian question by failing to recognise the past history of Serbian suffering under the Ustashe genocide of the 1941-45 war. Cosic (1993) continued to argue that, in fighting for their land and freedom, Serbians living in the region had been erroneously demonised as the aggressors:

> Serbs have lived in a single-state-Yugoslavia ever since 1918. Overnight, because the republics of the former Socialist Federal republic of Yugoslavia were recognised as independent, they found themselves residing in three states-the Federal Republic of Yugoslavia (Serbia and Montenegro); Croatia; and Bosnia-Herzegovina. It is very hard for the Serbs to accept this, particularly as no one ever asked them about it (and) this does not make them the aggressors. None of those who have lived on this land and defended it for centuries can be considered an aggressor.

The important point here was that the links between massacres and 'ethnic cleansing' in Europe during the 1940s, and present day conflict in former Yugoslavia, were much more than just mere thoughts occupying the mind of Serbians in the region and Australia. As seen through the preceding discussion and analysis, they were events and issues that highlighted a very real and powerful force to inform what people actually did, thought and felt in the 1990s (Benson, 1991; Connor, 1993; Eagar, 1993 and Zametica, 1993). They were historical events that created and reinforced difference and boundaries *between* people. They were the effective histories, first introduced in chapter 3, emanating from the region over centuries of conflict. And this carried with it a sentiment of enmity between Slavica Potrebic and her husband (and others), who began this chapter. In addition to this was the question of how the history of Serbian people (genocide at Jasenovac, broken trust, domination by the Turks, negative media reporting) had encouraged participants to *watch me* very carefully.

Historical events from the region were more than a determinant of people's physical security and wellbeing. This past has also revived questions of personal security in Australia. Gordana spoke of a recurring nightmare over a 12 month period that centred upon her family's suffering in Croatia during World War II:

I have this Serbian cousin who lived in Croatia between [19]41 and [19]43. She had seen the Croatian Ustashe come into her house where they shot her father, shot him in front of the whole family. His wife (my cousin's mother) tried to protect him and they practically chopped half of her arm off. The next day they [the soldiers] came and collected the mother and three of the brothers, one of the brothers was a Serbian Orthodox Priest, they put him on the spit and baked him on top of a fire and they killed the rest, indeed they did hundreds of people.

This nightmare, like the memories of the past for many of the participants of this research, were not limited to personal wellbeing and security alone. Stories of the recent past also reflected current thinking about the political and regional security in Europe. In an editorial published in the French newspaper *Le Monde* on November 8 1996, the author expressed 'astonishment and indignation' at Croatia being admitted to the Council of Europe. The editorial alleged that recognition of Croatia was undeserved because:

...of the Croatian Government's non-co-operation with the International Court in The Hague, the support it is giving to Herzogovinian Separatists, the banning of an internal opposition party from taking it's place in the Zagreb Municipal Council, and [government] initiatives that appear to be an attempt to rehabilitate the 1940 pro-Nazi regime.

It is this history of ethnic and racial conflict and hatred that could not be separated from people's minds in the 1990s. While this is important in its own right, it also serves to illustrate an important conceptual issue that brings together the contents of this chapter. It demonstrates that events of the 1940s generate issues of trust and mistrust, wellbeing and enmity, between people at a local level in Australia. At an even deeper level, events of fifty years ago have served to inform others about European political stability in the 1990s. What is particularly interesting about these seemingly unrelated fields of study *vis a vis* personal boundaries, conceptual maps and trust between people in Australia, and stability in Europe, is that each are united through a common historical underpinning. The point I am making here is that the distressing memory of Jasenovac Concentration Camp graffiti on an Adelaide church (chapter 2), and the fears and memories of 'a new generation of European families', as Ascherson, (1992) refers to them (see quotation in chapter 1), can be traced back to the potent symbolic memory of the Nazi occupied independent state of Croatia of the 1940s. In other words, the situations that the participants were describing in Australia, the former Yugoslavia and Europe were matters of personal and regional safety and security that are rooted in the recent and distant past.

Conclusion

This chapter, like all of those contained in this study, is predicated on the belief that Serbian Australians were self-interpreting individuals who made meaning out of their situation, whether or not they were physically in their ancestral homeland. It is clear that, from the ideas and interpretations given that when I had crossed over the 'boundaries' put in place by factors within and/or beyond my control, that I did not do this alone. No boundary so far examined in this study existed apart from the interpretations that I and participants attached to it.

This chapter has also developed ideas introduced in the first three chapters of this study. The boundaries of the research 'act' were a means of allowing participants to access and relate to me in a particular way. The inter-subjective information about who I was and what I was doing during the research journey, included participants wanting to know something about my ethnic and cultural heritage; I saw this as their attempt to place me in some sort of context. This interpretation was also influential in understanding how participants began to address larger questions of Yugoslavia in Europe, that is, it became an interactive means of interpreting how participants situated themselves in relation to the world around.

Having a boundary and map to follow as a guide offered participants insight and direction as they recast their lives in relation to people they had contact with in Australia. My view of this was that the newly defined boundaries of Central and Eastern Europe enabled participants to see and believe things that they wanted to see and believe in that region and Australia as well. Issues of national and cultural identity in the recent and distant past gave shape to their way of life. The 'sense of Serbian self' was created and sustained by the newly defined (Serbian) way of seeing things, and a particular point of view. When I began to draw a particular map of the Serbians in the former Yugoslavia and Australia, this picture was liable to be confused by participants with the hostile perspective of the news media, leading to both great outcry and cautious suspicion of my motives. As we have already seen, participants spoke of their anger and disgust at the media 'telling lies,' as well as displaying a careful concern for the 'story' that I was about to tell.

For reasons and in ways that I hope to have made clear, the more I learnt about the Balkan war and the Serbian Australian experience, the more conscious I was of the boundaries I needed to cross, as well as the boundaries I should not cross. The fascinating paradox for me in this journey was that, the more the Serbian Australians allowed and facilitated my study into the situations they faced in life, the more I seemed to be simultaneously crossing some boundaries and avoiding others that came my way in the process.

The idea that participants would no longer identify as Yugoslav (the identification then becoming Serbian), meant that newly defined ethnic identity was something to be proud of, something to be made prominent in communications with others - a self experience that was a true means to feel better about their situation in Australia. With an increased sense of the self, participants came around to the idea that the meanings given to their own ideas, feelings, interactions and involvements with others were contingent upon a new found sense of belonging to all that is Serbian.

Consideration of these issues sets the scene for the remainder of the study. In the *next* chapter, for instance, I am concerned with issues of bonding, belonging, national and cultural identity. The idea here is that health, as a process, can no longer be seen as a localised phenomenon - it must be seen as something that transcends both the body and the national settings within which people live. Exploration takes notions of health and healing beyond the specific care of physical conditions bound up with local circumstances, to consider the effect of long distance grief and devastation. In the next chapter, I also turn my attention to the mental health problems of Serbian Australians trying to make meaning about where they feel they belong in the world. Their stories and the circumstances in which they unfold form the substance of my interpretation.

Notes

1   A plaque had been placed alongside this fence. It read, 'Committee of the Serbian Church St Sava Plymouth and Serbian Sisters Association have built this fence 1996'.

2   Once again I am careful not to exclude the range of opportunities for data generation and interpretation (Lincoln, 1992).

3   Philip Mosley (1992) examined the ethnic history of soccer in Australia and postulated that European, post-war immigration had the most profound effect on Australian soccer. The soccer ground was a place where nationalistic loyalty also

played a part as a club victory could take on the stature of a 'victory' for the homeland and vice versa. Writing in the same volume as Mosley, Stoddart (1992, p. 133) points out that soccer in Australia 'has always been calibrated by a foreign trend, an ethnicity of some kind at every given point'.

4 By using the term 'boundaries' I am thinking of the geographical, racial and social boundaries between ethnic groups and individuals, in the former Yugoslavia and Australia; borders and boundaries between myself and participants, as well as boundaries between people of Croatian and Serbian descent in health and helping relationships in Australia.

5 In 1991, for example, the New South Wales Soccer Federation ordered that spectators with ethnic links to the former Yugoslavia be banned from certain matches to avoid violence, and there were rumours that plain clothes police were mingling with the crowds that did gather. Team names were also changed in a bid to avoid friction (Hill, 1993).

6 I make this point believing that the needs of different language and cultural groups in Europe are highly diverse and complex and therefore in need of multi-disciplinary perspectives.

7 There is a catalogue of border disputes and breakdowns between peace-keepers, governments, military and para-military groups in the Balkans. Many of these disputes took place over the recognised and makeshift borders of former Yugoslavia. During the week ending August 13 1995, for example, up to 400, 000 Serb refugees were expelled from the disputed Krajina region of Croatia. The expulsion of the refugees was preceded and followed by fresh fighting. On this occasion, fighting had erupted within hours of a United Nations brokered cease fire agreement that could have assured safe passage of Serbs into northern Bosnia. See Vulliamy (1994, pp. 67-8, and 299-303) and Bell (1996, pp. 170-180).

8 Chapter 6 of this study is devoted to more detailed discussion of participants' experience of events occurring simultaneously in the Balkans and Australia.

9 For further details of Molotov Cocktail attacks on Serbian Orthodox Church, people and property in Australia, see Illic (1995).

10 Trlin and Tolich (1995), in their study of New Zealand Croatians, report that the concealment of ethnic origin, anonymity, even being mistaken for an Italian among this group was preferable to being Yugoslav.

11 It is interesting to note that, in what was perhaps the most delicate mission of his pontificate, Pope John Paul II delivered an impassioned plea for unity, harmony and forgiveness during an open air mass in Croatia in 1994. In his sermon the Pope was reported by Traynor (1994, p. 1) to have said, 'My thoughts fly with nostalgia to the times when all believers of this region were united... the present tragic divisions and tensions must not cause us to forget that there are many elements uniting the nations who are now at war'.

12 Usually in the form of prescribed drugs and a secure environment for a person with a mental illness who requires immediate treatment in the interests of her/his health and safety and/or the protection of others.

5 Towards a New Blood and Belonging

I've lost my country, I really have lost it because I've always dreamed of going back and I've always kept it in the back of my head so that I can keep away from it. I was waiting to return one day but I know now that it would break me up and I would die (Radoika, a 52 year old Serbian Australian participant).

We only ever wanted to be Yugoslav but now I just don't feel Yugoslav anymore. I just want to be Serb. Now I am only a Serb (Persida, a 37 year old Serbian Australian participant).

Introduction

In the previous chapter, I examined how newly constructed boundaries and ethnic identity bonds had been developed by Serbian Australians in the shadow of the war. I also developed the metaphors of boundaries and maps to help interpret the implications of my combined roles of researcher and mental health professional. Through this interpretation I found that the origin and veracity of boundaries constructed by participants were reconfigured under the impact of war through historical traditions, and by means of cultural and nationalist networks.

This chapter extends the issues raised in chapter 4, and sets the scene for substantive issues to be discussed in chapters 6 and 7. It explains the underlying principles leading to an analysis of coping with the Balkan war, and the health and helping interventions for Serbian Australians discussed in chapter 7.

The chief idea to be explored in *this* chapter is how a sense of bonding, belonging and purpose in Serbian national and cultural activity was a means for participants to interpret and manage distressing events in the Balkans and Australia. 'Sense of belonging' in this chapter refers to a feeling of valued involvement and participation in the experience of being needed and accepted. This involves a self perception that is individually articulated, but which arises within the interpersonal milieu in which Serbian Australians live. For Milica, her sense of belonging was heightened or even re-created from a feeling of sadness and loss:

In this war I have lost my homeland, I am sick of the sensationalism being done to the Serbs by the Australian media, and I feel that even my new country - Australia, has let me down. This is a sad fact, it is how I feel, *(pause, crying)* I feel completely displaced and I feel as if I don't belong there any-more, that I have really lost my country there and lost my country here. I just feel that nobody cares and nobody wants to know *(pause, crying)*, no-one wants to hear about what's really happening and it's easy for people to accept what's dished out to them on TV. We only ever wanted to be Yugoslav ...but now I [only] want to be Serb.

Having a sense of belonging to Serbian ideals meant that participants experienced a fit or congruence with people, groups and organisations that contained elements of their spiritual and cultural dimensions of identity, through shared or complementary characteristics (Hagerty, et. al. 1992). Experiencing a fit or congruence with others was aligned with a feeling that life problems brought about by certain social circumstances (for instance, pain arising from the conflict) may be helped by feeling part of a group or community (Hagerty, et. al., 1992 and 1996). It was at this time that I identified 'sense of belonging' as being implicated in the way that participants coped with the upsetting and overwhelming aspects of the Balkan war. The Serbian Australian medical practitioner Dr Zdravlje explicates this from the point of view of people coming together as a community, at a time of experiencing the demonisation of being Serbian:

> The one good thing that is coming out of this war is the cohesiveness of the Serbian community. We started to realise that without coming together and working together we cannot survive and that realisation came also after the attitude of the Australian government and international community [they] put so much rubbish on to the Serbs, blamed the Serbs throughout the media.

Illustrating the sentiment that the Balkan war had brought people closer together, Dr Zdravlje referred to a split within the Serbian Orthodox Church in Australia during the 1970s, which was based along central administrative lines:

> In the churches, there is a coming together of people interested to meet and go to each other's church picnic or their gatherings and mixing freely and ... there is that sense of cohesiveness among the [Serbian] community and they are trying to be more polite to each other although there are some old

people in the high echelon who are a little bit wary of the younger ones. But the general feelings of the old split between the churches is that it was nonsense and now they have come together a lot more.

There is, in this sense, a new feeling of being unified with others who describe similar feelings, frustrations and problems of living-in Australia. I identified these as issues contributing to mental health and wellbeing because rather than isolation from others, there is a coming together in a local ethnic 'community'. This means rather than feeling isolated, vulnerable and weak, there was a feeling of being with others, able to face the pressures of living that someone else also understands. My conceptualising of health through a sense of Serbian national belonging means that negative and positive factors in health as a social process could no longer be seen as a localised phenomena; they must be seen as something that transcends the national settings within which people live. Zorica explains:

> It [the Balkan war] affects my health inadvertently by moving dormant feelings [of 'Serbianness']. It [the Balkan war] is a stress, it interrupts my daily life. Imagine that you don't like spiders, all your life you don't like them, they scare you. Then one day, a spider falls right on you. So that's very stressful, it has suddenly come to the foreground. [This incident] challenges your whole coping means, you have a distant fear of spiders, a distant fear that you can manage. But now it's a new extension of this fear, a new level of discomfort. There have always been tensions in you about spiders, and the tensions between Serbs and Croats is like this spider, [and] the war is like the spider landing on me. That's the best way I can explain it, since you're not a Serb.

This quotation draws attention to ethnic linkages that suggest that changes to mental health and wellbeing are achieved through individual cultural and historical connections. As previously mentioned in chapter 2, exploration of these issues takes health issues beyond local boundaries, to consider the effect of global circumstances. The combination of the issues being raised in this and previous chapters, lead to the view that what it meant to be a Serbian Australian and what was perceived to be sacred about this meaning was a fluid and evolving process.

Behind the arguments within this chapter lie the seminal formulations for chapter 7 where I am concerned with health and community processes that helped participants cope with feelings of distress and frustration. The health and community interventions for participants were part of a process linked to a changing national and cultural identity, relationships with others and the pursuit of life goals, in a way that affirms people and their purpose.

Serbian nationhood as experienced through participant observation

As seen in chapters 1, 2 and 4, the boundaries crossed to create interpretive connections with Serbian Australians included the ability to engage family, cultural and religious activities that few non-Serbians could access. As previously demonstrated, there was emphasis, in the research process, to try to establish reciprocal relationships between myself and participants. On this basis I was invited to a celebration of Serbian nationhood by a research participant. The telephone rang one evening with a call from Ljubo. He called to ask me if I would like to accompany him and his family to the Serbian Church hall for a celebration of twenty five years of Serbian radio in New South Wales.

When I arrived at the Serbian Church I immediately sat down at the table, ready to begin conversation. On the table there were two video cassettes detailing the lives of the indicted war criminals Radovan Karadzic and Ratko Mladic. The cassettes belonged to a person seated across from me. The other people seated at our table included men and women I had previously seen but not spoken with.

The evening began with the entire room rising from their seats to a standing position for a short prayer and a minute's silence for 'the souls of those Serbian men, women and children killed during war in Yugoslavia'. The ceremony of prayer and silence was facilitated by a Serbian Orthodox priest, who began and ended the ritual by making the sign of the cross. Making the sign of the cross is an expressive means by which to identify himself as an Orthodox Christian who was dedicating prayer in response to events in the Balkans.

As a participant observer I watched carefully how others around me made the sign of the cross. Similarly, I made the movements that followed as closely as possible behind the people I was seated with. Followers of the Serbian Orthodox faith make the sign of the cross by bending the small and ring fingers of the right hand while joining the tips of the other three fingers together. With the tips of these three fingers the person makes contact with the top of the forehead to 'dedicate his mind, his thoughts and self to the first Trinity: God, as the absolute thought' (Bulich, 1985, p. 94). Then the right hand is lowered to chest level and across to lightly touch the right hand side shoulder and then the left one. The shoulders are considered as symbolic muscular forms representing individual strength and power. The hand motion from the right to left of shoulder is to indicate that Christ came from the right side of the Father and has overcome the devil who is represented by the priest's left side.

Immediately after this prayer, the Serbian national anthem was played. As soon as the anthem was announced, people throughout the room stood in silence. The national anthem served to situate what was to come later that evening. The atmosphere was thoroughly absorbed in national and cultural traditions with frequent references to the war in former Yugoslavia.

At the completion of this anthem, people resumed seating and began to eat. During the meal Serbian folk ballads were played through the loudspeaker. The ballads were recited with the accompaniment of a single stringed wooden instrument called a *gusle*. The conversation between people seated at my table was mostly about the Balkans war and the way in which the Bosnian Serbs in particular had been misunderstood by their former allies Britain and the United States. Others spoke angrily of feeling betrayed by the President of Serbia, Slobodan Milosovic. When I later asked Zorica seated at my table what has been her experience of the evening, she replied:

> It is cause for me to feel Serbian. A reason to feel Serbian. My feelings were hidden, sleeping away in me, but now the environment of war evoked, threatened and challenged them. They were always there, but the war brought them out in the open. I'm showing it. It's not appropriate to go walking around in Australia being a nationalistic Serb. But it's still there and here [the Serbian church and hall] it's OK.

The remainder of the evening was dominated by the outpouring of historical information about the Balkans, the playing of old songs, and storytelling of myth and historical anecdotes. The stories were set against a continuous background of traditional folk music.

The people seated at my table also told me that the background music served to re-awaken individual memories of early family life.[1] For the participants with whom I shared the evening, this music was a catalyst to generate conversations about the historical situations it evoked. Music at this particular time transported people from the western suburbs of Sydney, to focus thought and attention on their homeland. One participant at my table spoke of the music as 'a joyful expression, a pleasant feeling reminding them of where they were born'.

As the evening progressed, a number of songs from the 14th and 15th Century were played on the gusle. These songs seemed to cover the themes of war, death, heroism, and affection for the homeland. With the songs came an enormous range and depth of historical information about the Serbians from the people seated at my table.

Towards the end of the evening, two young girls stood at the speaker's podium to tell their story of how they had experienced war in the former Yugoslavia. A child aged about 12 from Sarajevo spoke about the day her father was killed. It was at this moment that several people in the room began to cry.

But the climax of the evening was a live-to-air war report, broadcast from Bosnia, and a simultaneous telephone link up with a Bosnian Serb radio station. In this particular instance, a live radio program was being broadcast from Bosnia to an audience of about 600 in Sydney. The radio broadcast contained information about the war, and the fate of Serbian refugees from villages and towns under siege. What was particularly crucial at that time was that the lives of people in New South Wales were being intimately connected with the lives of people in the Balkans.

Questioning and interpreting

From the preceding interpretation emerge much deeper questions and issues concerned with 'sense of belonging' as a vital mental health concept. The point being made here is that the feeling that one does belong to a group, a country, a people, and a culture, at a time when all of these cultural, social and historical products are under attack from inside and outside their geographical borders, is a significant human health activity. The feeling of being loved, connected, at one with and at peace with the national and cultural beliefs that make up 'all that is Serbian' were seen to enhance self esteem and provide a framework for attachment and companionship (Caroline, 1993; Little, 1993), and improve upon feelings of loneliness (Haber, Mc Mahon, Price-Hoskins and Sideleau, 1992). This interpretation is aligned with sentiments from Neda:

> Going to church represents my culture. It's comforting. People who go there speak my language. It's a mini homeland in the Australian environment. For two hours it's only Serbian, ...it's comforting, it represents pride, the Serbian tradition, makes people feel good, gives me a feeling of belonging, self worth and identity.

In this quotation there is reference to the comfort and freedom of being a certain individual whose identity is preserved and protected. It is possible to merge Smith's (1995, p. 145-6) conception of national identity with this sentiment, as the contextual issues of globalism are very much a part of what characterises contemporary national identity:

> [W]hat binds many people more closely to an ethnohistory and heritage that they feel is under threat [is] the sense of irreplaceability of one's own culture values. The desire to preserve ancient values and traditions is not antiquarian nostalgia; it is the spur to a restoration of a lost community, to reliving its 'golden age', to renewing the community by ...reappropriating its distinctive cultural heritage. [T]he secret of identity is [shared] memory of the ethnic past.

But if the objects that symbolise this memory are destroyed, there is a build up of emotional energy and anger that must inevitably break out somehow. The Serbian Australian medical practitioner, Dr Lekar, describes what he saw when symbols of belonging so loved by his patients were destroyed:

> It is really something that struck me. Those Serbs from Bosnia, I mean I knew that the mentality of all of the Serbs, but the Serbs from Bosnia, the Krajina Serbs, they got so angry, they were prepared to die without questioning. I mean that's something true for a lot of Serbs, but the Serbs from Croatia and Bosnia in particular, that I witnessed, I was amazed to see that people who came to see me from those areas living in Australia were so affected by the loss of properties, houses, everything [Serbian] ...they definitely were effected in emotional ways.

Alongside these processes of belonging and attachment were issues of national identity and belonging that revealed an interesting paradox. As we have already seen through the lives of Gordana (ch. 1), Verica (ch. 3), Javorka and Slavica (ch. 4) and others, there is a complex interplay between cultural and national beliefs that brings about a sense of belonging and bonding on the one hand, and a sense of marginalisation and mental distress on the other. Contained within this interplay is the view that feelings of friendship, commitment, wellbeing, purpose and belonging to all that was 'Yugoslav' had been replaced by all that was 'Serbian'.

The feeling of no longer belonging to what was previously known as 'Yugoslav' was made more complex by the perception that the Australian government had taken sides in this war by supporting economic trade sanctions against Serbia and Montenegro. Dr Zdravlje saw the personal strain of this on patients attending his medical practice:

> For the Government to pick on our side this way [they feel they] don't belong anywhere. ...in some way they are losing their identity ...[they] are either this or that and that has created tension within their personal life and relationships with other people, that's right. A lot of times I hear patients saying 'I don't feel like going anywhere, I don't feel like talking to people, I don't feel like going out or why should I go out, who needs to be happy'. I think that a big mistake was done by Australian government to Serbians, unnecessarily, unjustly.

As 'the military struggles on the territory of the disintegrated Yugoslav federation eviscerated any remaining support for Yugoslavism and the Yugoslav idea' (Cohen 1993, p. 228), the breaking away from Yugoslavism seemed irreversible. Once the military battles, and atrocities involving all sides, were on the territory sacred to Serbians, any talk of ethnic groups being equal and ethnic identity being preserved along with the Yugoslav ideal was rejected. The 'ideal' of a person self-ascribing as Yugoslav could not be easily tolerated.

As we saw, through the lives of Slavica and Gordana, their belonging to the Yugoslav motherland was itself suddenly shattered with the onset of war, and their emerging transition from Yugoslav to Serbian had been a significant health issue. This means that the Yugoslav ideal was replaced with a new Serbian cultural and national consciousness that helped participants develop what might be called a new nationalist psychic structure.[2] In the next section I examine the possible contents of this structure by looking at the intimate re-awakening and re-connection with what it means to be a Serbian, and what was perceived as historically and socially sacred about it.

Broken bonds: The end of being 'Yugoslav'

When the republics of Slovenia and Croatia announced their laws and government to be supreme over that of the Federal Assembly in Belgrade, so began the end of what was six republics making up the Yugoslav Federation. As political tensions boiled over into bloody conflicts between police and civilians, along ethnic lines, the Serbian authorities, and the Bosnian Serb leadership in particular, announced the protection of Serbian civilian enclaves as a priority. What had once been the Yugoslav idea of 'brotherhood and unity' was replaced with individualised nationalisms. Serbian authorities in the former Yugoslavia made it both clear and public that their main interest was to safeguard Serbian minorities in Croatia (and elsewhere in the region) and the integrity of borders that could only be negotiated through peaceful ethnic division.

As the conflict in former Yugoslavia progressed along ethnic divisions there were people throughout Australia who had re-aligned themselves with their Serbian heritage. The war had forced open a new identity in Australia and the timetable of this new nationalist psychic structure from 'Yugoslav' to 'Serbian' was dictated by what was happening in the Balkans. Giving up on the Yugoslav ideal was difficult, as Persida, whose voice opened this chapter, explains:

> I have always felt Yugoslav, we have always wanted to feel Yugoslav. With so many people living together in one place, the only one solution is Yugoslavia, we're all Yugoslavs, we are all under the same umbrella and we can all live together if we want to. My father always taught us not to discriminate between people and this is what is so hurtful now, that suddenly we should be fighting for all the same nation, the same land.

> Yugoslavia literally means the land of the Southern Slavs. It's a humanity embracing concept. Isn't that a beautiful idea? That we speak the same language, doesn't matter about our religion, we can and should all be living together.

This experience, along with her words at the opening of this chapter suggest that, as Persida became involved with events in her homeland, she transformed herself from Yugoslav to Serbian. In an ironic twist, the transformation from Yugoslav to Serbian in Australia was helped by media reports of human rights violations, ethnic cleansings, and other abuses against Serbians in Croatia. For some participants, newspaper and television reports of violations against Serbians were a reminder of World War II atrocities against Serbians, now undertaken by the same ethnic groups at war in the 1990s.

The comparison of events in the 1940s and 1990s inspired Yugoslav Australians to redefine themselves as Serbian. In the transformation from Yugoslav to Serbian were feelings of togetherness, security and identity that were being shaped by events in the recent and distant past. As a cultural group, Serbian Australians were being re-defined with their counterparts in the Balkans. All of this was being helped along by electronic and print media reports of atrocities from the region that further compelled participants to selfascribe as Serbian. Verica, whom I introduced in chapter 3, explains:

> Well it's an awakening of people to remember their roots because we sacrificed our roots and our heritage and our nationality for an international cause and that international cause was the creation of Yugoslavia. Now we must altogether stand up as Serbs. We must unite to defend our nation [and] cultural history.

The coming 'together' and standing 'together' meant a passionate investment in all things Serbian. As an awakening this meant a re-connection with the symbols of a new blood and belonging.

Symbols of a new belonging

The new belonging brought with it a resurrection of symbols of Serbian identity and the renewal of historical myth and storytelling. The use of three fingers salute, for example, become a symbol widely used in Australia and the former Yugoslavia to represent a feeling of unity, victory and in some instances, extreme nationalism. One participant explained his use of the three finger symbol this way:

> The three fingers symbol [salute] is like a representation of the people we are. It's like seeing our flag, seeing something dear to our heart. To me it is like the double headed eagle if you like. If you happen to see another person wearing that symbol, then you know that it must be a Serb who is wearing it. Three fingers is like the flag that represents our people (Djordje, a Serbian Australian youth).

The three fingers that comprise this symbol are the same three that are used when making the sign of the cross. The important point being made here is that the three finger symbol had become re-awakened, re-appropriated marker of the *new belonging* to Serbian nationalism. The use of a historical symbol (the three fingers symbol) had become a strong statement of belonging to Serbian nationalism; a nationalism that gave people a sense of identity. This means that national identity and mental health are interwoven by the twin processes of history and events in the contemporary world. Smith (1995, p. 155) suggests that such memories, myths and historic symbols are:

> ... ceremonies of nationalism that provide the basis for social cohesion and [are therefore able] to concentrate the energies of individuals and groups to feel they 'belong' [and] making its citizens feel the power and warmth of their collective identification. As a result, individual members come to perceive ...greater feelings of fraternity, heightened self awareness and social reflexivity.

Alongside the processes of historic revival and preservation was the way in which death was also been memorialised as a symbol of belonging. The former BBC war correspondent Martin Bell (1996, p. 103) tells of Serbians as 'Serbocentric, in a world that turns around them'. Bell made his point through the following anecdote:

> They like to tell the story of the Croat, the Muslim and two Serbs who found themselves on the moon. The Croat claimed it for the Croats, because he said its barren landscape resembled the mountains of Dalmacia. The Muslim claimed it for the Muslims, because its shades of grey were exactly those of the hills and escarpments of central Bosnia. One of the Serbs then took out his revolver and shot the other. 'Now the moon is Serbian,' he said, *'for wherever a Serb has spilt his blood or lies buried is for ever Serbian territory'*. (emphasis added, N.P.)[3]

To 'be a Serbian' according to the point that Bell makes, is to gain full ownership, history and authority over what is claimed. The historical consciousness of this is not restricted to living beings. It is an all consuming belief that inhabits the living and the dead, as Zorica continues to explain:

> The other day I was listening to the radio and there was a man talking about his attachment to the land. *He was talking about the land being more than just soil, it represents people's life and blood.* He was saying on the radio that it was a living thing, it's like it was not a dead thing. Like it breathed, it was alive and therefore you must treat it with respect. He said that when someone took it away from you they did something bad to it, it was like a personal attack, yeah, a personal attack. *I thought to myself that this man must be a Serb.* But at the end of the interview it turned out that he was an Australian aborigine. And so I think of that as being like me. *Land is to us [Serbs] like it is to the aborigines.* Land is like another representation of our culture. It's like kiflica, church, music, land is no different. (emphasis added, N.P)

The historical quality of Zorica's sense of 'blood and belonging' to the lands of the former Yugoslavia leads me to make two further points. *Firstly*, as we have already seen, issues that permeate beliefs and ideas about 'being' Serbian Australian come from a combination of world catastrophic events and the actions of people in the local (immediate) environment. Cultural and historical events regarding perceived wrongs against Serbians in the recent and distant past are cited as thought and belief expressive of this belonging. *Secondly*, the way in which Serbian Australians belong to what they perceive is sacred in their past has a lot to do with the meticulous way by which notions of history and culture have been used in meeting the challenges of daily life under the impact of war. They share a belief in Serbian 'blood and belonging' that has helped some participants cope with events in Australia and the former Yugoslavia.[4] That is, Serbian Australians have a belief, thought and feeling structure that informs their understanding of themselves as demonised and misunderstood by the West and others.

In Serbian speech there is an intimate feeling of being as one with the land and people who occupy it. In reaching an interpretation of what it meant for Serbian Australians to 'belong' to something in the world, there is a revelation that history is a key part of this place. As Gordana explains, there is, in Serb speech, a sense that life and blood are 'as one' within the land:

> This is how I feel for my land - it's my mother. It is my mother. To know that it has been cut up and so divided and [means that it has] filled with blood. *It is just so painful and I feel that I have lost my mother, suddenly your own country is not your country anymore.* And you feel that you have really lost it. (emphasis added, N.P.)

Having lost one's sense of self, both through war and through the process of re-defining oneself as Serbian, there was a new affinity with all things Serbian. Aligned with this idea of cultural and religious identification and belonging was the way this loss had been coped with. My view was that Serbian Australian mental health was facilitated through a sense of belonging to the *'motherland'*. This idea takes notions of health and healing beyond the specific care of physical conditions bound up with local circumstances, to consider the effect of long distance grief and devastation. This means that health as a process could no longer be seen as a solely localised phenomena. It must also be seen as something that transcends the national settings within which people live.

The death and burial of Milos

In analysing Serbian Australian attachment to land and sense of belonging as an indispensable mental health concept, I recall a moving funeral service in Adelaide for a man who had left Serbia in 1963 at age 17 to travel to Australia. He had never returned to his homeland, and he died in Sydney at age 50. I had first met Milos (the deceased) about ten years earlier at the funeral of his first wife. Since that time Milos had become my friend too. I last saw him alive on the evening before the day he died. On that particular evening, I thought that he looked rather tired, almost as if he had come away from an exhausting week. The next day Milos suffered a heart attack and never recovered.

Milos's funeral service began at the Serbian Orthodox Church he regularly attended in Adelaide. When I arrived at the Church there were several hundred people waiting outside the main entrance in anticipation of his arrival. The funeral procession was made up of Milos, his family, the priest and funeral parlour staff. The procession drew alongside the front entrance of the church. Once Milos's body was removed from the hearse and taken inside it was time for the people waiting outside to enter.

Women moved to the left and men to the right of the church, each remained standing throughout the service. Bulich (1985, p. 90) explains that, by standing in the church, Serbian Orthodox participants imitate heavenly powers who 'serve God standing around his throne, feeling as his children, who resurrected together with Christ, are trustingly and freely standing and facing God'. Standing then, seems to be a fundamental position of worship, whereby the Church recognises the importance given to the spiritual life of Christ. In standing and facing the front of the Church, participants were also facing the open coffin containing Milos. In doing so, participants were giving their full attention to his and his family's presence.

What struck me about this funeral were the conversations taking place between Milos's family inside the church and the family in Serbia. During the funeral there were person-to-person telephone links between Adelaide and Serbia to report on the progress of the funeral procession. I could hear descriptions being given by Milos's son to his family in Serbia about how many people were inside the Church, and the physical presence and positioning of people in relation to Milos, at various stages along the way. What was most remarkable to both myself and several other Serbians present that day, was that when the coffin containing Milos arrived at the

Church, a third telephone call was promptly made to his parents at a Church in Serbia. There, a simultaneous service was ready to commence.

After the Adelaide church service, the coffin containing Milos was put back inside the hearse and taken the short distance to a local cemetery. When the coffin was lifted over his grave, another telephone call was made to a cemetery in Serbia where Milos's family had re-convened with a priest to commence a second simultaneous service.

During the Adelaide, service Milos's son read into a mobile telephone a summary of his father's life and achievements to those present both in Adelaide and in Serbia. This means that Milos's son was speaking to both the Adelaide and Serbian funeral audiences (participants, really) at the same time. The information being broadcast included biographical details such as Milos's date of birth, his age when he first left school, details of his first job, his date of arrival in Australia, etc. This information included the statement that, 'my father loved Australia and loved the people who lived here. But he always believed that his home and heart lay in Serbia. His dream was to return after the war'.

Serbians believe in predestination in life and death. They believe in the power of the holy spirit calling all Serbians into life and determining the moment of departure (death). The slogan *Nema Smrti Bez Sudyena Dana*, (*There is no death without the appointed day*, translation N. P.) is used to refer to the belief that one is called by Christ when 'their time has come'. After death, the soul delays its departure from earth to the heavens until the expiration of 40 days. This was seen to be the situation with Milos. Forty days after Milos died, the priest, family and friends (including myself) returned to the grave where his body lay. I wrote the following in my field journal:

> Milos died 40 days ago today. I have returned to his grave for the Parastos (memorial service). There were about 60 people here, both men and women. It was a very windy day with rain threatening. The wind prevented the people gathered from placing lit candles at the head of the grave. It was also difficult to hear what was being said by the priest as he conducted the service. There were two priests present.

On the way to Milos's grave I met up with two men, Misha and Drago. They saw me from a distance and drew my attention by waving. When we finally met, they both welcomed me with a kiss and we walked together to the burial site. Sometimes it felt quite strange for me to kiss another man, but I knew it was *always* the right thing to do in these circumstances.[5] I saw my being kissed by another Serbian as a sign of respect and acceptance of me by the group. To my mind it was much more than a simple polite gesture; it was a symbolic metaphor stating that my presence in the field that day (and throughout the research) was accepted and respected.

After a short walk together we arrived at Milos's grave. The gravestone was covered with flowers, yet there was enough space to show that the grave headstone had the Serbian flag painted on it. What struck me about the flag was the brightness of its colour. I spoke with Milos's son who told me: 'mum wanted all the flag and stuff. I probably would not have gone that far. But mum really wanted it to be there.'

After the church ceremony there was a table set up with whisky and brandy, soft drinks, zito (a thickened wheat mixture) and white, oven baked bread. I drank two small glasses of brandy and ate two chunks of bread. The bread was broken off the main loaf by hand in varying sizes and left in a pile for the people to take. The food at the grave site was there to symbolise the life of Milos being raised into the sky, up into God's Kingdom. His spirit and memory was still considered alive in heaven in life eternal.

After the memorial ceremony was complete, we drove the family home. There, more than 50 people attended, along with one of the Serbian Orthodox priests. Before entering Milos's house we all stood in line to wash our hands in a bowl of warm soapy water. The tradition here was, as Drago told me, 'to wash our body of the death we'd just been touching'.

Once inside the house, the priest addressed the group that had gathered. He payed tribute to Milos's life and, on behalf of his family, thanked all of those for coming back to the house. During his address to the group he told the gathering:

> We (Serbs) have seen many dead over the centuries including those in this war. In this war there are orphans who need our love and support. Like the death of our people in this war, we know that we can rise up and make a new life for ourselves. We must know that in life there is death and it is through our remembering the death of people we love, that we also remember their life.

In the family home there were a number of photographs of Milos, from his migration to Australia right up to the year of his death. What struck me about the gathering that day is that more people came back to the family home on this occasion than I recall on the day of the funeral. Nearly all of them filed past the photographs and almost all of those did so in complete silence.

We then sat down for the meal. The man sitting next to me at Milos's home was one of the two men who had greeted and kissed me at the cemetery earlier that morning. I turned to him and asked why there was a Parastos 40 days after the death of Milos. He answered that it was a way of allowing Milos's soul to leave his body and enter into heaven. He continued to tell me that there was always going to be a body underground, but the soul and spirit of the body would always remain in heaven. As I continued in conversation with him, he also mentioned that remembering the dead at 40 days was 'a way for the community to come together and see each other'. Of all that he gave me in his answer, I felt that this last point was the one that seemed to be emphasised above all others that he made. He went on to say: 'It's a way for us to feel as a community. This is where I belong'.

Belonging at (to) the Soccer

Serbian Australians used a variety of means to bring about a sense of shared involvements with others. At the soccer ground for example, the excitement and energy of soccer acted as an expression point for the pressure and frustration felt by mainly Serbian men unable to cope with events in the former Yugoslavia. I believe that this contributed to an explanation of how many male participants used the soccer to feel bonded and close to each other, sharing common beliefs about the Serbian point of view.[6]

At the soccer too, there was a coming together of Serbian history and culture, and an explicit portrayal of the social heritage of the group. Whenever Serbian Australians gather at the soccer ground, customs, language and lifestyle, came together to form a kind of unity which was the result of shared similar background. Along with the unity of these qualities was a love of the game, and a network to find out what was happening in the former Yugoslavia. This informal news network formed purposeful bonds of belonging that may have also encouraged some participants to return each game. Djordje saw it this way:

> When I go to the soccer I can see all of my Serbian friends. I can find out what is happening in Yugoslavia. We are all *brothers together*. (emphasis added, N.P.)

The above quote emphasises that the soccer ground was an important meeting place for some Serbian Australian male participants to feel bonded with each other. The soccer ground provided a space for meeting with social and cultural contacts and knowing that common male bonds of culture and identity traces could be made. Moreover, there was also a common concern for the people and places of the former Yugoslavia that individuals may know. The individual problems of living, brought about by the Balkan war, had feeling dimensions attached to them and, being in the company of empathic others of the same culture may have contributed positively to the process of helping. The common bonds of culture become closely tied to the process of promoting improved individual coping in the face of external conflict and adversity. The weekly soccer game also appeared to be a means of helping to promote positive mental health and wellbeing by facilitating a release of tensions, and securing 'close-knit' associations over common interests. Viewed this way, male bonding, and belonging to the sport of soccer and the social interaction it brings, is an example of health as a social and emotional process, involving the sharing of recreational space with others.

Symbols of Serbian culture and national identity such as flags and emblems are essential to this aim and were often seen during the game on the clothing of spectators, for instance a T-shirt design, or a lapel pin. Several T-shirts were branded with the four 'C's ('S' in Cyrillic script). These four Cs make up the acronym of the slogan *Samo Sloga Srbima Spasava*. That is, *'Only unity can save the Serbs'*. (trans. N. P.)

The importance of T-shirts bearing symbols of cultural identity can be seen through the meanings attached to such property. At the completion of a soccer game during 1994, a fight broke out between Serbian and Croatian youth. Djordje tells of having his T-shirt ruined:

> I had a black eye and blood all over me and bruises everywhere. They tore my T-shirt, my favourite Serbian T-shirt, the one with the eagle on it. It was a pity as I really liked it. I bought it in Sydney when it was 600 years of Serbian history after the battle of Kosovo.

The above meanings attached to the T-shirt serve as a symbolic marker of cultural identity and belonging. The battle of Kosovo referred to by Djordje above, was fought in June 1389 when the Seljuk of Ottoman Turks led by Sultan Armarth fought a battle against Tsar Lasar in the Kosovo fields near Pristina. The battle of Kosovo - convincingly won by the Turks marked the fall of Serbian independence.   It has been memorialised by the Serbian Australian writer Kazich (1989, p. 21) as:

> ... penetrating the Serbian national soul. An event of the greatest military defeat, which the Serbian people transformed into their greatest moral victory. Serbians have drawn the spiritual strength to survive through the stormy history of slavery and even today remain ready through the contemporary warfare against to protect its very roots.

Many contemporary Serbian publications in Australia, depict the Kosovo battle as a noble military defeat which began their 500 years of slavery under the Turks.   More importantly, perhaps, contemporary interpretations of the Battle of Kosovo signify a spiritual victory which gave the Serbs the strength to survive as an orthodox nation and to prevail over the Turks and all future enemies. Glenny (1992, p. 182) cites Turgut Ozal, the then President of Turkey, who stated during a May 1992 visit to Washington that 'the fluid situation in the Balkans [at this time] is a once-in-a-lifetime opportunity for Turkey to restore its economic, diplomatic and cultural influence among Moslem vestiges of the Ottoman empire'. It was for this reason that United Nations plans for Turkish troops to conduct peace-keeping operations in the former Yugoslavia raised concern from the Serbian side. 'Like pouring petrol on a smouldering Serbian fire', as one participant told me. The Serbian side repeatedly argued that Turkish forces would be keen to enact revenge and domination of the region, from battles 500 hundred years ago, as a pro-Muslim force.[7]

Viewed this way, symbols of unity, belonging and bonding were both internal and external to individuals, and more readily experienced rather than explained. Like the Serbian T-shirt, the Serbian flag is, to another participant, a symbolic representation of:

> the Serbian people, our people only. No other nationalities wear that symbol. No others know what it means or feels like to have it. At the soccer match we are all Serbs and we are all proud to be there wearing that symbol.

For Serbian Australians at the soccer ground, cultural symbols of belonging also seemed characterised by social and spiritual features through the use of Serbian language by spectators, and the availability of Serbian food and drink such as *chevapcica* (a small skinless sausage made from beef and spices, usually cooked over a charcoal grill and served with chopped onion, potato salad and cabbage), *slivovica* (a strong spirit fermented from plums) and *kolac* (cake). During fieldwork at the soccer ground, I made the following reflections in my fieldwork journal:

> I can see how important it is [for participants] to share national identity and sentiment with each other. For those participating at the soccer, there is an inside feeling and affirmation of valued involvement both on and off the soccer ground. Through the soccer, I could see how important it was for participants to share national sentiment with each other over what is currently taking place in Australia and former Yugoslavia. The pressure of events, the pressure of media reporting, the pressure of national sentiment, all must be going somewhere. It is almost as if it is travelling from their hearts to their mouths.
>
> The sum substance of which seems to be forcing them to come together. The soccer ground is a perfect place for Serbian Australians to gather, to talk and express their concern and angst over these issues. The ground is Serbian territory.

Through the above reflection and interpretation, there was a suggestion that the national and cultural identity of homeland events embraced people's sense of the local situation. I see this as an important means through which people experience, define and defend their community sense of belonging. Whether or not participants are team members, or on the sideline cheering, the experience of having your contribution to the day feeling valued, needed and accepted by others helps the overall articulation with the environment in which they live. Through attending and participating in soccer matches, the person experiences a fit or congruence with other people, groups, objects, symbols and dimensions of the Serbian bonding. Moreover, there can be a proud display of symbols of 'all that is Serbian'. These points are illustrated in the following quote from Djordje:

> (Soccer) it's the number one sport in the world. *When it comes to soccer, when it comes to the Serbian community, the majority of males will follow soccer. They (males) are so into it.* When we meet we all talk about soccer, the game last week, everything that happened. We get into it, *it's a Serbian bonding kind of thing.* I've done it ever since I was a kid. It has always been my father's number one thing. (emphasis added, N. P.)

What struck me about this young man's point of view was the way he seemed to merge soccer, men and bonding as if each of these three things were synonymous. Attending the soccer and talking with other

Serbian men was a ritual that served to consciously affirm his sense of belonging to other Serbians. Such an interpretation may illuminate how bonding and belonging at the soccer has acted as a release valve for some Serbian Australians. This may also explain how the majority of this group have avoided violent clashes and property damage with other groups from the former Yugoslavia who also live in Australia.

Blood and bonding to accept or punish others

The idea of particular actions by individuals and groups as personal forms of emotional release of tension, brought about by the inter-ethnic conflict in the Balkans, was also associated with the drive to accept and/or punish others in Australia. Participation in the so called 'Serbian bonding thing' for example, meant an explicit acceptance of individuals and groups willing to entertain the Serbian point of view. Against a background of Serbia being seen as the main perpetrator of the Balkan conflict, any individual, group, or country perceived by Serbians to be sympathetic to the 'Serbian side' was almost always well received. As Marija told me, this idea also meant that people from the former Soviet Union and Greece were seen as allies to Serbians in Australia:

> Last week on the news we saw that Russian soldier going over to Yugoslavia to help out the Serbs. When we saw television film of the soldier boarding the train, I felt something in my heart straight away. My mother and I were watching the news at the time and I saw my mother put her hand on her heart, and she said 'that's a nice thing to see'. I knew straight away that this guy is one of our people.[8]

In a separate interview, Marija spoke of a kindred spirited reaction to being entertained by people thought to be ethnic Russian:

> I took mum to see Torvill and Dean. Now they're Poms. There were a lot of others in the actual show, 8 other women and 8 other men, and when they were getting introduced by name at the end of the show, we found that there were a lot of Russians and a lot of Ukrainians in it, and I said 'gee, that feels nice'. It's like if they said a Serbian name very similar, because Russians have, like us in a way, in a lot of ways, we believe in the same things, we've got very similar traditions, very similar cultures to us, like were cousins ...[the] closest thing to Serbs.

This extract and the previous one suggests a fundamental affinity for the perceived ethnic identity of others. Participants now locate the source of compatibility between historical and national tradition as somewhere deep within themselves. Such a belief was despite individual participants never having direct or indirect contact with those they have associated themselves with.

Elsewhere, Serbian Australians who were identified by their own group as either un-supportive or un-sympathetic to the Serbian point of view were known as 'plastic Serbs'. That is, people who at a superficial level 'claimed to be Serbian, but did not stick together with others over the Serbian cause in Australia, [or] did not donate food, money or other items for Serbian refugees in the Balkans'. Being labelled as a 'plastic Serb' in Australia meant, in effect, that an individual would be the subject of negative gossip networks and other informal means whereby they could not be valued or respected. So-called 'plastic Serbs' were not welcome among groups of participants who worked for what has become known throughout this study as 'all that is Serbian'.

Rejection of people assumed to be enemies of the Serbs, such as Croatian Australians, was carefully monitored by the Serbian National Federation of Australia, as the following excerpt from *Srpski Pregled* (Serbian Review) (April-May, 1993, p. 8) explains:

> It was in Adelaide that Australian Serbs first learnt of the planned visit of Dobroslav Paraga, notorious leader of the neo-fascist Croat militia known as HOS. Ironically the source of this information was the Croat radio program which had announced on-air the intended visit of the infamous Paraga. The following day, after receiving confirmation of the proposed visit, the Serbian National Federation filed a formal protest with the relevant federal authorities pointing out the real potential for ethnic unrest of such a visit. Following the protest action, the Serbian National Federation was informed that Paraga's visa application had subsequently been rejected.

Here there was a deliberate protest by the Serbian National Federation of Australia against allowing a symbolic Croatian political figure into Australia on the grounds that he may be the catalyst for ethnic clashes and unrest. In addition to this was the way in which the war between the two groups in Australia was being played out.

Take as another example of punishment and protest the case of the Australian federal election of 1993. In this election, the Serbian National Federation of Australia began a nation-wide 'Put Labor Last' campaign 'for discriminatory policies towards Australian Serbs' (*Srpski Pregled*,

Vol. 1, No. 2, 1993, p. 5). Once again, Serbian bonds were being used to vent frustration and anger brought about by the war, and in this instance towards groups who 'did not listen to or support the Serbian people's point of view' (p. 5).

In the election, Paul Keating won his first victory as leader and this also saw the Australian Labor Party (ALP) enter its fifth consecutive term.[9] While there was a national swing to Labor of 2 per cent,[10] Labor lost the seats of Adelaide, Grey and Hindmarsh.[11] It was these seats that the Serbians had been targeting with a view to defeating the Labor candidate. In the seat of Hindmarsh, the Serbian National Federation recommended a first preference vote for the Liberal candidate (Ms Chris Gallus) for she 'had previously demonstrated her willingness to listen to the Serbian point of view and had actively assisted the [Serbian National] Federation in pursuing certain matters' (*Srpski Pregled,* Vol. 1, No. 2, 1993, p. 5). In addition to this the Serbian National Federation provided logistical support and organised the distribution of pamphlets and how to vote cards in the marginal electorate of Kingston on behalf of the 'pro-Serbian candidate, Mr. Egils Burtmanis [who] deserved such support'. The Serbian National Federation felt that, while the shift in the Serbian vote cannot be held totally responsible for the loss of three Labor seats, their efforts did offer something to help the Liberal party take them from Labor:

> The coherent bloc that is the Serbian vote was a substantial portion of the margin of victory in all of these three seats. Any shift in the Serb vote back to Labor will make these three seats difficult to retain for the new Liberal members (*Srpski Pregled,* Vol. 1, No. 2, p. 6).

Through the use of aggressive political campaigning against the Australian Labor Party, the Serbian National Federation set about the fight to destroy what they believed to be a force oppositional to Serbians worldwide. Having established a collective identity, the Federation moved toward helping those who they believed had helped them. This was done on the Australian battleground, where the territorial claim was for a Serbian voice to be heard in such a way that the Australian government would listen and act. Serbians who participated in the distribution of pamphlets were given the physical means to do something about their frustration and anger. This meant that there was, for some, a clear sense of direction in where to take the case of the Serbian point of view. For many, this was a welcome cause of mental relief.

Conclusion

The discussion generated in this chapter has centred upon issues surrounding Serbian bonding and belonging in Australia. The issues raised suggest that, what participants believed it meant to belong to national and international Serbian interests, and what was sacred about these involvements, became entangled in historical and cultural beliefs from the recent and distant past. These beliefs, mediated through the Serbian Orthodox religion, local sport and recreational settings, politics at a federal level, and family grief, were guided by global and local pressures and frustrations. As the old verities of 'Yugoslav' identity fell apart, participants engaged a new ethnic Serbian consciousness that helped preserve the social life and cultural meaning of individuals.

Also explored in this chapter was how a sense of belonging, bonding and purpose in Serbian national and cultural activity was a means for some participants - mainly males - to interpret and manage emotionally distressing life events in the Balkans and Australia. Through analysis of what participants said of their experience, this chapter has revealed that health as a social and emotional process could no longer be seen as a localised phenomena. Rather, the health effects of the Balkan war on Serbian Australian participants must be seen as something that transcended the national settings within which they lived. Physical and mental health issues for participants were revealed as part of a process linked to changing constructions of Serbian national and cultural identity and relationships with symbolic events of the recent and distant past.

Viewed this way, the sense of belonging to the Serbian nationalist culture and tradition was an important element in the mental health and wellbeing of some individuals. According to this analysis, sense of belonging was an experience that was not limited to local situations: the experience of being valued and involved in activities in Australia was interpreted in direct reference to issues of European ethnic identity. In this respect, sense of belonging to a situational event such as the Balkan war was made more powerful when ethno-historical connections were interspersed with contemporary events and issues.

We also saw how campaign strategies to reward and punish political parties in the lead up to a Federal election gave a heightened sense of meaning to the Serbian community. With this level of support, some individuals felt confident to generate new community resources to benefit the Serbian cause. In this situation, Serbian Australians responded favourably to politicians who, they perceived, both valued and believed in them. This means that, in circumstances where Serbians felt they had a positive self image in the political arena, they were prepared to accept and support those who offered public support.

The selection of themes for discussion in this chapter acknowledges the suffering of participants in multiple ways. In the next two chapters we move to consider the wellbeing of participants as they try to cope with emotional stress, anger, anxiety, fear, guilt, poor sleep, feelings of frustration and of becoming out of control, as these problems were framed by newly defined personal and cultural boundaries and sense of belonging in the context of local and global processes presented so far. In moving deeper into the discussion of health and cultural issues in the life of Serbian Australians, we must also move closer to interpreting the ferocity of the armed conflict in the Balkans and violence in Australia.

Notes

1   It is interesting to note the call for a historical emphasis to help with the plight of Muslims in Bosnia. Akbar Ahmed (1993, p. 11) writing in the *Arab Review* argues that until the Bosnian Muslims become more aware of their history they 'will continue to suffer unless they inform themselves better ...they need to know the roots of what is happening [that] are embedded in encounters that took place centuries ago'.

2   Here I am thinking of the great mass of human consciousness that is beyond my reach. Nevertheless, the items that characterise psychic structure are made up of Bollas (1992, p. 38-46) describes as hermeneutically dynamic forms of experience and other 'mental contents that help express thinking and individual meaning'.

3   Julian Borger (1996, p. 4) of the *Guardian Weekly* newspaper presents a variation of this story as a joke circulating in Sarajevo during 1995. Borger tells of a Croat, a Muslim, and two Serbs arriving on the moon. The Croat points at the lunar mountains and says: 'Those are like the Dalmatian hills. This must be Croatian land.' The Muslim argues the cratered surface resembles the shell-scarred roads of Sarajevo, 'so it must be Muslim'. One of the Serbs pulls a gun, shoots the other dead, and says: 'A Serb died here. This is Serb land'.

4   The idea of identity and belonging helping Serbian Australians to better cope with events in the Balkans and Australia, is explored in more detail in chapter 7 of this study.

5   For the person who initiates the kiss, the correct procedure is to kiss the right hand side of the face first, then the left, then finish off with a third kiss to the right hand side once again.

6   Here it seemed that the sport of soccer reflected the masculinist assumptions and interests of mainly male Serbian Australians.

7   See also, *Spruiks Zaidnica*, May 1994; *Serbian National Federation of Australia Media Review*, No 4 (Early May) 1993; and Fisk, (1992, p. 1).

8   Australian, American and British mercenaries with and without ethnic ties to the former Yugoslavia have fought on the various sides. At the signing of the Dayton Peace Accord in December 1995 an estimated 1,000 mojahedin volunteers from

Afghanistan, the Middle East and Africa were thought to be active around the Bosnian towns of Zenica, Tesanj and Zavidovici.   See also, Borger, (1995); Donaldson and Coverley, (1992); Doyle (1992a); and Doder, 1994.

9   Paul Keating had dislodged the previous prime minister, Bob Hawke, 15 months earlier in a Party coup.

10   Antony Green (1996) estimates that 80 per cent of the Australian electorate have a primary political allegiance to one of the major political parties and the other 20 per cent are the so called 'swinging voters' that candidates dedicate so much time and effort to attract. At most elections in Australia the final outcome can be decided by as few as one voter in twenty.

11   All three seats have a long history of association with the Australian Labor Party (ALP). Up until the 1993 election, the ALP held the seat of *Grey* for almost all of the preceding 50 years. The seat of *Adelaide* has almost always been held by the ALP since Australia's Federation (1901), and the seat of *Hindmarsh* was lost by the ALP for the first time in its history.

6 The Experience of Long Distance Devastation: Globalisation of Worry

One issue concerns all Australians about the countries emerging from the former Yugoslavia: the appalling loss of life and suffering taking place there. Australians have been touched by it. We understand the pain the conflict causes citizens of communities with links with parts of the former Yugoslavia. With the suffering and horrors which have been deeply felt here, it has been a tribute to those of former Yugoslav descent to not allow the pressures and tensions of this appalling conflict to spill over into this country (Paul Keating, Prime Minister of Australia[1]).

If this group [alleged Croatian attackers] 'takes out' the Serbian church, they'll get all the Serbs against them. It begins as a feeling of hurt, then turns into a feeling of aggression. Blowing up [our] church is like trying to wipe out the Serbian race (Serbian Australian male youth speaking at the scene of property damage in Adelaide).

Introduction

At about the time when the Hon. Paul J. Keating spoke the words that open this chapter, I had come to more fully realise the suffering being felt by Serbian Australians, and indeed all Australians from the former Yugoslavia. Clearly, as will be demonstrated in this chapter, I had seen many Serbian Australians during the research who had told me of their worry, anger, suffering and anguish. But the Prime Minister's remarks confirmed a phenomenon, both national and global in its ramifications, namely, that people were being caught up in and consumed by events in the former Yugoslavia to the extent that this was threatening the peaceful stability between groups with links to the region.[2]

This chapter is primarily devoted to an interpretation of what participants did and felt in response to violence, destruction and upsetting events occurring simultaneously in the former Yugoslavia and Australia.

It will be argued that the prolific and repeated reporting of the Balkan war collided with participants' memories of the region. This experience gave rise to feelings of hurt and devastation, and involved bouts of extreme emotional distress, as people tried to live amid the carnage. Whether or not participants had migrated from Serbia proper, Bosnia Herzegovina, the disputed region of Krainja in Croatia, or had ever actually set foot in the Balkans, there was both a willingness and, it seems, a need to talk with me about the experience. In particular, participants wanted to talk about feelings of frustration, emotional stress, anxiety, anger, worry, fear, guilt, not eating, and, not sleeping. At this point I refer back to chapter 1 where we first learned of Gordana's mental distress and torment. Below is an example of how she expressed her feelings:

> ... I so desperately feel the need to bear my soul, overflowing with grief, to someone who may take the trouble to hear. ... When Yugoslavia came to its fall and destruction, my whole world seemed to have fallen apart as well. I could never imagine that it would bring me such heartache and have such a traumatic impact on me. ... It [the war] has brought me and some of my close family living here enormous pain, as at times I get to the point of breaking. Always a very happy and outgoing person, I have now lost all joy and sense of fun, wishing no company, finding no diversion in friends and outings.

Later, through what *I* describe as palpitations; feelings of being distant and unable to concentrate; feelings of frustration; severe emotional exhaustion; feelings of becoming 'out of control'; and an urge to get violent towards other nationalities and groups from the former Yugoslavia living in Australia, I will endeavour to show how these problems of living have been framed by local and global processes. Before turning to these areas however, two background issues that have emerged from the data must be noted. These are what I call *long distance devastation* and *local and global hurts*.

The twin processes of long distance devastation and global and local hurts

Long distance devastation may be thought of as the unpleasant experience of watching from afar as homeland people and places are being destroyed. In this case, the memories of the people and places of one's birthplace and childhood are caught up in the destruction brought about by the Balkan war. It is made worse by not having contact with friends and family and/or not being able to help and comfort family should contact be possible. The

Serbian Australian medical practitioner Dr Zdravlje, (first introduced in chapter 4) describes the mental distress and worry of patients attending his general practice, when trying to cope at great distance from the devastation occurring in the Balkans:

> All the time they lose their sleep. Some don't have contact with the family for months and don't know what is happening to their parents or their brothers and sisters and all they heard on the news was that one of their first or second cousins was killed ...And then you have the reaction in the beginning of the war when the skirmishes began last year, their was more anxiety, more agitation of not knowing what might happen, where the skirmish might end up.

Similarly, Ratko expressed his distress at being distant from his family and friends:

> ... it's heart breaking (because) you see your friends and families going through hard times then having problems and not having any money, job, school life. It makes you feel very uncomfortable just being there watching [the television]. We still have some contact with some of our friends that are still fighting there. When they come to their families they ring up and it's hard for me to cope with that.

These quotations emphasise the powerful and ever-present linkages present in participants being caught up in the experience of loss and long distance devastation.

Marcus (1995, p. 116) considers the apparently increasing global integration of people's lives as 'intimately becoming more integrated and this, paradoxically, is not leading to an easily comprehensible totality but to an increasing diversity of connections among phenomena once thought disparate and worlds apart'. I consider this argument to have very important practical and theoretical implications in the development of this chapter, because of the ways in which participants were being caught up in the experience of loss and long distance devastation.

Like many of the people with whom I talked about the impact of the Balkan war on their lives in Australia, Dr Zdravlje described what he saw as creating significant linkages between the two regions. Below, he tells of the health effects brought about by the Balkan war, and the Australian government's decision to support economic trade sanctions against the former Yugoslav republics of Serbia and Montenegro:

[The patient's] stress has been made worse by sanctions. [Patients] would like to send some money and some things across to their family. *They feel cheated and abandoned, ...cheated, angry and bitter.   Bitterness is something that eats away at you. [They are] very bitter, and angry [and] that creates a lot of psychological problems in people.* They have lived here [Australia] for many years and now feel outcast. My general feeling is that the Serbian community has a great sadness. (emphasis added, N.P.)

Zorica, a 36 year old married Serbian Australian, expressed her sentiments about this issue:

It's a worry if they [her aunts, uncles and cousins] are OK. [It's] a fear about if they are dead or alive. Not being able to contact them is a worry. I worry about them being so far away. It's times like these that it hits home how far away they really are. And that makes it sad too.

They tell me on the phone 'We are short of flour, we can't buy bread, we can't do this and that', and like many times I want to send money over there and I cannot because there is a ban on all dollars. You cannot send money, you cannot send food and you know your family is in strife and you can't help them and you can't help them because this Government is doing these bad things to us. After I get off the phone it comes to the point of, I think like oh God, you just want to explode you want to scream, *[Zorica's eyes go skyward and fists clench at this moment]* but that doesn't help you ...You almost could hit somebody; the tension is really there.

The continuing power of long distance devastation is apparent, as the mental health of participants seems interlinked with historical and cultural factors. This can lead to complex processes arising from the emotional pressures previously described in the context of some individuals seeing themselves only in relation to what is happening in the Balkans.   From this perspective, Serbian Australians weave into consciousness the events they see on the television, hear on the radio and read in the newspapers, which leave them in an almost perpetual state of worry and guilt. An important intervening factor in this situation is a sense of powerlessness to help members of their own family caught up in the war.

These situations appear to be made worse by two intersecting issues. *Firstly,* there is a preoccupation with the (often) unknown fate of friends and/or family living close to fighting, as Darko and Nenad, two adult males, both of Adelaide, explain:

I worry since I have family over there. Naturally enough I worry, you know. I started regular ringing over there, every day and that was very costly, two dollars a minute, and when you ring a few members of your family each day it mounts up. And my niece at school over here, she worries about her parents, as she thinks that a lot of people over there will start to arm themselves. 'What are our family going to do?', she asks me. I was worried that if somebody, my brother, cousins, goes off to war what will happen to them? Yeah, there was quite a bit of worry about this. (Darko, a 55 year old Serbian Australian)

I worry, of course I worry, I have five people in my family in the war. We know that one is dead and the other four have disappeared. We do not know if they are dead or alive. They are my cousins mainly. My brother has my cousins living with him, seven people living in a one and a half bedroom flat. I worry about this because I don't know what to expect. I have spent 30 years in this country but I still can't forget that country over there, [the] mother country. (Nenad, a 57 year old retired Serbian Australian)

And, *secondly,* memories of interethnic events of the past intersect with contemporary events, as Darko explains:

(B)ecause I knew soon that if somebody [government officials] starts to call the shots with ethnic identity cards, ethnic and religious information then the same thing that happened during the Second World War will happen again. And I say God forbid if they [Croatians] implement that - that would be a real tragedy because the Serbs will not stay quiet this time [they] will not allow anybody to rule them or take away their rights like before during the last war. Somebody will start to kill somebody and then it will all begin just like before. It just spreads more and more. ...It's not just a possibility, it's a certain future.

Clearly then, these issues of long distance devastation disrupted and led to a break down in health and social wellbeing. It is from this interpretation that the term *local and global hurts* evolves. Local and global hurts were situations in which the individual impact of the Balkan war, and the mental health of Serbian Australians, are interlinked; this might lead to biophysical and social pressures that would bring about a feeling of distress, leading to a range of problems of living. People caught up in the process of long distance devastation entered into a period of being completely absorbed by feelings of anger, frustration and powerlessness. This period of immersion in devastation in contemporary social life gave way, in and through time, to the feeling that something must be done. In the course of doing something about their situation, there was emotional exhaustion, sadness, withdrawal, and a feeling of being 'hurt' by what a person saw and heard from the electronic and print media. These feelings of hurt were caught up in the framework of local and global processes and a reappropriation of the Serbian past.

In demonstrating the concept of *local and global hurts,* I refer back to Zorica, a 36 year old Serbian Australian welfare worker, as she expresses her frustration about the television news:

> ... just too distressing to watch. Too reinforcing of the feelings of worry and concern even more. It makes me feel powerless. It is all going on over there, and there is nothing I can do about it. I didn't watch it [the television news] because it was a visual immediate representation of what was going on. Seeing it was worse than thinking about it. You think about it but when you see it you get more [of the] reality of 'over there', over here.

This quotation reveals that the reality of war is not prevented from entering into life in Australia. As Verica told us in chapter 3, there was a sense of how *physically* participants are here, but *mentally,* they are over there. This situation is aligned with what Giddens (1996, p. 22) remarks as an important feature of globalisation: a condition that 'no one can opt out of'. It is an 'in-here matter, which affects, or rather is dialectically related to, even the most intimate aspects of our lives' (Giddens, 1996, p. 51). It is part of our personal and social lives, and must be recognised as such, both in human relations and empirical research (Robertson, 1992).

Clearly then, both long distance devastation, and local and global hurts were influenced by a powerful and ever-present international media, a clear sense of national and cultural identity and, as seen through participants' lives, a deep feeling of loss and powerlessness to intervene.

The perspective taken in this chapter

As indicated throughout this study, I have taken a particular kind of global perspective to help me interpret the ways in which Serbian Australians experience life in the shadow of the Balkan war. In other words, local situations in one part of the globe, under conditions of international migration, affect conditions elsewhere. Diasporic nationalism is one aspect of this. As Anthony Smith (1990, p. 22) has emphasised, the 'globalisation of nations and the nation state is complete, there is no area unaffected by nationalist protest free of the nation'. Here, as seen throughout my journey, participants' interpretations of the past were an active element in their living the present. In formulating this chapter, I refer back to the description of early morning property violence against the two Serbian Churches in Adelaide. This event was marked by participants' interpretations of a Croatian Nazi past. As I walked around the Church to photograph the smashed windows and doors, the death threats and the accompanying graffiti, I came across the source of the second quotation used to open this chapter:

> If this group [alleged Croatian attackers] 'takes out' the Serbian church, they'll get all the Serbs against them. It begins as a feeling of hurt, then turns into a feeling of aggression. Blowing up [our] church is like trying to wipe out the Serbian race. (Serbian Australian male youth speaking at the scene of property damage in Adelaide)

I took the above statement, said to me in English, to mean that local Serbs were emotionally hurt by the continued accusations about their ethnic and religious identity. As will be further outlined in this chapter, local hurts were also manifest on talkback radio, letters to newspaper editors, graffiti attacks on private property, as well as other more serious violations, including death threats against Serbians, decapitation of Serbian statues and other incidents. One participant, the owner of a city hotel, told me during an interview that he had received several anonymous bomb threats, by telephone, telling him 'you've got two hours to evacuate the hotel you Serb bastard'. Despite the local police urging him to do so, he never went ahead with an evacuation of the hotel. Instead, he claimed that, 'they won't ever get me this way; I have my pride. I know who these guys are and I won't be intimidated by them'.

To further emphasise that globalisation of the Balkan war meant that it implicated events at a local level, I refer to the sentiments of two Serbian Australian church men, Peter Radojevic and Bogdan Bolta (1992). In an 'open letter' sent to the central governments of Australia, England and the United States, they described their 'pain' about the Balkan war in this way:

> *We have been morally and nationally hurt* by your Government's decision and the manner of recognition of the republics that broke away from the Yugoslav Federation. *All Serbians in Australia are greatly pained by the new spilling of blood in our own homeland and believe that the division of Yugoslavia should be conducted according to the will of the people,* expressed by voting referendum, in a peaceful manner and by consultation, just as it was first formed in 1918.[3] (emphasis added, N. P.)

Such sentiments encouraged me to explore *what people actually do and feel during heightened frustration, anger, hurt and emotional distress as these feelings relate to events both local and global.* As will be demonstrated below, this enlargement of focus led me to search for the meanings Serbian Australians gave to their encounters. This, in turn, led me to consider the meanings of symbols long forgotten, and interactions between participants and the larger world.

Welcome to hell

The formulation of interpretation in this chapter was also influenced by two still photographs of Sarajevo war scenes on the cover of *Seasons in Hell: Understanding Bosnia's War,* a book by the British journalist Ed Vulliamy. This contains stories of violence, atrocity, horror and in the most explicit detail, what the author describes as 'the failings of humanity to make any difference.[4] Perhaps more than anything else, it is an eyewitness account of military, civilian and humanitarian efforts in the former Yugoslavia during the course of the war. From this perspective, Vulliamy's (1994) insights provided contextual information about the conflict, and thus served as an important resource and reference point for interpretation. The distinctiveness of Vulliamy's writing about these issues is situated in how he adroitly shifts between being the narrator of events and a sometimes impartial participant in the lives of people caught up in the horrors of the war.

At the Omarska Detention Camp,[5] Vulliamy (1994, p. 113) recounts conversations with surviving prisoners who had been witness to the constant beatings and murders of fellow prisoners and, in the same section, with almost cynical reluctance he tells of the 'media circus' that quickly formed outside the camp gates, eager to send the first pictures of this horror back home. Later (p. 242) he tells of how his fear of being killed when driving a 'soft skin' (not armour plated) vehicle at high speed under constant arms fire did not really matter to him until long after the incident. His proximity to the centre of events, and skills employed by Vulliamy, inevitably led him to examine a range of complex and paradoxical situations.

But the main significance of the book *Seasons in Hell: Understanding Bosnia's War,* for this chapter, is the photography on the front and back covers. The *first photograph* is an 'up close' colour image of dead girl child, aged about 12 years, who appears to have been mutilated by shrapnel. She is lying on a green canvas stretcher with eyes and mouth slightly open. Upon careful scrutiny of the photograph, the most apparent wound sites appear to be her neck and upper right arm. My brief analysis of the nature of these wounds suggests that they were caused by a jagged edged projectile with a strong blast effect, leading to extensive injury (this seems particularly true in relation to the wound in the region of the girl's neck). The projectiles that I imagine to be most likely responsible for this damage are pieces of shrapnel from bomb casing. The child's eventual death looks to have been caused by prolonged bleeding, suggesting that her life might have been saved by expert medical intervention.[6] The only information provided by Vulliamy comes from a brief cover note saying, *Victim of the night's shelling, Sarajevo, Bosnia.* Perhaps this is an early morning photograph.

On the back cover of Vulliamy's book is the *second photograph*. It is of an armed gunman, aged about 20 years. He is standing slightly stooped wearing fashion pleated trousers and a multicoloured jumper. Both jumper and trousers appear to be new, and in very good condition. This man looks more like a potential job seeker, inadvertently caught up in the conflict while on his way to a job interview in a Sarajevo department store. The point is that he looks nothing like the experienced armed gunman or paramilitary soldier sometimes seen on the television news from the region. His dishevelled appearance and tired facial expression suggest that he has not washed or slept in recent days. His eyes are looking downwards and squinting slightly. For protection from incoming gunfire he is standing behind three waist high sandbags. To his left is a concrete wall with the graffiti WELCOME TO HELL[7] daubed across it in bright red paint. The caption beneath this photograph reads, *City under siege, Sarajevo, Bosnia.*

My view is that these photographs represent defining moments of a different kind to those expressed above. They are graphic illustrations of the ferocity of the armed conflict in former Yugoslavia, that both destroyed human life and caused people in the region to get caught up in war, without any time to prepare themselves for the true nature of their involvement. Clearly, the armed gunman was not dressed for war (in camouflaged greens and a flak jacket), and the dead child certainly should not have been killed. If the world, as witness to events in the Balkans over the past five years, had not realised this at the time these photographs were taken, then the mass production of them in the form of a book cover would certainly tell that story. After all, it is difficult to see how this photograph of the dead child could not move the most seasoned viewer of television war violence.

In an epoch of global international media and telecommunications the events of Bosnia arrived on Australian television screens as fast as they unfolded (Poggioli, 1993).   News-television and news-radio revealed 'breaking-news' events as if they were occurring just a kilometre away from our homes. Events in Australia - what I term the 'local world' - such as drive by shootings in Queensland, destruction and desecration of Serbian and Croatian church property in Sydney, Melbourne and Adelaide, death threats against Serbians, and street marches in Canberra, Sydney, Melbourne and Adelaide, were always influenced by 'local' events in Australia and 'global' events in the former Yugoslavia. My point here is that the linking together of the 'global' and the 'local' in the lives of participants was amplified by media presentations that, in turn, had been used to devastating effect.

Like the thousands of hours of interview and participant observation data that I generated during the course of the conflict, television images, news-bulletins, documentaries and special interviews were all 'objects' that served to augment participant interpretation of what was going on in the Balkans, and what the experience of this actually felt like.   These images were not pleasant to look at and, in the case of Vulliamy's book cover, I could not look at the photograph of the dead child without feeling sick in the stomach.

Like a bullet to the head

With the conflict marked by ongoing and ever-present transmission of images, I found it important to explore more deeply the impact of the media. It is arguable that the inclusion of photographs and film of armed and maimed civilians engaged in the war had only a small part to do with the story the news item was intended to tell. With regard to the contents of Vulliamy's book, I believe that these photographs were placed on the cover because it was the publisher's decision to market the book in this way.   As in the electronic and print media industry, these photographs acted in similar ways to a newspaper headline or a 30 second television 'sound bite'. They were a sort of 'photographic headline' designed to attract and retain a worldwide audience (Turner, 1993) and, if possible, to agitate them into some sort of response.[8] Darko explained his 'frustration' about this type of media, in the following way:

I know that everybody in Australia listens to the news, radio talkback and a few other things. If I have some time when I am at work I listen at my desk. I listen to the radio and read the newspapers. I hear and see a lot of comments from Australians and they start accusing the Serbs of this and that and the Croats accusing the Serbs, and the Australian media accusing the Serbs, everybody accusing the Serbs and nobody seems to me to be saying anything in support of the Serbs and I become frustrated! Are we really that black? A few times I ring the radio station and get on to 'talkback' and say that 'nobody is saying anything else but blaming us'.

This quotation highlighted a feeling of demonisation experienced by some participants, in the process of trying to find out as much news from the region as possible. Nenad, a 57 year old retired male Serbian Australian, elaborated further on this issue:

When I watch the TV news I feel so angry. You know why? Because every [television] channel, especially SBS, they lie. They say that so-and-so is a Muslim fighter, but people in Australia they don't know how he dress. They are Serbian fighters who have been killed. They say that people are suffering because of the Serbians, but they show like Muslims and Croats making war.

As with the previous sentiments about radio and the cover of Vulliamy's book, could it be that television news from the Balkans was designed to grab the attention of viewers rather than attempt to summarise the complete subject matter of the story contained within it (see, Bonney and Wilson, 1993; Hartley, 1982)? This would mean that words, phrases and images had been carefully selected and designed to make an impact on others, that is the viewing audience.

The use of shocking images from former Yugoslavia to jolt a reaction in the mind of local and overseas governments and interest groups was the focus of a BBC Panorama program by British war correspondent Martin Bell. It was, as Simpson (1993, p. 19) explains, '50 minutes of clearly labelled private opinion... a clearly labelled private and personal view to get something done about the situation'. Of similar sentiment but with much less circulation potential were publications by the Serbian National Federation of Australia (Media Reviews, mid-May, 1993, and early September 1993, in particular) and the University of Zagreb Medical School. In the University of Zagreb *Croatian Medical Journal: War Supplement:1*, the editor Matko Marusic (1992, p. 1) wrote:

This (journal) will witness and document medical data on the war in Croatia ... The crimes committed by the enemy against civilians and those wounded and captured, the brutality with which they attacked churches, schools and medical institutions, villages and cities, historical monuments and every facet of the Croatian culture, identity and its very existence.

Like the cover of Vulliamy's book, the Serbian National Federation of Australia's publication, *The Unseen War: Croatian Land Grab in Central Bosnia,* and numerous articles contained within the *Croatian Medical Journal* carry photographs of mutilated and tortured human bodies. In each of these publications there are photographs of civilian and military personnel, with entry and exit gunshot wounds to the head, trunk and extremities. In the *Croatian Medical Journal* photographs are accompanied by commentaries such as '...a female, aged 16, from the village of *Gornja Budicna* killed by 10 erratic gunshot wounds on the right side of the trunk and extremities' (Kovacevic, 1992 p. 25). Another reads '...this male was executed by two gunshots in the head. Forensic expertise showed that the contusions and lacerations found on his body were inflicted by blunt mechanical force, suggesting that he was beaten before execution' (Marcikic, et. al. 1992 p. 33). In the Serbian publication there are eyewitness reports and photographs of similar atrocities in central Bosnia. Even more disturbing are photographs of Serbian children, as young as six, with bullet wounds to the head and smashed skulls. Sadly, these events and images, and the horrific stories that surround them, were repeated many times over during the course of the conflict. Night after night the world was offered a diet of violent television in real life settings with grizzly voice-overs.[9] In the following extract, Gordana speaks about the hurt of losing her homeland village, or town, and seeing the images of it on the television screen:

The same thought was going through my mind, night after night I can't sleep, I asked the Lord, 'after all these years, why must my holy ground, my motherland, fall apart?' The motherland, like a beautiful rainbow of diversity and it was the colours that made it so beautiful, now it's being pulled apart. Brother doesn't like brother any more and the motherland is pulling the brother's hands, legs, arms in different directions. Like the people who's bodies are being ripped apart by shrapnel, she's [motherland] pulling apart my homeland.

My interpretation of what was hurting Serbian Australians involved an understanding of the physical and emotional distress they felt as they tried to live amid the carnage and devastation. Whether participants were at home with friends and family, watching the television news, attending high school, at the work place, or at the soccer ground, they were *experiencing* the Balkan war at various levels. Participants saw the Balkan war on television and read about it in the newspapers. They were hearing it being talked about on the car radio, at church services and at cultural gatherings. One measure of how prolific and extraordinary the coverage of the Balkan war was, when compared to other crises around the world, can be seen through the following example. *The New York Times* newspaper from January 1991 to June 1992, carried around 50 reports on the crisis in Somalia, the Armenian-Azerbaijan civil war, and the Georgian civil war. Over the same period, *The New York Times* carried in excess of 500 reports on the Balkan war (Source: *Serb Net*, Washington DC Chapter, p. 3).

Clearly, it would be wrong to think of news-radio and news-television from and about war in the former Yugoslavia as only impacting upon people *inside* the borders of Europe.[10] As demonstrated by the participants' voices revealed so far in this chapter, the prolific and repeated reporting of this war collided with individual memories of the people, places, and childhoods tied to the region, the frustration of losing these, and feelings of hurt when speaking with others about the impact of the conflict.[11]

My analysis of these issues has led me to conclude that disturbing images of the war in former Yugoslavia were a palpable cause of distress for people around the world with cultural, familial and spiritual ties to the region. Herman (1992) discusses the impact of the stress of seeing images of war in Vietnam on soldiers who fought in it, arguing that the post war experience of seeing images of fighting and destruction keeps the distressed person confronted with the trauma. Poggenpoel (1995) describes a similar finding in relation to people living in 'black townships' that surround Johannesburg in the Republic of South Africa. There, Poggenpoel argues, people living in townships who were witness to ethnic and racial violence on a continuing basis, were often left in a perpetual state of mental distress. Similarly, Ratko explained:

> I'm always feeling 'on edge'. I am constantly thinking about what is happening overseas. Every phone call, every ring of the telephone, I become edgy thinking it's news from home, that something has happened.

The distress described in South Africa, and in the post-Vietnam war period is aligned to the experience of Serbian Australians. It reveals that, for participants, what they saw and heard from the 'motherland' was more than isolated incidents of violence in far away places. As the participants whose voices occupy this chapter tell us, they sometimes lived in a helpless and perpetual state of not knowing if and when someone they knew would eventually fall victim to a beating or murder, to ethnic cleansing or to rape.

This situation was made worse for participants when footage from the region was run and re-run over several evenings. For Desa, a Serbian Australian Community Welfare worker, based in western Sydney:

> The media is changing the average Australian's perception of the Serbian people. I have Australian friends who I have been very close with, they have known me for more than 15 years. I have been here for 22 years and they are people who know me very well through my work and therefore know the Serbs. The thing is that [I need to tell them that] Serbians have not terrorised any country or nation. They [Serbians] have a good record here in Australia. Now if you look at Croatians, they try to poison the dams, they have had their military training camps in the bushes, they have had something that the Serbians have not had. Australian people are good people but they now have their doubts about us. There are now doubts from what you are hearing on television or radio or seeing or reading. It's what they have been fed.

Is it likely, or indeed possible, that the 'average Australian' had a particular perception of Serbians before the war? If so, what might this perception have been? While it is near impossible to know the answer to these questions without some kind of systematic research, it has been possible to speculate on the impact of Serbian 'bombardments' of Sarajevo that were portrayed on the television news almost every evening for more than three years. In *War and the Media: Propaganda and Persuasion in the Gulf War*, Philip Taylor (1992) argued that television war news revealed that there were two wars going on during the period of the Gulf War: the war itself, fought by the United States led coalition against Saddam Hussein's forces, and the war as portrayed by the media. The war was 'live to air breaking news' and the news was 'live to air entertainment', that taking a strong priority over advertised program schedules. The Australian media commentator, Philip Adams (1996, p.

54), speaks of today's commercial news as being loaded with value judgements and manufactured to entertain:

> If someone's has got a home video camera when Los Angeles cops are putting the boot into Rodney King (an instance where being black enhances the story) it will occupy an immense amount of air time as it's lovingly lick-lickingly re-run, complete with slo-mo and freeze frames. *News is driven by visuals, by ten second grabs, by simplifications that have to be instantly comprehensible.* Forget complexities, subtext, contradictions, shades of grey. You'll find them if you're lucky, in print. (emphasis added, N. P.)

During the course of my journey, the six o'clock news became the place to see women weeping in front of television cameras; at the same time, television stations ran and re-ran footage revealing graphic and deeply disturbing descriptions of people being brutalised. One Bosnian woman told of being raped by a neighbour, and urinated on in the face (Goytisolo, 1993); another spoke of watching her sons dragged from their beds, forced to lie prostrate on the ground outside the family home to be killed with bursts of automatic gun-fire in the presence of family and other witnesses (Loyd, 1993). A participant attending a family gathering told me of her feelings and experiences of these and other, similar incidents:

> It [the killing] tears me apart completely. I can't watch the television as it makes me physically sick. It's too upsetting to watch. This war has torn people apart completely. I feel that there is such an injustice being done here to innocent people, it's terrible, really terrible seeing this.

For some participants the images of dead and injured also served to fuel the bitterness and hatred they had for the other factions caught up in the war. This applied to all the groups involved. The television images were a graphic reminder that the dead and mutilated child, the homeless family, and the orphaned pets on the roadside could have been the niece of a Croatian Australian, the former neighbours of a Bosnian Muslim Australian, or a much loved family pet of any such combination.

While reliving the trauma may provide an opportunity to deal with it in a positive and productive way, participants in this study dreaded the fear of seeing the war over and over again on the television screen. Gordana expressed her experience of watching the television images in this way:

> *It hurts me so much to see this land destroyed this way. It's devastating to see this* land which is so beautiful be destroyed so badly. *It is devastating*

to see the faces of children crying, doesn't matter who they are, Moslem or who they are, they are innocent children and they have no idea why this war is on and *it's dreadful to see this.* (emphasis added, N.P)

Notwithstanding the newsworthiness or otherwise of this material, these media images served to augment the viewer into a perpetual state of mental distress and hurt that was constantly being propelled by the television screen. Herman (1992, p. 42) points out that:

Reliving a traumatic experience, whether in the form of intrusive memories, dreams, or actions, carries with it the emotional intensity of the original event. The [participant] is continually buffeted by terror and rage. These emotions are qualitatively different from ordinary fear and anger, outside the range of ordinary emotional experience [they] provoke intense emotional distress.

For Drago, intense emotional distress in the form of 'depression and anger' went 'hand in hand':

I started off as really depressed, but now the depression has gone into anger. I'm just so angry all the time, angry at the world, angry at everyone, angry at a presenter on television that I've liked for years but now they talk in the light that they all talk about the Serbs in, and you suddenly hate the presenter. I switch him off, it's no good but I have to do it. It's the same thing night after night.

Viewed this way, television images of war from the former Yugoslavia were much more than the mere 'vision' that accompanied the reporting of a news event. The conventions used in shooting television pictures, the use of 'close up' shots, the editing and construction of relations between shots, and continual reminders from the soundtrack to pull viewer attention back from other activities (Turner, 1993), were crucial to my understanding the way participants felt. Unlike cinema film, television is in the domestic environment and therefore brings world events into the living room, the kitchen and, perhaps, even the bedroom and bathroom.

Emotionally and physically distressed by the war as participants may be, there was a certain paradox about this situation that must also be discussed. Despite knowing and experiencing the impact of war scenes on the television, people continued to watch the evening news. It was at this point that I asked myself, *While the news made people very angry, why was there a sense of urgency and desperation to see the next bulletin?* I was struck by participants who ate their meals around the time the television news went to air. Some even refused to answer the ringing telephone or a knock at the door. With such a commanding influence over information from the region, the television news became an important reference point in practical terms for conversation with others. As Zorica told me, people constructed their conversations with friends and relatives, indeed arranged their very lives around what they saw on the television news:

> I can't stand watching the news. It hurts me to see all those people suffering. It makes me sick, ill. But I have to watch it because I need to see if there is anyone I know, a relative or someone like that on the news. I have to know what's going on. I have to talk with others to see if they saw what I saw. I know that it makes me sick to see it all but I have to see it anyway.

As I moved in conversation with Zorica, I interpreted her as being like the many voices that make up this study: physically, Serbian Australians were 'here', but emotionally and spiritually they were 'over there'. This suggests that the interpretive context was an amalgam of local and international conditions (Robertson, 1992). Television images and radio broadcasts of the conflict, letters and telephone calls from home, served to connect Serbian Australians with the greater world. This immediacy of things global in local situations is viewed as a reaction to the greatly increased compression of the world that involves the simultaneity of the universal (Balkan war and catastrophe) and the particular (Serbian Australian experience). At a deeper level, I sensed that Zorica had feelings of powerlessness to help her family who were caught up in the war:

> For the first time, since the beginning of this tragic civil war, I feel completely helpless and without hope. With the fall of Krajina, I have crossed the threshold of the soul's innermost pain and have no tears left to cry. The happy memories spent around my grandparents and the many members of our extended family, sharing countless, precious events of my childhood in the large family home in Knin, keep flooding back with the full knowledge that it is no more and that all of the remaining members of that beloved family have now left the security and warmth of that home with no hope to ever return. Besides the personal tragedy of my closest family, I share completely in the plight of the entire 350, 000 Krajina Serbs stripped of their dignity, their lands, their heritage, without friends, without future, without hope.

This quotation draws attention to way in which the life-situations Gordana and others had lived, were bound up with circumstances that existed both inside and outside of Australia. In addition, her feelings of powerlessness to intervene and support her family was made more challenging by 'not knowing' anything of their whereabouts or wellbeing:

> ... there is an anxiety one goes through with not knowing what is happening to relatives. I have no idea if they are dead or alive. There is that balance one is playing with all the time and the frustration and anxiety that comes not knowing what fate has befallen them. That is a real pressure that I have on myself. They are the sorts of mixed feelings that certainly go through me.

For another Serbian Australian participant, Ilia, a 44 year old accountant, the nightly news of the Balkan war was nothing more than images that 'misrepresented the Serbian people', to the extent that the media was perceived as telling lies:

> You don't know the actual truth of the matter, and now when I watch the news, I honestly don't anymore, I mean I watch half of it and I always get upset with what they're saying. I'll abuse the news reporter and things like that. I'll say all sorts of things about it, because I know in my heart, I know it's not the truth, and if I am wrong, so is the Serbian community more or less here, because they don't believe any of it either.

Another participant, Desa, spoke of what she saw as the 'one-sided' nature of the news reporting against the Serbs, thus casting doubts on its credibility:

> It all feels one sided and biased! I never believed it! Where is the evidence? How can they support their claims? I believed that there were always two sides to the story. I believed that it was almost always first and second hand news ...always the media's interpretations of what was going on.

Darko reinforced his rejection of print and radio news by calling it 'rubbish'. At the same time he told me of the cumulative effects of having his family caught up in the war, and the frustration of not being able to help them in their the situation:

Nobody is saying anything else but blaming us. They say to me that 'You Serbs are trying to find a way to excuse yourself from wrongdoings'. They are always looking at us as the guilty party. It's like I'm killing myself to get the message through to them. I am frustrated by all this. I cannot bear those accusations that are thrown over the radio and newspapers and everything. I don't like those stories because I know that those stories are not true. It's a certain pressure building up in me and it's always in me. I worry about what our family are going to do...It's always on my mind. Whatever I am doing, it's always there. Whenever I do my work, I always think about it, what's happening over there and I think, 'My God, what's happening over there'. Many times it almost comes to tears on you. It comes to the point that is really pressure building on you. The most difficult thing is the frustration you can't do anything about.

As Darko spoke of his experience of conflict through the television screen, he gave me some insight into how these images of people committing atrocities against innocent others were perceived as atrocities 'wrongly attributed to the Serbs'.

Certainly, and alongside other groups, Serbians were suffering too. In mid 1993, for example, relief agencies had estimated approximately 600, 000 refugees from Bosnia and Croatia were displaced in Serbia, living with host families, many of who were not related (*The Economist*, October 31, 1992, p. 50). Darko went on to tell me that:

True

The Serbs are not getting recognised for looking after so many refugees. We only hear about the Serbs having these death camps, for the starving Muslims and Croatians. They show the same thing over and over again, the same footage of these camps, yet in the distance you could see a Croatian soldier guard walking around.

Along with these issues was trying to cope with 'all that is Serbian' being demonised in the media, popular opinion and children's literature (see Mattingley, 1993) as criminal and barbaric. Perhaps the most outstanding example of demonisation of Serbians through misinformation was spread by a United States based public relations firm on behalf of one of the warring factions in Bosnia Herzegovina. During 1992 a 'report' was sent to international news agencies that told of the deliberate killing of children by the Serbian Army. This false story claimed that Serb soldiers were being paid 300 British pounds for every child they killed. The story told of how the Serbs '... target the children because they are easier to kill [and] with their small size, the bullets make a bigger mess' (*New Statesman and Society*, 30 July, 1992, p. 12). The story was spread widely

What about freedom lie?

throughout Europe and North America before it was found to be completely untrue.

Clearly then, the sentiment surrounding the use of national and international media to emphasise human tragedy in the Balkans cannot be overemphasised. In 1992, Penny Marshall, of Britain's ITN television, beamed the first pictures of people being held in the Trnopolje 'death camp'. Her powerful images of near naked, starving Muslim men and boys, held by their Serbian captives behind barbed wire, were as graphic as those seen during the Holocaust. The images of men with ribs starkly prominent changed United States and British foreign policy towards former Yugoslavia, as Philip Knightley (1993, p. 11) explains:

> Beamed around the world on Thursday, August 6, 1992, the film's impact forced newspapers to emphasise the link with Nazi Germany. In Britain, two papers labelled stills from Marshall's film 'Belsen 1992'. Another said: 'A grim vision of a new Holocaust came to our TV screens last night.' In Germany, a Berlin newspaper declared: 'In Bosnia today, a new Auschwitz is beginning.' In the United States, ABC television said: 'To see adults starving was like a throwback to the death camps of war-time Germany.'

> Fewer than 20 minutes after Marshall's report was broadcast on American TV, President Bush had changed his policy towards Serbia. In Britain, Prime Minister Major recalled his cabinet from holiday for an emergency meeting which decided to send 1,800 ground troops to Bosnia. Within weeks the detention camps were closed, but the picture of the emaciated Bosnian Muslims had entered the iconography of war, and any sympathy the public might have had for the Serbs in this bitter civil conflict evaporated.

Whereas for Gordana, the repeated use of dramatic images from the detention camps served to demonise the Serbs:

> The media keep showing us the bodies, with shocking things having been done to them. They were saying that they were bodies left by the Serbs, but I know that they were mutilated Serbian bodies, mutilated by the enemy. *And this is what's so hurtful, it's so hurtful to suddenly feel so Serbian through all of this and I do feel Serbian,* and then read in the paper once again that 'Serbs in Australia should feel ashamed of themselves, they should come to their senses and try and influence their Serbian brothers over there'. *Well this is so hurtful because I am not a savage* [moving closer to me she screamed into my face], 'Am I a savage who would kill others'? (emphasis added, N. P.)

From the above quotations I concluded that the denial of atrocity or morally culpable behaviour by one's own group, was one way of coping with long distance devastation. In Victoria, for example, radio broadcaster Bob Radulovich was disciplined for breaching SBS program standards for 'certain' comments[12] allegedly made 'on air' that might exacerbate the 'Yugoslav' crisis locally. In response to this, about 500 Serbian Australians rallied outside radio station 3EA to have him reinstated. At the rally, Petar Zukanovic of the Serbian National Council of Victoria addressed the crowd saying that local Serbs 'felt discriminated against and starved of news from their homeland' (Masanauskas, 1991a, p. 6).[13]

When people's sense of belonging to the war region was combined with allegedly false news reports of fighting, rape, ethnic cleansing and property destruction, significant mental health problems emerged. In addition to this was the added difficulty of participants unable to help, either because it was too dangerous to so, or because there was not enough household money available to donate to the region.

Health effects described by participants thus far in the situation included sleeplessness; irritability; inability to concentrate; feelings of frustration; loneliness; anxiety; and intrusive thoughts. As we saw in the case of Darko, in the previous section, there was a preoccupation with the unknown fate of family trying to survive in regions in or around fighting particularly when telecommunications had also been lost. Television pictures were almost always seen to be a source of great distress.

Following on from this was his concern that television pictures and other media were almost always seen to be a source of great distress.[14] Television pictures represented violence and destruction that was qualitatively different to violence described using words. From this perspective the photographs and news footage touched more closely the mind of Djordje:

> That's why they keep showing us this stuff. They keep showing us the dead children, the burnt out houses [because] they show us the stuff that sends a message back home to people. You see things like Rwanda and things like that, they show little children starving because more people feel sorry for them [the children] than the adults. It's like that with churches, house, schools a lot of things like that. They show us the things that get a lot of people very upset, more and more upset about it.

The key reference points for these experiences were the emotional connections with people, places, memories and portrayal of the homeland. The images that participants saw were images that gave the only representation of what was actually going on 'over there'. They were the 'celluloid reality bites' of how the situation had changed from simply being a 'Yugoslav' to that of multi-ethnic war.

As another participant, Milka, a 44 year old woman, expressed it, the media images from Yugoslavia were proof that 'they [Serbs and Croats] hated each other', a hatred that seemed to be leading to inevitable death and destruction:

> I don't have anything to do with my family any more. I've lost touch with them and I don't know where they are. I just go on my own way. I read everything I can get, everything, every single newspaper that comes along. I am completely absorbed in the war. The hatred I have for the [enemy] is destroying me. *I know that hatred destroys a person and I know that this is what is happening to me. I know that I am angry [and] I know that this is pulling me apart from others,* [making me] pull away from others around me. (emphasis added, N.P)

Every news report that came into the home was in addition to the one from the previous night and the night before that. Yesterday's news was combined to last years news, and this led to a range of issues and stress reactions that became compounded and largely unresolved. To Serbian Australians they were living the effects of long distance devastation through the constant stream of images of a destroyed homeland. They were constantly thinking about people lost and left behind, constantly mulling over who was responsible, often to the point of having difficulty getting to sleep at night. This situation was made worse by the experience of recurring nightmares about being attacked.

Milka also spoke of her sister's reaction to the collapse of the former Yugoslavia and ongoing media reports of the conflict. The participant's sister was, before the war:

> ... very Yugoslav, she adored Yugoslavia and that's why she's so hurt. She just cries all the time. She started off depressed and now the depression has gone into anger with her. She's just so angry - at the world, she's angry at everyone. A presenter on television for instance, as soon as he talks against the Serbs, she really hates him. She feels enormous pain and just can't cope with it.

The decision for some Serbian Australians not to watch the television news was brought about by not wanting to once again experience the pain that they felt yesterday. Zika, a 79 year old Serbian Australian, responded to the news media with the following sentiment:

> They (media) are only talking about one side of the conflict. At this moment there are some 16, 000 or 17, 000 Serbs on the run, families from three regions, three town that are being run over. Nobody talks about that, nobody is running over there with Red Cross or anything else to help them. Many times I decided that I was not going to watch television any more, nor listen to the radio. Why, because often I can't sleep. Why, not because I am feeling guilty, but because I am feeling very, very, angry, much disappointed that the world media at the moment is one sided and I said no more, but then as soon as 6 p.m comes somehow, I don't know how, I go to the television, but I end up switching it on again.

A complicating factor in the nexus of local and global hurts is that the experience of hurt and devastation is amplified by the repetitive nature of the image being portrayed, as well as by the cumulative effects of the distress it represents.

Getting into fights and disputes

For Djordje, whenever there was footage that he found upsetting of fighting or devastation in the former Yugoslavia, he would react very angrily. 'I just want to go and hit somebody', he told me. On one occasion there was a fight between Serbian and Croatian youth in a city nightclub:

> I can't honestly say there is one good reason for the fight happening. I think it has a lot to do with what's going on over there [former Yugoslavia] and all the injustice of it. It upsets me, and after I see something on the news about what Croatians - they might have taken another village, it might touch me personally because I might have someone from that village or something like that. After seeing the news I go outside with feelings of hatred towards them, feelings of aggression, and I want to take that out, I will do it on a Croatian who provokes me. Anyone, even my neighbours.

The anger expressed above, and described throughout this chapter, indicates the strong linkage between hurts, both local and global. However, it would be wrong to view them as not relevant to children of school age. For Darko, his concerns were made worse by many adolescents around the age of his daughter coming to him for 'advice':

We Serbs have a problem with the second generation Serbs not born here, who end up seeing this news. They are mad because of what they have seen, what they see everyday on television about their own ancestors, we have trouble to keep them calm. Otherwise there'd be a bloody war. We have cooperated with the police, we invited a police officer to come and have a talk with them, to tell them to be quiet, not to explode. We tell them that sooner or later our time will come, the truth will prevail. This is why we didn't have any trouble here.

This process of younger Serbian Australians being drawn into the vicarious effects of the Balkan war appeared motivated by the anger and frustration arising from long distance devastation and local and global hurts. In addition to this, there was a mix of symbols, memories and traditions passed down from generation to generation, woven into contemporary Serbian Australian social life, that were being destroyed. There was, as Smith (1995, p. 80) puts it, '...a rich harvest of symbols and memories, traditions in which epic battles were fought... handed down from generation to generation as living cultural traditions', that were being subjected to a hostile environment both in the Balkans and in Australia. The process of having frustrations invoked in Australia can be seen in the quotation below. Here, a year 12 high school student tells of being 'provoked' by her class teacher's 'joke' about the Serbs:

'Hey! Slobodanka!', she called me over to her in the [school] yard at lunch time, 'Do you know why Serbs have got flat foreheads', she said, and I go 'No, I don't', and she goes, 'because every time they don't know something they hit themselves in the forehead'. I was angry at her because this is just not on. ...I came home to try and talk about it with my father ...I just felt like hitting someone, I just feel like screaming in a loud microphone, that's what they're making me feel. Why should I put up with that?

In the same interview, the participant spoke of her anger at being 'devalued' by her teacher, and bullied by other pupils as they taunted her with the following, 'Serbian butchers, what are you guys doing killing little babies like that'. Another student explained to me how her teacher challenged her ethnic identity during a classroom discussion about world customs and religions:

This teacher told me, 'You're not a Serb Mila! How can you be a Serb when you're born here in Australia?' I just sat there feeling like I was worth nothing. He just cut me off. One of my [Serbian] friends used to get really upset and skip lessons because of him. I told him what I thought. Australians to me have got no customs, no religion, nothing. Straight away this teacher and I had this big barrier between us. But it didn't bother me. After a while it got really bad, I said 'I am what I am and you are what you are, and you don't know what you're talking about with the Serbs'.

Mila was more vocal than others in articulating her opposition to the teacher's approach to her Serbian self. In her own words:

If I can confront the person rather than avoid him. Avoiding the issue, letting people rub it in about the Serbs, that's what hurts.

Conclusion

The focus of this chapter has been to build upon the idea that war in former Yugoslavia had not only been a tragedy for its people and the world community, but has disrupted the health of people living in Australia who ascribe to being Serbian. We have seen how participants' experiences appear to fall within three broad areas: (i) *attempting to obliterate upsetting realities of the war by reiterating that Serbs are 'always the victims'*; (ii) *withdrawing from others*; and (iii) *openly challenging the perceived stereotypes of Serbs through outspoken means*. All of these issues are based on data generated from participants, and emerge in response to coping with the problems of living, brought on by the Balkan war.

Analysis of these situations shows that conditions both near and far influence the process of health and wellbeing. This suggests that health is a process framed by both local and global circumstances and events, and the experience of long distance devastation opened up a multitude of potent health and lifestyle concerns. Coping with the effects of long distance devastation was helped along by an intimate examination and re-examination of perceived cultural and historical roots.

Consideration of these issues has led me to situate health and wellbeing as local and global processes. My construction of *Long Distance Devastation and Local and Global Hurts* takes into account the events that generated feeling in Australia (local) and the Balkans (global). As previously discussed, taking a global perspective in this journey helped me to see that Serbian Australians exist in the local world with historical, ethno-nationalist and cultural sentiments that originate from, and are integrated with, homeland events. Viewed this way, globalism is a contextual organising concept, rather that the subject of interpretation *per se*. Health, therefore, must be seen as a global and local phenomenon influenced by the powerful elements of identity, belonging, bonding and a historical consciousness that transcends nations and communities where people live.

Consideration of such issues prepares for the discussion of health and community interventions for Serbian Australians in the next chapter. What do people say and do for each other, having just experienced the loss of an entire village where they spent their childhood? How might they empathise with another person in this situation? How do they help someone who is trying to come to terms with what they see happening thousands of kilometres away? How do you help someone who has withdrawn from all others? In the next chapter, I draw from the actions and experiences of participants to consider what help was being offered to such people.

Notes

1   From his address to a luncheon in honour of Dr Franjo Tudjman, President of Croatia, Parliament House, Canberra, Tuesday 20 June 1995.
2   This was despite Australians of Croatian and Serbian origin gaining attention about their individual suffering through national and international news-media (Fabris, 1991; Hill, 1993; Stone, 1992; Strong, 1991; Totaro, 1991), protests to the Office of the Australian Prime Minister (Radojevic and Bolta, 1992) and the Office of the Minister for Immigration and Ethnic Affairs (*Srpski Pregled*, 1993, p. 11).
3   With the collapse of the Axis powers in November 1918, the first Yugoslav state was established with King Peter I of Serbia becoming the first Monarch on December 1.
4   Vulliamy was the first print journalist to report from inside the Serbian held detention camps. He also had extensive experience of reporting for *The Guardian* newspaper from the many battle sieges and makeshift hospitals. He was obliged to testify as a witness for the prosecution at the War Crimes Tribunal in the Hague, at the trial of Serbian café owner Dusko Tadic, one of Omarska's convicted torturers and killers.
5   Known around the world as concentration camps reminiscent of Jasenovac, or the Third Reich, it is alleged that thousands of mainly Muslim civilians were tortured and exterminated by their Serbian captives. The team that uncovered the Omarska and Trnopolje camps in North-Western Bosnia was made up of journalists from *The Guardian* newspaper, and two ITN television crews.
6   Here I am using my nursing expertise as pre-knowledge in a very different sense to how I used it when participants' mental distress and frustration were being interpreted. In interpreting situations of gross mutilation of human flesh, I have drawn from domains of anatomy and physiology, that feature significantly in physical health assessment.
7   Capitalisation as per original photograph.

8   John Simpson (1993), writing in *The Spectator* magazine, remarks that the very worst news from Bosnia was deliberately run night after night on television screens, to provoke viewers into saying to their local politician that something must be done to stop the war.

9   There is no way of knowing the cumulative and enduring effects that television violence of this kind had or could have had on viewing people of any age (Friedrich-Cofer and Huston, 1986).

10   The impact of catastrophic television images from afar on other countries is not new. Perhaps the most striking example was when Kenyan cameraman Mohamed Amin brought to the world images of Ethiopia's famine in 1984. His film of the starving and dying was soon to be known around the globe as the 'celluloid seconds that stabbed a billion hearts'. The film footage led to an international humanitarian relief effort and the Bob Geldolf *Live Aid* concert that raised millions of dollars for famine relief.

11   Images of the Balkans devastation also impacted on Croatians and Serbians in the United Kingdom (Cohen, 1991), the United States (Stone, 1992), and Arab and Islamic countries like Turkey (Glenny, 1992, p. 182; 1994), Saudi Arabia (Ahmed, 1993), Iran and the Gulf States (*The Financial Times*, 6 November 1992).

12   It was alleged by *SBS Radio* that Radulovich had suggested in his radio program that, if listeners were not 'satisfied' with either the Labor or Liberal Party response to the Serbian cause in the Balkans, they could consider an informal vote at the election ballot box.

13   See also Masanauskas, (1991b).

14   There are a few exceptions to this. In July 1994, Paul Johnson, writing in the *Sydney Morning Herald* Newspaper, used the title, 'Stop behaving like a Serb, Rupert' to describe the Murdoch empire's drive for a commanding share of British news media as aggressive, destructive and bellicose. Calling for Murdoch to 'stop behaving like a Serb' implied that Serbs were acting in the same way, and with the same goal of encroaching like a predator over their prey. Ilia Glisic, President of the Serbian National Federation of Australia, responded to Johnson's careless use of language as a 'racist slur'. Glisic (1994) argued that this dangerous throwaway line was both offensive to Serbian Australians and clearly 'misrepresented the true nature of Serbians who had been trying to defend their homelands'.

7 From Trauma to Re-Affirmation: Health and Community for Serbian Australians

It's something that builds up [inside of me], it's a build up and I have to take it out somehow. Some days I feel that I want to take my anger out on something, so I might go down to the gym and work-out. Or it might be that I go for a walk and clear my head, or go down to the beach, or get stuck into fatty foods and think that this is bad, but it makes me feel good, you know. Other times, I just sit there and watch TV or listen to music and just get completely off, off my train of thought. You get yourself off into a different sort of feeling. I can't always use fighting as the solution - you can't always use aggression to cope with these feelings (Djordje, a male participant aged 19).

Introduction

Directly or indirectly, many of the substantive issues developed so far in my journey represent participants' struggles to cope with the influence of the war on their life. In the previous chapter, for example, we saw that as the twin processes of escalating anger and frustration gathered momentum, participants had their lives suddenly thrust into situations that challenged their health and wellbeing. In this chapter, we shall see how this led in some cases, to a fragmentation of social life, in others, to social withdrawal and in a number of cases, to greater public involvement with the Serbian cause. As war continued throughout much of the former Yugoslavia, life in Australia became increasingly difficult. Moreover, the participants' sense of individual personhood was subject to hardships that could not be divorced from the power of long distance devastation and hurt.

This consideration has significant, although complex implications for the analysis contained in this chapter. Within this perspective, the experience of Serbian Australians involved aspects of what Robertson (1995, p. 30) describes as the concept of glocalisation. For Robertson, glo*cal*isation is the 'simultaneity and the interpenetration of what are conventionally called the global and the local'. The compression of the world, Robertson continues, 'increasingly invokes the creation of and incorporation of locality processes which themselves largely shape the world' (p. 40). In relation to the life of Serbian Australians in the shadow of the Balkan war, Robertson's formulation speaks to the emphasis being placed on the local condition and local situations of participants. This view of glo*cal*isation incorporates the health and wellbeing interests of participants because the Balkan war, as we have already seen, was becoming increasingly visible through global media and tele-communications and, therefore, was becoming part of the social life of participants at the local level. This means that, in the lives of participants, interest in contemporary global and local world geopolitics, as well as Serbian cultural and historical perspectives were brought to bear on individual health and wellbeing. It is for these reasons that substantive issues of a global-local nature, and the discussion of health and community interventions for Serbian Australians are both complementary and deeply penetrative.

My interpretation of global forces impacting on health and wellbeing in a local context takes into account Giddens' (1996) sentiment, previously examined in chapter 4, that nobody is outside the influence of the global in social life. As Giddens (1996, p. 125) sees it, 'everyone throughout the world has to filter and react to many sources of incoming information about [and affecting] their life-circumstances'. Such information comes to Serbian Australians at a rapid pace across various mediums where it is 'not simply part of the 'external world'. In their reactions to and usages of information, participants 'construct, reconstruct and deconstruct their environments' (p. 125).

From this perspective, a number of issues became relevant to the contents of this chapter: how did Serbian Australians cope with living side-by-side with their Croatian and Bosnian counterparts; how did they cope with feelings of anger, hurt, frustration, isolation and perceived betrayal by the media; how did they cope when church and community property was vandalised or destroyed or when they received death threats; and, how did Serbian Australians help themselves and each other to cope with the effects of long distance grief and devastation?

These issues, marked by events unfolding in the Balkans and Australia, intersected with the delivery of health, as well as community interventions for participants within their sphere of influence. This chapter is dedicated to interpreting what participants did for themselves and their community to cope with the impact of the Balkan war in Australia. Impelled by events in the former Yugoslavia, participants established a means to cope with situations in Australia. It will be argued that, as social life became more difficult in Australia, and as participants tried to cope with this, the more they became distressed by their experience. To help overcome the hurt and devastation, many sought each other out, looking for re-connection with their historical and cultural traditions. The outcome was, put simply, an emotional bulwark in the face of long distance devastation, global and local hurts, and perceived and/or experienced demonisation by media and popular opinion.

Orientation to health and helping interventions

In the exploration of health and community interventions for Serbian Australians, I inevitably brought into play my experience and background as a mental health nurse. With my identity as a nurse and health researcher being inextricably related to the world I was studying, I found myself wanting to respond to the distress that I saw and heard, as if in the mental health nursing role.

The more I experienced the personal and social impact of the war on Serbian Australians, the more I felt it necessary to bring my professional nursing background to the interpretation of participants' lives and wellbeing. But clearly, this was not a study about nursing, *per se*. Instead, nursing, like globalism, provided a contextual reference point in this study, which illuminated my interpretation of health and community interventions.

Two main issues led to my constructing interpretations using nursing as an influence. *Firstly*, nursing is concerned with the multitude of events impacting on a person's life, and their health in particular. This study was, in part, a response to recent calls for the development of health and nursing scholarship to incorporate critical global events, globalisation of concepts (Hutch, 1995), and collaboration across cultural divisions within its scope (Gortner, 1992; Meleis, 1992, 1995; Parker, 1996).

Secondly, nursing is concerned with the care and comfort needs of *all* people, including those for whom issues of war and ethnicity are salient for their health status and needs. This focus was particularly relevant to Serbian Australians, a group believed by major world opinion to be the main perpetrator of the conflict and the key obstacle to peace negotiations. As the focus of this attention intensified around the world, I became concerned with the social, health and community relationships of one of the world's most demonised ethnic groups.

To accommodate these contextual influences, I took the view, as seen in chapter 3, that nothing in the social world speaks for itself and that the beliefs and ideas the participants and I brought to the research context should be worked out interpretively. As a researcher, I chose to elaborate upon the beliefs and ideas I brought to interviews and participant observation without the use of 'bracketing', so that the Gadamerian notion of effective history was part of my interpretation.[1] This approach was also informed by reflexivity in ethnography, described by Marcus (1994, p. 571) as:

> ... foregoing the nostalgic idea that there are literally completely unknown worlds to be discovered. Rather, *in full reflexive analysis of the historical connections that already link it to its subject matter,* contemporary ethnography makes historically sensitive revisions of the ethnographic archive *with eyes fully open to the complex ways that diverse representations have constituted its subject matter. Such representations become an integral part of one's fieldwork (and) define not only the discourse of the ethnographer, but his or her literal position in relation to [participants]* (emphasis added, N. P.).

Although Marcus is conscious of the 'self' being engaged in ethnographic work, I have further explored the idea of 'historical connections' in this study. In the previous discussion of what Gadamer (1975) defined as the concept of horizon (see chapter 3), interpretation in this research journey has also been subject to the way in which participants interpreted me as a health professional and health researcher, and therefore is reliant on what they told me. Consideration of this perspective means that the work of the ethnographer was not the only influence in establishing health and helping interventions.

The difficulty with finding help

Data gathering in this aspect of the study was difficult to obtain. Very few people could/would speak to me about how they were managing their health, and health issues, under the impact of war. I began by framing my questions to Serbian Australian participants in a very general way: Are you having any health problems at the moment because of this war; What are your main worries about your family, parents, sister, brother in Bosnia doing to your health at the moment; What worries/concerns you most about the situation in the former Yugoslavia; and, what aspects of the situation in the former Yugoslavia have most impacted upon your life/health/stress levels in Australia?

Whenever I began asking questions about these issues, I was told, as by one family, that, for instance, 'nothing can be done by us. It is up to the Australian government to help us. But they [the government] had better be careful about things. There are many Serbs here who would retaliate if they are pushed any further'. When I first came across this point of view, I thought it might be best described as the politicisation of health concerns, as contrasted with the medicalisation of political concerns. One Serbian general medical practitioner, Dr Zdravlje, expressed the following about participant frustration at the (in)action of the Australian government:

> If I had to summarise the general feeling about the whole situation within the Serbian community and how it affects a certain individual, my general feeling is one of great sadness at what is going on first of all and anger at the world community and Australia. What is sad is that the Australian government needs to say to Serbians who are also Australian citizens that Australians of Serbian origin are decent people and that they condemn the actions of other communities here and over there who do things against the Serbian people. We never asked the Australian government to take sides or to pick our side but to be even handed and to react to certain Serbian individuals (Milosovic, the Communists) and not go for all Serbs, the Serbian nation or the Serbian country. That and the sanctions[2] against all the Serbian people has created a lot of anger problems. People feel that they are Australian citizens but also feel cheated, abandoned. ...they came here years ago and have tried to be part of Australian society... [but now their] citizenship rights have suddenly altered.

This data reveals that participants had a double exposure to the problems of living in the shadow of the Balkan war. Interlinked with the anger directed towards the Australian government, there was a feeling of not belonging to either Yugoslavia or Australia. At the same time, there was a renewed feeling of wanting to be closer to what they believed to be the Serbian cause. In addition to this, there was an emphasis, as placed by Dr Zdravlje, on the nexus between this situation and issues of ethnic identity:

> ...and there are people who feel ill with psychological problems of stress and worry [and] they feel alienated not only from the [Australian]

government and the Anglo-Saxon population in Australia, but they feel
alienated from the other country too.

With their identity being unsettled by the simultaneous unfolding of
events in Australia and the Balkans, participants came around to the idea
that their coping would be helped by returning to their historical situation.
This meant that participants' obeisance to the Serbian past was an active
element in the scenario of Serbs-helping-Serbs in the present. As will be
discussed later in this chapter, many participants began to value and talk
about the heroic efforts of Serbian folk heroes. I saw this as a means of
coping with, and maintaining their individual and community life in
Australia. But what lay behind this situation? I began by asking myself:
What could explain the relationship between events in the past and current
health issues; and, What issues could possibly lead people to seek help for
their breakdown of feelings in relation to war, by interpreting their culture
in a historical context?

At this time, I was also struck by the comments of one participant, a
woman who's name I did not know, who approached me stating:

> [I] want and need help, psychological help. I keep asking myself; Why am I
> still here? Why haven't I lost it completely, to a point of no return?
> Because, I'm really finding that, with everything that is being said in the
> media about me, I'm being pushed to the limit in this war.

Increasingly throughout this journey, I was able to recognise that the
suffering of participants was quite intense. As seen in the previous
chapters, for example, participants spoke of their emotional breakdown
after hearing that the place of their childhood had been overrun and
destroyed. In these instances, I empathised with the situations being
presented, and encouraged participants to make contact with their family
physician or local community health centre. It made no sense to me to
pursue data generation from a person seeking psychological help.

Upon hearing these sentiments, it became clear that there was no
real gain in being overly investigative about these issues. In fact, it now
seemed to me to be very dangerous to do so. From my point of view, there
was a strong probability that the collective frustration and emotional
devastation of Serbian Australians could explode at any moment. Put
simply, the Serbs had had enough, and my asking them about the
experience of this could end up being a catalyst for verbal and/or physical
aggression towards myself or others.

Coping with feeling abandoned

While the Australian Government had attempted to keep the politics of the Balkans out of Australia by calling upon European and United States interests alone to settle the war, there were instances that distressed participants. The April 1993 issue of the Adelaide *Srpski Pregled* (p. 5) explains:

> Australian Serbs are appalled by Keating's call for sanctions against Serbia and Montenegro in response to the Sarajevo bread queue bombing. Keating seemed to be intent on unilateral Australian sanctions (even though Serbian forces were not responsible). ...In December 1992 the UN General Assembly passed a non-binding resolution calling for the lifting of the arms embargo on the Muslims and the use of international force against the Serbs. This resolution which was sponsored by the Islamic states was supported by only three western countries-USA, Austria and Australia. Australia now had the same foreign policy as Iran. ...Australia's decision to allow visa applications to go ahead for Croatian and Muslim soccer teams and politicians while Serbian politicians such as Dr Plavsic had been denied entry is a blatant act of discrimination against Australian Serbs.

Elsewhere, the President of the Serbian National Federation of Australia, Ilia Glisic's comments in *Novosti* on May 18 1994, illustrate the common theme of Serbian Australians feeling betrayed and abandoned:

> A matter of intense distress and dismay has recently come to the attention of the Serbian-Australian Community. We refer to the alleged participation of a RAAF pilot Lt. Gavin Phillips in an abortive bombing mission against Bosnian Serbs as reported in the press recently. ...The Australian Government has repeatedly stated that Australia has no vital interest in the Balkans and consequently Australian military officials testifying before parlimentary committees have rejected the participation of Australian service personnell in UN operations in the former Yugoslavia. ...We would consider this yet another discriminatory act taken by this Government against the Serbian-Australian community.

The accusation by participants was that such acts were making them feel like 'second class citizens'. This in turn made many Serbian Australians very angry, because they felt abandoned and betrayed by the Australian Government, as Misha explains:

It's impossible to separate myself from what is happening to our people here and in Yugoslavia - it's like cutting your roots. And you just can't do that. You see, I listen for fresh news. *Sometimes I have a sleepless night when I hear something that's unpleasant.* I try to find a solution, to not wanting (sic) to know so much but I am a powerless man here in Australia. I really can't do anything to help myself. We are just not supported by anybody. *We are just left alone. We feel deserted, discriminated against by the Australian government and its media.* (emphasis added, N. P.)

The main problem for this participant was that the war in former Yugoslavia had led to a series of other battles and conflicts in Australia. As we saw in chapter 6, for instance, the war had disrupted one participant's sleep, had given him to focus on issues outside his relationship with his wife, and had brought about a sense of powerlessness. His feeling and frustration was brought about not only by his perception of the situational factors already outlined, but also by his bond to the Serbian people of Australia and the former Yugoslavia.

In light of these circumstances, I came the realisation that the mental strain being experienced by participants came not only from the war and its media reporting. In an interesting paradox, the objects and people used by participants to feel better about their situation - historical reference points, Serbian churches and community centres, giving humanitarian support for Serbian refugees in former Yugoslavia - were also the subject of stress, abuse and destruction, both inside and outside the borders of the former Yugoslavia. As this chapter will show, this made the suffering of participants even more profound.

The frustration of feeling destroyed

It is almost impossible to discuss participants' feelings of abandonment and frustration without considering the expressed need of some participants to become violent. As demonstrated in the previous chapters, this situation was made worse, as a number of anonymous bomb threats, abusive telephone calls, graffiti attacks, death threats and fire attacks were being made by unidentified others. These events in the local and global world led some participants to feel that there was an attempt being made by the Roman Catholic Church, the United States, Germany and Croatia to 'bring about the elimination of Serbians from all societies around the world', as Nenad explains:

There is a three point plan by Germany, United Nations and America to destroy the Serbian territory in Bosnia.   German fascism will never die [and] the five million Serbian people don't want fascism.   That's why there has been fighting since [the Second World War].   Serbs want to keep the energy, the energy to keep the gun up.   Serbs have learned to keep up their defences, to keep smarter than them.

As a result, some participants wanted to join in retaliatory violence, both in the former Yugoslavia and in Australia, despite the risk to their personal safety and wellbeing.   During a visit to his workplace, a participant told me how an episode of 'pay-back' property damage by Serbians in Adelaide was prevented, following a vandal attack on one of their churches:

> The bastards have just done over our church again. Swastikas, death threats and shit like that. They [attackers] just want to kill us off, destroy us. We were all ready to go and get them back. We were all due to meet in the [location] and do a graffiti job on them. Stuff the Nazi bastards! ...But the phones were running hot the night before. They [names] were calling up everyone. ...We were being told not to go ahead with it. [Name] rang everyone up who he thought would be in on it and said, 'Don't go. Just don't go and do anything to anyone.' (a Serbian Australian small business operator, male aged about 30 years)

The motivation for Serbian Australians, in planning revenge attacks was sparked by the attempt of unknown others to destroy all that symbolised the Serbian tradition.   In this sense, the attempted destruction of the Serbian church was seen as an attack upon that which Serbs hold as most sacred, in the religious, social and cultural sense.

A similar interpretation may be made of the impact of graffiti. Here, the violation against Serbian Australians lay in the meaning of the symbols that were used to violate their property.   The Croatian Nazi wartime slogans and symbols were in this sense, seen as a form of symbolic violence, leading to death and destruction.   In situations where there was graffiti only, this also signalled to some participants that much more damage could be done, and perhaps might be done in the future.

Elsewhere, participants saw themselves as the victims of property damage, and this brought a pressing need for violent retaliation.   There was, for example, a need for revenge, power, and forceful control (retribution) towards others from the former Yugoslavia that they believed responsible.   It became the role of the Serbian Orthodox Church to persuade people not to retaliate. I attended a church service on the morning of the graffiti and property attack. During the *sluzba* (service) the priest made a particular point of asking people to show restraint: 'You [people assembled] must not go and do anything that breaks the law. Do not interfere with this process. This will only bring more violence to Adelaide'.

The difficulty with this situation was that there were many present who later voiced their frustration with what was seen as an us-or-them proposition that could only be solved using force. Others stated that there was no use in thinking that the Australian Government and South Australian Police would intervene, for 'they did not care about the property of Serbians [and] the Serbian people'. For these people there was a feeling of having been let down by the authorities. This meant that, for many, there was no faith in legal networks to help resolve their anger.

With little or no faith in the viability of help from structures outside the Serbian community, participants saw it as their only way, to resolve issues within Serbian networks. This helped relieve feelings of frustration and powerlessness. Here I was reminded of Giddens (1996) earlier sentiments, outlined in chapter 4 of this study. Violence and death threats against the Serbians living in Adelaide had led to feelings of retaliation and aggression, as well as physical withdrawal and protection. In my interpretation of a three metre high fence being erected around the Serbian church and community centres in Adelaide, I made the point, in chapter 4, that the Serbs had tried to avoid violence with Croatian Australians by altering the material conditions used to enact it - in this instance the church structure, including its windows and plaque - in an attempt to reduce the likelihood of damage to it. In this discussion of political and cultural violence in contemporary human affairs, there was emphasis on the idea that 'no culture, state or large group can with much success isolate itself from the global cosmopolitan order ...while exit may be possible for some individuals, it is not available for larger social entities' (Giddens, 1996, p. 238). I concluded that it was for this reason that many informal networks became established in and around the Serbian Orthodox Church, to help calm people and prevent an escalation of violence.

Physical activity was one means through which to overcome aggressive feelings. Nenad for example, took it upon himself to collect money from fifty-six Serbian households within ten kilometres of his house. This money would be given in donation to refugee Serbs who had escaped areas besieged by fighting. The collection of this money was on a purely voluntary basis and it was transported to refugees through official

Church networks. What struck me about Nenad's collection of the money was the way this activity released his tension and frustration:

> I feel aggression all the time in my heart and in my heart I must say sorry to others about this. [The Serbian Australian] people's lives have changed, in my case I am impatient to get myself out and collect money. There are six men who do this [and] I just got myself involved. Everyday I put in five dollars myself and every month I go to fifty houses and collect fifteen hundred dollars from people because I know that they are angry too. We see that there are Croats helping Muslims but nobody's helping [the] Serbs.

> What pushes me to walk 100 kilometres a week is inside of me. Ninety-five percent of the Serbs are like me, they see that people have taken houses and freedom from Serbs in Yugoslavia. I feel so proud to do something. I do it to help get myself out, to do something.

In addition to this, I saw supportive networks with leadership by men and women, trying to engender a sense of calm amongst people who wanted to turn violent against anyone they believed responsible for hurting them. The efforts taken by the church to be active rather than passive in the face of difficult times was also undertaken in the form of peaceful street demonstrations, and in the establishment of humanitarian aid for refugees in the former Yugoslavia.

Since the outbreak of war, all Serbian Orthodox priests have included extra petitions in their church services, asking for 'God's mercy on all the conflict in the former Yugoslavia, and all those who have died in the name of their faith' (Ilic, 1995, p. 1). The message emphasised during church services to persuade people against losing control in the face of extreme mental distress, was a plea for calm through prayer. Elsewhere, there were anti-retaliatory messages such as 'You live in Australia first, you must think of your life and responsibility to your family here first'.

As the Serbian Orthodox priests in Adelaide tried to calm people into a co-operative, peaceful spirit, their words were sometimes punctuated by the myth and storytelling of heroic sacrifice related to the recent and distant past history of the Serbs. Kazich (1989, pp. 6-7), in a summary of the developmental relationship between Serbian history and religion, sees these political, historical and religious developments as inseparable:

> The Serbian Church acquired its inexhaustible strength during the Middle Ages, when the state and Church were one and when she was entrusted with the educational and spiritual development of the people. It was then that Orthodox Christianity became a philosophy of life for the Serbian people

and although there were times when it was repressed, *in historical periods of enslavement, it always triumphed as a resurrecting life force, which gave re-birth to entire generations and which remained implanted deep in the hearts of the Serbian people to this very day.* (emphasis added, N.P.)

As a consequence of this, Serbian Australians were encouraged by the Serbian Orthodox Church to avoid physical clashes, property damage and violent acts towards other former Yugoslavs living in Australia through the spiritual qualities of suffering, self-sacrifice and forbearance to tolerate others. Randon Ilic (1995, p. 1) outlines the Church's official response, quoting the head of the Church, Patriarch Pavle:

Lord stretch forth your hand to us that we remain your people according to Faith or Deeds. *If we must suffer, let that be in the way of Your justice and Your truth. Let it not be because of our injustices.* Lord protect us from hate and evil deeds and help us to abide by the truth and justice of the Kingdom of Heaven. (emphasis added, N.P.)

Clearly, the role of the Church in helping to create informal, calming networks, designed to achieve restraint, was instrumental in helping people to cope with their hardships and deserved closer scrutiny. An intimate part of these networks was the strong sense of belonging to symbols of Serbian national and cultural identity. Smith (1995, p. 156) suggests that the phenomenon of national identity is certainly powerful enough to do this:

National identity is often powerful enough to engender a spirit of self sacrifice on behalf of the nation, in many, if not most, of its citizens. This is especially true of crises and wartime. Here one can witness the degree to which most citizens are prepared to endure hardships and make personal sacrifices 'in defence of the nation', to the point of laying down their lives willingly.

As applied to this study, Smith's argument alerts us to the way in which some Serbian Australians have derived their power and strength to cope with the effects of the Balkan war, through a combination of processes derived from history and national identity. Collective religious, cultural, national and community identity was helping people reach a peaceful resolution to their inner angst and frustration. Serbian historical and national identity was, in this sense, a means for participants to protect and maintain their emotional wellbeing and help prevent further feelings of alienation and demonisation. The same processes may have also helped prevent retaliatory violence by Serbians against others with cultural links to the former Yugoslavia. This was particularly important when negative perceptions and popular opinion against Serbians world-wide had gathered momentum.

'I need someone to talk to, someone who understands my situation'

Individual frustration and anger brought about by the Balkan war also meant changes in the nature of medical practice, as undertaken by Dr. Zdravlje. With the onset of war, it became necessary for him to talk more with patients about their situation, and to offer more counselling and reassurance to those who sought it:

> It's definitely been evident in my practice that I have to spend more time with my patients. I have less patients but I spend more time with them. I am spending more time with them because there is the time to spend and there is a necessity to do it. The reason being is that almost everyone is affected in one way or another and that is particularly showing in my patients from Croatia, Bosnia-Herzegovina because they have family in those places and that creates a lot of problems.

> It [the medical consultation] starts off by them not telling me straight off about their problems with family over there, occasionally they do, but they complain of say headache, dizziness, occupational stress, they become intolerant, impatient, and different. All sorts of these problems and on top of that they worry about paying the Church and the family over there donations and help.

> ...after a while you scratch a bit and they all 'open-up' and things start pouring out. In this process their problems actually end up becoming clearer ...then they are definitely aware how they have been affected by the war. But they still think about it all the time that they lose their sleep.

Here the opportunity to speak with someone who cares about a particular situation has led to the outpouring of emotional information related to the impact of the Balkan war on Serbian Australians. Consistent with the experience of the general practitioner, my interest in the Serbian Australian experience, as a known health professional, stimulated many participants to speak with me about their feelings, as Marija explains:

Well, personally, I need to speak with you ...I think that it is a really good thing, for me and our people. It gives us a chance to express our feelings, our opinions, on what's going on. Our situation is not just over here but over there. [We] can talk [with you] about our feelings, our fears, and what we are like as people.

Another interviewee and study participant, Ljubica, resumed contact with me after a break of more than six months. She came to see me, 'to talk with me' about her 'depressed mood and withdrawn behaviour'. She had just been living in the 'longest six weeks ever, it felt like an eternity'. The reason for feeling this way was that her region of the former Yugoslavia, the Serbian Krainja, had just been overrun by Croatian forces.[3] She summarised the post-Krainja period in this way:

When I first heard of this, I was just hysterical. I just had to do something, so I started to do the dishes really quickly to expend some energy. My sister, who knows how I feel about our family over there, she just suddenly started to look at me and like, I'd just burst into like uncontrollable heaving crying. I became really nervous, for days and days afterwards. For seven days I just lived for the news, the TV, I would get up at 7.00 am in the morning and catch the news, lie down again, catch the 11.00, the 12.00, catch the 5.00, catch the 6.00 and the 7.00 news. It was just a constant thing for days... you did not know what the story was so you just kept going on. Then, one Tuesday, we were watching the news, and I saw my auntie, on TV in a refugee camp. When I saw her I jumped out of my seat, nearly onto the TV, it was not something that I was really aware of, just an automatic reaction. After that, we just went into a frenzy for as much information about the refugees as we could.

As Ljubica continued to tell her story of immersing herself with television and radio news in an effort to find out about her refugee family, she also told me of her gradual withdrawal from the world around her, into a space that was focused only on the war in former Yugoslavia:

I just watched the news. I did not turn on any music [it] got on my nerves. I didn't go outside, didn't go to the shops, I didn't have any contact with anybody. I just watched TV, listened to the radio, sat by the phone. I read every paper I could find, anything to get information about what was happening over there. I just tried to get myself out of all of this but I could not.

As the ongoing conversation developed between us, it seemed that her withdrawal from everyday life was becoming more profound, right before my very eyes. This process may be interpreted as her grieving and needing to come to terms with the experience of losing her homeland. She continued to tell me about how she avoided her Serbian friends:

> I withdrew from everybody. I found that what happened in Yugoslavia was always in the back of my mind. I have less to do with the Serbian people because I need to maintain my sanity, you know. I didn't want to see them because it was always their topic of conversation. I couldn't deal with it. Everyone was going through it in their own way.

Here we see a contrasting situation where, rather than affiliation with others, there was a need to withdraw. That is, in a situation of traumatic loss, a feature of the individual coping was by shutting others out of her life. As she put it, 'push them out of my life to keep in control'. Her reaction was marked by an avoidance of things that were reminders of what she loved and believed in. The 'shutting out' of others, and the trauma of re-experiencing news from the region, left Ljubica in a distressing situation. She had become incapable of living with others in her household. She had stopped talking with those she loved and lived with, in an attempt to cope with her sadness and despair. Moreover, at the same time she was desperate for *any* information of her family, and yet, she was becoming increasingly upset by the repetitive nature of re-experiencing the trauma of seeing Serbian refugees on the television screen several times over each day.

Ljubica's situation was made worse by her memories of 1990, when she had lived in the former Yugoslavia. In addition, the constant rumination about and visualisation of the people and places she fondly remembered, was itself important. For Ljubica, these images and memories were now haunting her day and night. As this situation in her life reached a climax, she told me of her frustration at trying to get 'professional help' for what she called her 'nervousness':

> I wanted to go to a counsellor, a psychologist because I knew that things were not going well for me. I though I was going to 'lose it' completely. Go to the point of 'no-return'. I didn't know if there was going to be a time when I would ever feel happiness, openness, a carefree heart again. So I went to a doctor, I wanted to see if he could give me something, because it was getting really hard for me to cope. He started to write a few things down and then he started to give me his version of things over there. You

know, about how important America is for negotiating peace etc. I just told him that America was just playing a super-power and helping the Croatian army to crush us.

At this point of the interview I could sense myself moving into the mental health nursing role, in order to find out more about her coping. I also began to look at ways to bring about more of an emotional catharsis in her as she told her story. This would involve what her feelings were actually like, and how these feelings made her feel 'inside'. I sensed, that for this participant, emotional expression and personal disclosure might be an effective means of coping with the trauma (Minas and Klimidis, 1994). While this might be important for her health and healing following a traumatic event, it was outside the professional ethical bounds of this study, to act in this manner. When I realised that I was becoming professionally involved, I simultaneously turned the conversation back to the main purposes and aims of the research, while directing her to professionals available in her local area who I felt might be able to help her situation.

In a very real sense, the fieldwork involved two simultaneous dimensions: a qualitative inquiry into the Serbian Australian experience of Balkan war, and a thoughtful and delicate act of trying to encourage appropriate help and support for others.

Serbians helping Serbians

For Zorica, talking with people in the networks she had established among her Serbian friends made her feel better. She spoke of her frustration as an 'all consuming annoyance that just kept coming into her life'. To cope with the situation of seeing something on the television about the conflict in former Yugoslavia, she would:

> ... talk with people who are willing to hear me out, people who understand me. I do this to cope with the lies over there. It's all bullshit. I find my mother to be a good person to talk with about things. I can't go and talk to Australians because they don't understand my situation. The only people who seem to understand the Serbs are other Serbs. The real problems are still there, the feeling of hurt and pain are still there, but it's a more diluted feeling, it's not as bad. The important thing is that I feel a lot better after I talk to somebody who understands [me] and listens to me.

This 'talking' seems to be a short term intervention devoted to getting rid of anger and frustration, as Dr Lekar continues:

> [T]he best way is to talk to other people, to gather together and to cough it out of the chest and talk to someone and if they learn that somebody else within the community has similar problems, similar thoughts, they feel in some way easier than before. In the way that they are not alone. They have to go to someone who can understand and this is the only way as far as I can see that they are trying to help themselves by listening to one another, the other talking. But this is not ever going to be enough for them as there are some who are developing serious problems, some of them purely can't talk to me, [they are] just asking for something to settle their nerves. Some tablets is all I can give them, because they can't sleep, being awake at night, thinking about problems with family and friends.

Here, as seen in chapters 5 and 6, the process of talking with others is one which may lead to greater acceptance as a Serbian by another Serbian. The sentiments expressed in conversation with another Serbian also tended to be about issues to do with media reporting of the conflict, the right of Serbians in the former Yugoslavia to have self determination without oppression from past enemies, and frustration with the Australian government.

Other study participants such as Gordana (chapter 1), Radojevic and Bolta (chapter 6) wrote letters to State and Federal Government politicians and media outlets to tell people what was going on in the Balkans from their point of view. This writing down of feelings was accompanied by a sentiment that 'it [writing] probably will not help change the situation, as one voice cannot help my cause, but I feel that at least I've told them, I've told them of my pain and it's been therapeutic for me'. This feeling gave way to sense of sadness and dislocation that was sometimes more difficult for people to cope with. Participants who reached this point spoke of feeling frustrated, angry and helpless; they were worrying if they had lost people, asking international aid agencies if they were they still alive, or if they were being tortured: 'Are the children alive and will we see them again'?

While talking about the frustrations and anger generated by war brought some relief to people, for others it raised anger and created further uncertainty. The anger was directed at the world for failing to intervene to stop the war, and the media for being perceived as biased in its reporting. These feelings became internalised and, during some periods of the research, there were reports of attempted suicide by Serbian Australians, as one senior male member of the Serbian National Federation, Dushan explained:

> I had a woman telephone me at 3.30 in the morning telling me that she was sitting in her backyard with a can of lawn mower petrol and a cigarette lighter ready to blow herself up. She told me that she can't take it anymore. She just can't take seeing her family being forced off their land that they had held for hundreds of years and now she just doesn't know were they actually are ...if they have been captured of even killed.

> I just talked her through all of this. I knew this was difficult for her and I knew that my helping her was due to her having the same feelings and frustrations that I have. (I've got a brother you know in Sarajevo that I have not heard from for months, I don't know if he is dead or alive.) I asked some of the women from the church to come around and see her, get her to go out more with them and I found out that [they] helped her a lot.

One of the important things to recognise in the above situation is that there was an intervention to save the life of the suicidal participant through an awareness of the underlying issues of her problem. There was no attempt to make her try and feel less suicidal. Rather, there were efforts being made by others for her to feel understood. The factor that helped her through this crisis was that she felt listened to and acknowledged by someone she knew understood and identified with her feelings. This acknowledgment appeased her suicidal thoughts and gesture.

It is possible to interpret the suicidal thoughts that occupied this person as a need to seek some kind of end to suffering because her psychological pain and torment had become intolerable. To escape this situation meant that she must end it with whatever was available. The intended use of lawn mower fuel suggests the spontaneity of her desperate act.

Within the process of Serbians talking to Serbians, community leaders played a significant cross-generational role as another senior Serbian National Federation official, Darko explained:

> A lot of young Serbs about 20, 25 or 30 years of age are coming to talk to me. They are full of frustration about the situation (and) even though a lot of them are born here, they still feel that they are Serbs. They said that their family and relatives have been slaughtered over there and it's against Australian law to go to fight but they are frustrated and say they want to go over there.[4] They say that a lot of Croats going over there to fight and they say to me, 'Why shouldn't we go there to fight to defend the country?'

I have a lot of problems when I say to them, 'boys this is not the war we should fight physically because you boys, you are mostly born in this country, and you must obey the Australian laws'. I also tell them, 'be more politically active here, be more active in our Serbian organisations, organise nice dances and try to do more to raise money for our people'. But they say back to me, *'We don't feel like dancing, we don't feel singing, we feel like fighting'*[5] (emphasis added, N.P.).

I'm not a professional person who can give them advice. I say to them 'go take your energy outside go watch the football, go to dancing groups and go and have a picnic out and even have a nice day out so it will help you forget a few things ... go get easy on yourself'. They are starting to go and do these things [that I suggest], but still there is frustration about it. You can't do much about their anger, but we try to organise ourselves. We send a lot of letters and put a lot of energy into proving to the media that they are telling lies about us. And now, thank god we are coming to see a little bit truth about the Serbs, bit by bit. It is creeping in slowly but it's coming back.

It is difficult to overestimate the importance of the informal work being done to persuade Serbian youth, the group considered by some in the community to be most 'at risk of losing their self control', not to engage in violence, either in Australia or in the former Yugoslavia. One Serbian Australian welfare organiser (Slobodanka aged 36 years), known for her efforts to solicit help from Serbian youth to coordinate humanitarian aid for refugees from Serbian Australians, described her experience of this:

From my interactions with people around the country there seems to be a large number of younger people quite appreciative of what I have taken on and, what the committee here has taken on. I am getting a lot of approaches from younger people saying that we are doing a good job. They look up to us as they have got a lot of respect and trust in us. I have had many calls offering me assistance and certainly offering me their moral support.

The support of people in Australia for refugees in the Balkans war has also been an effective means to persuade some participants to avoid involvement in physical violence. At the same time, effective use of nationalistic pride and cultural heritage among participants led them also to dis-engage from this process; some participants gave over more time to religious and spiritual identification, and others emphasised their learning and/or re-learning of the Serbian Cyrillic script and greater use of the Serbian language.

Doing something to help the refugees

As we previously saw with Nenad, there was considerable activity 'on the ground' with sustained efforts to collect money and possessions for humanitarian relief for displaced ethnic Serbs in the former Yugoslavia. By August 1993, the Serbian Orthodox Church Saint Sava Association had sent three aid missions to the former Yugoslavia, with particular efforts being made for nine hospitals in the *Republika Srpska* and *Republika Srpska Krajina.* By this stage over one million dollars worth of aid had been distributed by the Church in Australia (source: *Srpski Pregled* Vol. 1, No. 3, July/August, 1993, p. 6). Upon gaining news of this, I attempted to interview one of the Melbourne-based Serbian Orthodox priests responsible for organising shipments of humanitarian aid. Before turning to the contents of my interview with him, I will briefly describe the context in which it took place.

I had come to see Fr. Dobrocudan at his parish shortly before lunch on the day of interview. He suggested, 'Before we get down to business, let's go and get some lunch' (when told this I sensed, from the size of his abdominal girth, that he quite liked his food!). He also told me that his church had been the subject of recent vandal attacks and he and his family had received death threats. This meant that he would only agree to being interviewed in a discreet location. What struck me about this was that, despite the death threats, he and I walked the city streets to a restaurant in an ethnically mixed city suburb to eat lunch. During our walk together to the restaurant, several Serbian people approached him, shook his hand, while others acknowledged him as they passed by along the street. He told me that, despite also walking past several groups of Croatian Australians, he did not fear for his life: 'The threats against me make me more determined to live my life in freedom this way, with my people. I'm not here to be hidden away, intimidated'.

Once we arrived at the restaurant we went to a table at the very back, away from the main street front entrance. The interview began with questions from Fr. Dobrocudan about what I was trying to achieve and, whether I planned to talk with others in the community. After sharing as much as possible about my research with him he proceeded to tell me about the humanitarian relief that he had organised on behalf of the

Serbian Orthodox Church community in Australia: 'A massive relief convoy, with an accompanying media contingent, to deliver food, medicine, sutures, bandages, blankets and clothing from Australia to the regions where there were Serb refugees'. He went on to describe how the help he and others had become involved in had prevented mental health problems in Australia:

> One of the reasons that I encouraged so many people being active [in the project] is to vent their anger and frustration in a positive way. I am, for example, trying to be constructive about it, trying to assist the community over there [former Yugoslavia] through moral and humanitarian support. The humanitarian support that we are sending off is of fairly great significance to the Serbian communities over there in the conflict. It's also being done for the moral support that they are getting from the fact that they know that they have people barracking for them here. So that sort of helps me not to get into deep depressions.

While Fr. Dobrocudan was able to use his energy to prevent himself getting into 'deep depressions', there was also a feeling of doing something to help people caught up in the war - both here and in the former Yugoslavia. Aggressive feelings and death threats in Australia were being managed by the Church's representative in a productive and assertive way. In this situation, the priest had provided both physical and spiritual leadership through his decision to remain focussed on the needs of the Serbian people, in Australia and in the former Yugoslavia.

As we saw earlier in this chapter, with Nenad, another focus of the Church's practical response to the conflict was the collection of cash donations from parishioners across Australia. Donations were called for and received during and at the end of church services. By the end of 1995, a total of $790, 000 had been raised and delivered to the Serbian Orthodox Patriarchate for use in its humanitarian aid programs (Illic, 1995).

A participant who had been involved in the organisation of a relief convoy, told me that the giving of time and money was a burden that could not be easily shouldered by her household. Nevertheless, in the choice between doing something or doing nothing, voluntary work gave her time to network with others over common areas of concern. How then were the frustrations of this situation, of not being able to help more directly, experienced and coped with? I was told that there was still some room for doing things for Serbian refugees as a vicarious means of 'self-help', but there was also the need for 'friendship with others in the Serbian community'. I wanted to know what friendship meant to her, and what it was that helped her cope with her frustration. A good friend, she told me was:

> ... someone who is able to listen to me and the part of Serbian friendship that has helped me cope is in the history of the Serbs. In [our] history all great leaders, people of religion, were all saying that Serbs need to get together, get along with each other, so no-one can harm us. If we are not all friends, all of us together, if we are not all together, the Serbs won't exist all that long because we are not all that much a big nation as some other, as some Islamic world nations.

The complexity of wanting friendship and belonging through linkages of ethnic identity linkages is evident in the data above. The historical and cultural dimensions of national identity are being drawn from as a source of strength and emotional support. In this consciousness, there is a sense of security and safety in the experience of others that is contingent upon 'getting along together'.

This interpretation contrasts sharply with the use of national identity as the ultimate means of affiliation and security. Serbian national identity during the Balkan war has been seen by many commentators as responsible for social breakdown and mass genocide. While some might argue that the agony of those left behind in the former Yugoslavia has been appeased with a sense of national identity, it is the same kind of nationalism that has been identified as the principle agitator of ethnic cleansing (Goytisolo, 1993; Amnesty International Report, AI INDEX: EUR 63/03/93:2) and civilian massacre (Vulliamy, 1994). As Ignatieff (1994, p. 186) suggests, individual rights and nationalism in the Balkans is:

> ... a form of speech which shouts, not merely so that it will be heard, but so that it will believe in itself [where] the quotient of crude historical fiction, violent moral exaggeration, ludicrous caricature of the enemy was in direct proportion to the degree to which the speaker is aware that it is all a pack of lies.

In this instance, it is argued, people such as those in the former Yugoslavia, have 'the right' to self determination and territorial claim with heroic sacrifice against enemies both internal and external (Ignatieff, 1994, p. 3).

Elsewhere, Ed Vulliamy (1994, p. 43) sees Serbian nationalism as a force to bind Serbians together to ensure their physical as well as racial purity. This is a nationalism that draws upon past history of Serbian sufferings that becomes 're-planted as a neurosis of threatened common identity upon which Serbian nationalism feeds and transforms into a psychotic means of justifying violence'. This is powerfully put, and leads Vulliamy to conclude that the Serbs 'make good friends and awesome enemies'.

Nevertheless, not everyone uses nationalism this way. It is important to stress that the relationships and connections between nationalism and inner sense of wellbeing, as I have interpreted it, were crucial elements in shaping the way participants coped with life in Australia. There was, as Graham Little (1993, p. 137) explains, the need for people to look for friendship in the form of 'the company of people, who are true to themselves, with a strong sense of the self'. Analysis in this chapter shows how nationalist rhetoric can lead to affiliation, and something of an inner feeling of sincerity and bonding. As soon as friendship and companionship were reached emotional discomfort would be alleviated. The important point is that friendship-as-help, for the participants, was through a network of Serbian cultural connections, linking the events of the present to those in the past.   Such analysis of nationalism, bonding, belonging and sincerity, gives rise to an understanding of how participants coped with events, despite the distance between the Balkans and Australia - a distance that could never be physically overcome.

Moving forward from the hurt: on becoming more Serbian

As participants found that they were able to help others and themselves at the same time, there was a transition from feeling traumatised, to recovery. This again drew on their cultural and historical background. Notwithstanding the degree of severity of the traumatic event (birthplace being razed to the ground; family becoming refugee or slaughtered; a perceived negative bias in the media against the Serbian people), it became increasingly clear that, for some Serbian Australians, the only way they could feel better about their situation was to become 'more of a Serbian'. To illustrate this important point, I return to Ljubica. Here she is telling me of how she managed to 'feel better' again:

> I realised that when people asked me my nationality, I was telling them that I was a Serb. I used to get a variety of mixed reactions and I could see people going, 'oh, you're one of those, you're the bad guys'. People just

saw [Serbs] us as trouble makers. Now, after all that I've been through, I never say that I am Australian. I always say that I am Serbian. I say it over and over to myself, more and more that I am Serbian. And more and more I think it is important to say that I am Serbian. I think that I am a good model for the Serbian people. I am a good Serbian. I think that the more people know that I am Serbian, the better I feel. I am not ashamed at being a Serb.

At the same time I stopped looking at the television. Every time the war came on TV, I either changed the channel or left the room. I removed myself from this space I was in when the war came onto the screen. If I left the room I made sure that I could not hear it [the television], so I would close the doors. I would then go and sit down and give a sigh, a breath out to relieve my tension. I needed to let out all of the strain, like a good massage. I knew that if I did not relax I would get really sick, I would mentally break down. During all this time I did not eat and I knew that I was heading for a mental melt down.

At this point of our conversation together Ljubica went on to thank me for the help that I had given her during previous meetings. In addition, she continued to tell me about what had helped her to cope with life over the past three years. It was, as illustrated by the above quotation, a renewed feeling of Serbian national identity.

In reinforcing the self-as-Serb, there was a simultaneous development of what I call the 'Serbian self' as a means to preserve and protect one's wellbeing. The Serbian self acts as an emotional bulwark against the pressure and frustrations that actually emerge from being Serbian in the first place. This was also apparent during our interview together:

This war has torn me apart completely. It has torn people - Croats and Serbs apart. They may not hate each other at all, but there is a certain feeling of injustice between them and it tears you apart from each other. *It's dreadful and I am sure that there's a lot of people devastated in a very nationalistic way.* For me its the devastation of what it has done to my life. ...[A]nd now, *because of all of this, I am a Serb. I am no longer an Australian. I only call myself a Serb. I am a Serb who lives in Australia.* (emphasis added, N.P.)

Through this process of being a renewed self-as-Serb, there was an opportunity to bring about a working through of issues such as emotional pain and loss of homeland. Relationships made during childhood, and their memories, are also inextricably linked with re-developing a national and cultural identity in the shadow of homeland devastation. The transformation from the 'old self' to the 'new self' has a character of its own. At the same time, the process of helping Serbian refugees has helped people into a re-connection, and re-awakening, with all that is Serbian. Zorica describes her experience of this as something:

> ... inescapable, a natural thing to happen that is to become - if it's possible, to become more of a Serb. I am more of a Serb from the point of view that I have been exposed to our community activities; to our community needs far more (and) therefore, things like having to use the Serbian language far more frequently and reading material in Serbian has of necessity made me more tuned-in if you like, or closer to the community... although I have been extremely close in my heart and own spirit to my cultural heritage all the time.

The important point to emerge from the discussion above is that, with the dissolution of what was Yugoslavia, the Serbian Australian experience of long distance devastation, and events in Australia, became shaped by the cultural, social and spiritual life of 'being' Serbian. While some participants sought comfort from others outside the Serbian community, there began a network of supportive friendships and relationships that expressed empathy with and support for each other, and with those made homeless by the war. The frustrations of wanting to retaliate in kind to property violence, death threats, and the destruction of Serbian held territory in former Yugoslavia, were held back by a determination to remain calm. At the very heart of these efforts was the Serbian Orthodox Church as a presence representing local security and stability.

The Serbian Orthodox Church demonstrated a restrained approach, despite their property and parish members being the target of violence and death threats. Under these circumstances, had there not been this kind of support and restraint, it is almost certain that there would have been much violence in Australia that would have required high level strategic police intervention. As legitimate bearers of authority, the Serbian Orthodox Church have proven themselves to be more than effective as a calming influence on Serbian Australians.

There is, a need for some caution in analysing the complex way in which this operates; after all, little is known outside this study about the relationship between the teachings of the Serbian Orthodox Church and the lives of people living outside of the former Yugoslavia. However, Bulich (1985, pp. 2-3), for example, has undertaken a qualitative inquiry into the relationship between the Serbian Orthodox faith and the mental health of Serbian Americans. He found that personal engagement in and experience of the church service liturgy equipped and enabled people to feel:

> comfortable about oneself, to relate and share with other people, to cope successfully with daily life tasks and demands, to have full and wholesome life, to think and feel about himself not as an isolated individual but as an integral part of the community. This person has a strong sense of believing and belonging, (and) has meaning and purpose.

In the case of shifting identities and boundaries from Yugoslav to Serbian, participants were situated to embrace their new sense of belonging. The testimony of Verica, first introduced in chapter 3, explains what happened when being helped by fellow Serbians at the time when the house she was born in was taken by the enemy:

> I never really thought about it before but, I would do anything to help the people who have helped me. It shows in the war, because I think before the war no-one actually needed that much help. But now, during war everyone helps each other and [this shows] the real true connection of the Serbs.

National and cultural identity is at the heart of what it means to have real connections with Serbians. Having a cultural and national identity with others gives rise to a sense of belonging, that is, as evidenced by this research, inextricably linked to a human affinity and 'being' a particular person. Verica continues to explain this connection:

> When my home town was taken over by the Muslim army, I felt very sad. *It's something that I felt was tending to ruin my health. I had a strain in my heart.* But when [Serbian] people treated me as they did, they just wanted to help me, I just felt alive again. You feel that you need to be well and be alive so you can return them that friendship, you can help them sometimes. *My health comes from my heart,* or your brain ...[I]t's really hard to express these things in words. (emphasis added, N.P.)

The important point to emerge from this material is that the Serbian culture and nation that participants feel they belong to in the world, is interwoven with their mental health needs during times of personal crisis. This situation suggests that Serbian cultural, religious and language traditions are re-affirming of individual identity and belonging. In this way, participants experiencing the episodes of long distance suffering and devastation described in chapters 5 and 6 of this study, are being helped to cope with feelings of worry, hurt, isolation, frustration, sleeplessness and emotional exhaustion by discerning individual meaning in life through cultural and national identification.

The Serbian Orthodox Easter 1995 and the re-affirmation of Serbian identity

I was told by a number of participants 'When I need to feel closer to my people I go to Church'; so I naturally undertook to do some fieldwork during the Serbian Orthodox Easter. On the day I arrived to generate the data, I was struck by seeing more younger people present that day then I had seen on previous occasions.

A section was set aside at the rear of the Church for burning candles. These candles were being lit by a continuous stream of parishioners in respect for living and deceased friends and family. The collective presence of the icons, candles, participants and priest created an environment whereby in this space, at this particular moment, the living and the dead were as one. The candles were being monitored by an elderly gentleman. Many of the candles had drooped over and lost their flame. I waited as my friend Saveta purchased candles and, once she was free to move through the masses of people present in the Church, she handed me two candles. I watched carefully as Saveta made a sign of the cross and lit each of her three candles. Saveta inserted two candles in the top tray and one below. The top two were for her son and daughter-in-law, and the bottom candle was dedicated to the memory of her late husband. She told me later that the ceremony of the candles was a means for her to remember people, past and present.

I followed as closely as I could the actions of what the others present in the Church did with the candles. Before lighting each of my candles I crossed myself with my right hand, lit the candle and placed it in the sand - one candle in the upper section and the other in the lower section (the latter section in memory of the deceased). Once I had completed this I turned to face the front of the Church, to watch the priest make his moves and perform the ceremony.

There are no chairs or pews, except along either side of the Church and these had been reserved for the elderly. Bulich (1985, pp. 85-86) remarks that the lack of pews serves to ensure that participants stand close to each other:

... thus enabling them to feel more keenly the sense of community of believers, belonging to a community and also helping them not to be necessarily conformed in their actions. The presence of children, including babies contributes to this atmosphere of informality, feeling of belonging to the family, being at home.

What I experienced in the Church was the coming together of formal ceremony and the informal means by which people conducted themselves. On the one hand there was a well structured process of liturgy in progress, involving singing and speaking by the priest and a small choir, and yet, throughout, there was a continuous array of 'other' activity. Throughout the service there was a trickle of people entering and leaving the church, as well as occasional conversations between participants and children moving about freely inside the Church. These conversations appeared largely the result of people newly arriving at the Church greeting those inside. From time to time there was a low-level hum of voices brought about by small pockets, mainly of men, in conversation, at the rear of the Church. These men were expressing their disapproval about others in the doorway leading into the Church who were also engaged in conversation.

The distribution of people was sharply along gender lines, men on the right hand side of the Church and women on the left. Occasionally, a sprinkling of mixed gender would appear on either side, and this appeared to be associated with a connecting family member.

Being in the Church that day had, for those with whom I spoke, a feeling of intensified community that could not normally be found elsewhere. Bulich, (1985, p. 82) remarks that:

> The Church is both visible and invisible, both divine and human. It is visible, for it is composed of concrete congregations, worshipping here on earth: it is invisible because it also includes the saints and the angles. It is divine, for it is the Body of Christ.

I left the 'field' that day with a strong sense of those whom I had met being a kind of metaphor representing all that is Serbian: Church, music, food, religious icon and language. That is, the Serbian Orthodox Church was a place of powerful symbolic element of life force and religious identification.

Conclusion

This chapter was primarily dedicated to understanding and interpreting what participants did for themselves and others to cope with the distress of distant war, and secondary events in Australia. Interpretation has revealed that the objects and people that Serbian Australians used to feel better about their situation - Serbian Churches, Serbian historical reference points, community centres, humanitarian support for Serbian refugees in former Yugoslavia - were also subject to threat and destruction. The deliberate targeting of these objects by people opposed to the Serbian point of view served to unleash their inter-subjective capability and in some instances served to precipitate the drive toward retaliatory violence. As social life became more difficult in Australia, and as participants tried to cope with this, the more they became distressed by their experience. The more disturbed they were by events in Australia and the Balkans, the more relations between Serbian Australians became orientated toward increasing emotional and spiritual support. To overcome the hurt, worry and a sense of long distance devastation, many sought out each other for support, friendship and reassurance, and for re-connection with their historical, cultural and religious traditions.

This support for each other in the face of increasing distress also served to counter their feelings of abandonment in Australia. There was a very real and powerful sense of participants being able to endure increasing hardships by, for example, giving cash donations to Serbian refugees, spending up to two dollars per minute on telephone calls to the Balkans region in an effort to try and located displaced family members, among other concerns. While being the source of considerable distress in themselves, such actions also served to give participants the power and strength to cope with the volatile impact of the war.

In the next chapter, I build on this and all previous interpretations to conclude my research journey. Through a review of the substantive and methodological issues emerging throughout chapters 1-7, I demonstrate that individual health and cultural processes in local circumstances could no longer be seen as separate from events in the larger world. This means that, rather than being peripheral to people's lives, events and processes in the larger world, in many instances constituted a reality that existed in local settings too. The result has been a theoretical and practical understanding of how information from participants was informed by the interactive and autobiographical elements of data generation in the shadow of a global catastrophic event.

Notes

1 As I have demonstrated throughout the research, there has been no attempt by me to withhold or suppress the Gadamerian notion of 'effective history' (chapter 3). This means that I have put to work my conscious use of personal nursing knowledge and practice brought with me to the research setting and have worked this influence out interpretively rather than attempting to withhold or suppress its meaning.

2 While the majority of sanctions against the former Yugoslavia were lifted after the Dayton peace accords on Bosnia were signed, the United States and the European Union preserved an 'outer wall' of measures, including exclusion of membership of international organisations. These secondary sanctions are only to be lifted once Serbia's central government meets several targets on human rights and democratic reforms.

3 At the fall of Krainja on August 13 1995, an estimated 200, 000 Serbian refugees were made homeless as this Serbian controlled region of Croatia fell to Croatian troops. Ian Traynor (1995, p. 4) of the *Guardian Weekly* said in his report from the region that 'this was the tragic ending of 400 years of Serb culture in rural Croatia'. All of this was despite the UN special envoy to the region, Mr. Yasushi Akashi, contacting the President Tudjman of Croatia in the days leading up to the assault, asking that he negotiate with Serbian forces.

4 Hill (1993, p. 38) quotes Alexander Pavkovic, Director of Slavonic and East European Studies at Macquarie University, New South Wales, as having calculated that approximately 7000 Croatians and 3000 Serbians from Australia have returned to fight.

5 *The Canberra Times* on July 14 1992, p. 3 carried a report that on the previous day, a Croatian youth was seriously beaten in Sydney while returning from a soccer match. The attack, allegedly by a group of Serbian youths, was said to be linked to a concern expressed by both communities, that, after the return from overseas of Serbian and Croatian volunteers, open fighting could erupt at any time.

8 Conclusion

Introduction

Central and Eastern Europe during the 1990s was a time of extraordinary change in every aspect of economic, political and social life and, perhaps above all, in inter-relationships between ethnic groups hostile to each other. The questions and issues that have occupied this research journey were derived in direct reference to contemporary European events, and the Balkan war in particular. A central theme of this research journey has been the impact of the Balkan war on the culture and health of people living in Australia who ascribe to being Serbian.

By engaging in a research approach guided by Gadamers' (1975) philosophical hermeneutics and Marcus' (1986; 1995) formulations of contemporary ethnography, this research journey showed that Serbian Australians suffered from sleeplessness, irritability, frustration, loneliness, sadness, worry, anxiety, anger, and bouts of extreme emotional exhaustion. The torment affecting Serbian Australians drew its influence from the simultaneous unfolding of the Balkan war and episodes of violence, unrest, and humiliation in Australia.

This final chapter examines the substantive issues emerging from the research. The question, 'How could this chapter best be constructed?', has been answered by taking a step back from what actually happened in the research to emphasise what the research journey revealed. This research is revealing of both the practical struggles endured by Serbian Australians and the appraisal of these social events along interpretive lines. For instance, this research journey revealed how war in the Balkans moved people beyond the borders of friendships and relationships built around ethnic identities from the former Yugoslavia in Australia, into a graphic re-awakening of individual thoughts of Serbian identity. The dramatic consequences of this on Serbian Australians was to have their thinking in relation to the Balkan war moved beyond their conceptual pre-suppositions. All of this occurred in the context of great personal sadness, historical resurgence, and personal and political uncertainty that inevitably led to dramatic changes in the way that health and cultural life was lived out.

164

From this perspective, the first part of this chapter centres upon the ways in which participants moved through the experience of re-evaluating and re-drawing their personal and social boundaries with others, and the emerging conflicts and tensions. Underlying this action was the need for participants to feel a sense of belonging and valued involvement in Australia, as well as a sense of historical closeness to people and places of the former Yugoslavia. The analysis continues by reflecting upon the dominant position of suffering, guilt, emotional hurt and irritability in the participants' lives, and the way these issues were coped with.

The final part of this chapter considers questions surrounding the methodological aspects of the research. As previously emphasised, while the experiences of participants were illuminated by the joint influences of philosophical hermeneutics and ethnography, this brought about a tension in the relationship between the values and knowledge of the researcher and the researched. For these reasons it is prudent to review how information from participants was portrayed in the research, and the means through which my understandings were transformed into text.

On the substantive issues of the research

It has become clear from the research that Serbian Australian culture and health during the Balkan war, 1991 - 1996, cannot be adequately described without reference to the shifting historical contexts given by those who participated in this research journey. My theme throughout the research period was to try and find out as much as possible about what it meant to be a Serbian Australian and what was perceived as sacred about this meaning. My efforts were illuminated and explicated through Gadamers' (1975) philosophical hermeneutics, Marcus' (1995) view of contemporary ethnography, and the development of a particular kind of global-local substantive position. The immediate context of my trying to find out about these issues was amid the dynamic interplay between the catastrophic events in the Balkans and the social life of participants living in Australia.

The conversations and observations reveal, from chapter 1 onwards, that the Balkan war was not only a tragedy for its people and the world community, but also a distressing life event for people living thousands of kilometres away. Serbian Australians were moved through a range of historical, cultural and emotional processes that involved them in coming to terms with the way they experienced guilt, worry, powerlessness, long distance devastation and suffering. This situation recognised both

Giddens' (1996) and Robertson's (1992; 1995) views that no one is outside the influence of the global in social life. The Balkan war effectively leapt over national boundaries and was seen as something directly impacting on individual health and wellbeing in local situations.

Because this research journey emphasised the individual experience and reaction of participants' experience in Australia, much was revealed in relation to feelings of anger, frustration and sadness, and how these experiences ultimately challenged their view of who they were, and to a lesser extent, the country in which they were living (Australia). The search for linkages, between the participant's experience of events in the Balkans and those in Australia, led me to the interface of Serbian national identity and the rejection of the old ideals of Yugoslav unity. As seen particularly seen in chapters 4 and 5, this situation led Serbian Australians into re-defining and re-negotiating the boundaries of their national identity along ethnic lines.

Serbian national identity was, for participants, inextricably linked to mental health and wellbeing, both directly and indirectly. In a *direct* sense, there was a human affinity and belonging that bonded people and gave them a sense of common purpose. With this purpose came a sense of renewed and highly valued involvements in Serbian culture, language and religion. In an *indirect* sense there was an decision being made by participants that connected them with two worlds: the world of belonging to the many aspects of contemporary Serbian national interests, and the world that acknowledged the broad historical events of the recent and distant past. By looking both to the past and present at the same time, participants were then able to integrate a more robust sense of individual coping into their social life. For many, the spiritual and cultural dimensions of Serbian life overshadowed the problems of living brought about by the war and its adverse media reporting.

The re-defining of individual identity was aligned with a resurgence of religious, historical and cultural beliefs and values that were almost always a constant companion during periods of worry, sadness and emotional exhaustion. As a researcher I found that, by becoming involved and immersed as much as possible in what it meant to be a Serbian Australian, and in what was perceived as sacred about this meaning, I generated new and deeply revealing insights about individual and community life. In their efforts to survive the distressing effects of the Balkan war, participants enhanced their wellbeing with a selective blend of factors such as nationalism, history, religion and a sense of belonging with names and places in the former Yugoslavia. As described in chapter 7, for instance, this gave rise to participants being able to interpret from each other a collective sense of re-building and re-affirming oneself as Serbian. In extreme moments of rage, anger and frustration, Serbian national identity in Australia was associated with participants believing in the justified use of violence in defence of their county of origin.

Since the war tended to vary in intensity over time, participants developed an ability to cope with the effects of stressful situations that were constantly being altered in the face of changing circumstances. These changing circumstances included confusion over whether certain relatives were dead or alive, when a particular village had been razed to the ground, and the arrival of erratic and fragmented pieces of largely unconfirmed news and information from the region. The central point to emerge from all of this was that, as participants were struggling to find a means to help themselves, and each other, to cope with the many health problems brought on by the war, they were also trying to cope with problems of living in Australia. And these problems in themselves constituted what social life in Australia actually was for them at that time.

With the conflict in the former Yugoslavia being marked in Australia by the twin processes of historical re-interpretation and a re-negotiation of relationships between ethnic groups in the Balkans and Australia, the task of participants trying to cope was not an easy one. While some simply cut off all communications and association with others, most appeared to reduce their social networks, in one sense, at the same time as expanding their involvements with others in and around the Serbian community, with mixed results. Slowly, as the negative health impact of the Balkan war was increasing, making social life even more burdensome and challenging to the individual, there was a steadily accumulating pressure coming from both inside and outside Australia to maintain effective coping strategies.

These considerations have significant, although complex implications for analysing the practical impact of the Balkan war on social life and health in particular. What this analysis achieved was to draw attention to two significant issues. *Firstly,* it raised important questions about the way certain individuals construct social and cultural realities, by separating themselves and their families from specific stressful events. This aspect of interpretation in the research journey helped me to realise that the newly created ethnic relationships and historical understandings brought about by disintegration of the former Yugoslavia were linked to the social life of participants in Australia.

Secondly, and partly as result of a critical reception by Serbian Australians to the Australian government's decision to support sanctions against Serbia and Montenegro, it became apparent that some participants had lost confidence in calling themselves 'Australian'. This connection between the implementation of economic and trade sanctions against Serbia and the participants' sense of an Australian identity was a potent and destructive mix. Behind the idea that participants would no longer identify as 'Yugoslav' lies a range of issues that helped guide them to feel better about their situation. As described in chapter 5, in particular, with an increased sense of a re-affirmed identity, participants came around to the idea that their involvements with others could only ever be contingent upon a new found sense of what they believed to be the Serbian cause.

The analysis of sense of belonging, as a vital mental health concept, in chapter 5, brought forward two important points that contribute to the discussion of health and cultural issues. The first was that, by moving forward the ideas of social and cultural boundaries described in chapter 4, participants had a map of 'the other' to follow as a guide during the transition from Yugoslav to Serbian. During the course of this process, participants were given some help in ending their Yugoslav identity, at the same time as they recast their lives in relation to events in Australia and the Balkans. This newly discovered map of self and others helped give Serbian Australians someone to blame, someone to hold responsible for their suffering. And all of this helped transform Serbian Australians, along with the country with which they held ancestral linkages.

The re-casting of a new found cultural identity, based upon centuries old rhetoric and tradition, gives rise to my second point. With a new found re-connection with the past as part of the symbolic construction of boundaries, the boundaries themselves became something that featured so strongly in the mental life of participants that they could not be ignored. From this moment, whenever participants spoke of the Balkans, both past and present, there was an active sense of identity and valued connection with their historical roots.

In searching for the meanings of identity and belonging, we heard from participants, in chapter 6, how the repeated television images of devastation and killing, reflected more than isolated life events taking shape in far away places. People were distressed and disturbed by these images to the extent that they suffered significant health effects. These health effects - sleeplessness, irritability, inability to concentrate, feelings of frustration, worry, anxiety, nightmares and intrusive pre-occupations with the fate (often unknown) of family lost in or around fighting -

demonstrate the complexity, and emotive connections, between increased mass media, literacy and advanced information technology. We saw how media journalists and reporters such as Neil Ascherson, Martin Bell, Misha Glenny, Mark Thompson, Mark Traynor, Ed Vulliamy and others, played a vital role in this process. They became, along with their editorial teams in the Balkans, England and the United States, the architects of a real and bloodied imagery of suffering and devastation. They became lead figures in what I have called the consciousness industry that manufactured particular ways of seeing the Balkan war. It became clear, in chapter 1, and through chapters 4, 6 and 7, that the beaming of certain images, and construction of carefully scripted voice-overs, could alter the course of people's lives in Australia. These celluloid seconds from another world moved people to see and feel the impact of a catastrophic event as if it were happening in their very own suburb. In trying to come to terms with these events, participants had a consuming need to hear and see, as much as possible, a tremendous amount of news from the region.

From this analysis, it appears almost throughout the research journey, that the repeated exposure to electronic and print media of the conflict was for some participants both disturbing and yet a vital means to find out what was actually happening. In this situation, participants were trying to find a means to reconcile their need to hear and see as much information from the region on the one hand, with trying to cope with the shocking effects of long distance devastation on the other. While radio brought up-to-date information about the conflict, numbers of dead and wounded, and the names of towns and villages lost to the enemy, television brought to life the graphic effects of the war. Some participants could not watch television, as it made them physically ill, brought on ideas of suicide and caused problems in everyday relationships with others. For others, the television news became a catalyst for them to want to take up arms and travel to the region to fight.

The trauma of seeing one's homeland destroyed, and the frustration of not being able to do anything to stop it, was made worse when friendships and family were lost, either directly through fighting or indirectly through the re-working of boundaries in Australia. The suffering and guilt being experienced by participants was an understandable reaction to a significant human loss of life. When participants' usual ability to enjoy and participate in social-life - everyday activities such as eating, drinking, sleeping and socialising began to be interfered with both day and night, it was clear that disruptions to health were an inescapable tragic consequence of the Balkan war. As we saw throughout the research journey, to cope with this situation, participants came around to the idea that it was important to become more Serbian, and to have the greater sense of the identity that this implies. This gave rise to a stronger sense of being a person with a sense of purpose, belonging, and valued involvement in the Serbian cause.

These were the main reasons for Serbians becoming more intimately connected with all that they perceived to be the Serbian cause. As a cultural and social process, this helped establish a coping connection with other Serbians and the Serbian Orthodox Church in particular. The Serbian Orthodox Church community confirmed Bulich's (1985) perception of it as a deeply engaging form of spiritual support and reassurance. The Serbian Orthodox Church was also responsible for the transmission of anti-violent messages being communicated person-to-person during church services and other group gatherings. Notwithstanding the feelings of emotional support this generated, such actions also helped calm certain participants and prevent violence erupting between groups hostile to each other in Australia. In addition to this, a range of new and largely informal networks and associations evolved in Australia during the Balkan war, and these had, to a varying extent, encouraged calm and peaceful demonstration and the rallying of humanitarian help for Serbian refugees.

The anger and disillusionment that followed the rejection, by the Australian government, of the humanitarian needs of Serbian refugees, and much of the electronic and print media about the war, leads me to speculate on the implications of social and family issues for health and helping professionals. The key reference point to engage in this discussion is the emotional connection made by participants with homeland people, places and memories, as well as family bonds. The cultural and spiritual connections made by Serbian Australians are private in the sense that they are difficult to access in interpersonal relationships, and complex in structure. Moreover, cultural and spiritual connections being made by such people are inclusive of ethnic identity, and belonging, and fluid geographical boundaries, that help give Serbian identity form and meaning. The purpose of spelling out these features is to make the point that homeland destruction, loss, uncertainty and communication breakdown, and family, are interlinked, leading to biophysical and psychological pressures that may not be immediately apparent in health and helping situations. This means that multiple losses may constitute the call for stronger national identity and religious affiliation by those affected. By calling on such national, cultural and religious commitments, there is also a calling on being an 'Australian', and, a reminder, that, first and foremost, 'you live in Australia'. For some individuals this strategy may bring about less mental distress and increased protection from unwanted feelings that emerge from the experience of long distance devastation. That is, an emotional bulwark is created, to obliterate the pain of the Balkans war on people living it from thousands of kilometres away. Having a sense of belonging and community may also help to release tension and frustration, thus directing it away from others from the region who also live in Australia.

It is useful to discuss on the implications of this analysis for professionals and authorities in Australia. There are wider implications, for example in the mechanisms used by Serbian Australians to help avoid physical clashes, property damage, and violence towards others from the former Yugoslavia living in Australia. Police and emergency personnel for example, will be better informed to cope with the effort needed to calm or prevent violence, following provocations of the kind identified in this research journey, by considering the global and local factors that trigger and motivate people to respond this way. These triggers include evolution and articulation of the nature of how individuals interpret the past, as well as events in the 'here and now' and projections into the future. Serbian Australians are seeking to establish themselves in a new world context through the re-awakening and re-locating of symbols and structures that once featured so strongly in cultural life, rather than abandoning the past. This reawakening and reconnecting is aligned with a blend of national and religious spirit and energy that is 'all me as an Australian Serbian'.

In this context it is important for professionals and policy makers to know something of the potential impact of distressing media reports, the feeling of betrayal by the Australian government, and loss of a 'voice' and audience in Australian society that encourages feelings of isolation, rejection and anger. Through an understanding of these conditions, social and legal authorities may come to realise that how individuals experience long distance devastation and hurt has a lot to do with the catastrophic and powerful mix of events in the global and local worlds. Such awareness may give rise to the realisation that, as life in Australia and the former Yugoslavia becomes more distressing, so too does life for the Serbian Australian individual.

In summary, the impact of the Balkan war has been directly felt here in Australia as a turbulent event with historical reference points. As a critical global event, the war has transcended the communities which are immediately affected by it, to disrupt the physical and mental lives of people living thousands of kilometres away. Regardless of the geographical distance between Australia and the former Yugoslavia, Serbian Australians have struggled to cope with the emotional disturbance caused by the ending of what was once Yugoslavia and the associated secondary events in Australia. All of this has brought about a new and complex re-affirmation of what it means to be a Serbian Australian in modern times, and what is sacred about that meaning.

On methodological issues in the research

Were the insights outlined above informed, or perhaps, as Giddens (1996) sees it, in some way influenced and interpreted, by the social scientific techniques used in this study? Is it reasonable to speculate that an autobiographical connection with the people and places of the former Yugoslavia, and many years as a mental health professional, may have had too much influence in developing an excessively personalised point of view about Serbian Australians?

In addressing these questions I must review the research processes that were deployed in constructing the text. To interpret the complex interplay between the tragedy of European war in the 1990s and the disruption to health and wellbeing for Serbian Australians living thousands of kilometres away, it was necessary for me to witness, interact, collaborate, absorb, engage with and disengage from the lives and beliefs of the participants. The techniques I used to do this - interviewing, participant observation and networking - had a lot to do with the symbolic interactive techniques informed by Denzin (1994) and Goffman (1989), and the experience gained as a mental health professional of more than 10 years standing. Central to the relationships I developed with participants was an inter-subjective appreciation of interpersonal dynamics at work.

The dynamic and interactive nature of fieldwork involved my taking personal and professional risks alongside the practical aspects of locating my substantial position in this research. From this perspective, consideration of Marcus's (1995) conceptualisation of local situations in the context of global impacting forces was combined with Giddens' (1996) double hermeneutic. The merging of these ideas caused me to become alert to the idea that the human inquiry I was engaged in was inextricably linked to the way I asked questions, and the way that global-local issues were part of this inquiry.

To help counter the tensions caused by my autobiographical connection with the Balkans, and the Gadamerian view of presuppositions as a mental health professional, was the construction of a global-local framework as a duel methodological and substantive position. As we saw in chapters 2 and 3, for example, these combined positions evolved, both situationally and through their intellectual frameworks. This analysis and discussion provided me with a sense of conceptualising participants in a global epoch, marked by a real change in the way contemporary understandings of the human health experience were currently framed. This means that the global-local framework, developed through the study, became something more than just a contemporary aspect of social scientific discussion: it was something that helped move me to consider possible intersections between culture and health in relation to the recent resurgence of religion, ethnicity and national identity worldwide.

With the generation of interpretation being inextricably related to methodological issues, it was sometimes a challenge to appropriately balance aspects of the methodological and substantive discussion. In earlier drafts of this research journey, I believe that Gadamer's (1975) influence led me to write a lot more on how I *did* the research in relation to *what* were my findings. I wrestled with this issue along the following lines of inquiry. Firstly, I wondered whether or not the balance might be justified, given that generating data also meant interpreting it. In other words, I had to encounter and actively negotiate the research environment, and this meant generating a method in specific relation to this. The way I did this had a good deal to do with the way participants responded to me and, in turn, how I responded to them. All of this became both a methodological and a substantive issue, as the global-local experiences of participants were interrelated with each other. So from this perspective I decided to engage explicitly the nature of methodological accounts and substantive issues each within the framework of the other.

One of the difficulties with the methodology chosen was, nonetheless, the trap of indulging in romantic over-involvement, such that with the 'I' of the research journey replaced the 'eye' of the researcher. To counter this, Habermas' (1994) critique of Gadamer's (1975) hermeneutics was enlisted to try to avoid an over-romantic indulgence with reflection and, similarly, over-involvement in the lives of participants. In doing this I sought to retain the belief that remained throughout the research journey: the belief that both Serbian Australians and I were self-interpreting individuals, caught up in the Balkan war, at the same time trying to make meaning out of the experiences brought about by it. To effectively counter romantic intoxication, and to avoid over-involvement with the idea of being both self-interpreting and at one with participants, I engaged J. C. Alexander's (1995) call to explicitly explain and apply qualitative material from participants in the situations both they and I describe. This led to the frequent use of quotations and participant observation data in the text, as a way of distinguishing their 'voices' from my own.

In practical terms, Alexander's (1995) influence and Habermas's (1994) critique of Gadamer's (1975) philosophical hermeneutics, led me to think very carefully about the way in which I, rather than participants, emphasised particular words, actions, and interactions that emerged during the data. This and the overall context and themes of the research are revealed in each of the chapters. I thought very carefully about the way in which there was a particular reason for my insertion or emphasis of quotations, and what this might imply in relation to the discussion being generated. I was conscious of trying to intermingle the voices and actions of participants as much as possible, while contrasting this with my own interpretation, analysis, and strategic footnoting. Providing information about those I observed and interviewed, the important point to be made about this approach is that the intermingling of voices did not lead to an incapacity to tell which voice was speaking.

There are some interesting linkages between the above issues and the conduct of qualitative health research. They begin with the researcher's own willingness to undertake fieldwork whenever cultural connections and affirmations are being made. As Serbian Australians come to terms with the widespread changes in their life, there is a commitment to objects that are familiar and 'safe'. As we saw in chapter 7, for instance, religious and cultural symbols such as churches, traditional dance, music and other celebrations were a means to reunite oneself with one's identity, and to re-affirm who one is. For the qualitative health researcher, this means that entering into such situations for the purpose of generating data requires sensitivity and empathy, whenever the emotional content surrounding the experience of, for instance, long distance suffering, takes hold.

Another linkage is the meeting of international dimensions of human suffering and global media in the local situation. As we saw, in chapter 6 in particular, the repeated display of electronic and print media from the region on Australian television brought both researcher and researched to the interface of feeling traumatised and saddened. Health researchers in search of descriptions of this experience are also witness to the trauma that recalling such material may bring. Sensitivity and scholarly understanding must be tempered with an appreciation that the mere presence of the researcher can bring forth material not normally probed for in the normal course of events that day. Understanding and respect for participants in the context of frustration, that increases when researchers are pre-occupied with their own interests, must be balanced with the desire to do no harm.

I believe that the sense of purpose and (mental health) professional identity I maintained during the research process helped reduce the possibly traumatic impact of my asking questions and observing participants. While not primarily a nursing study, my being a mental health nurse was, overall, beneficial to this study. This background helped me be alert to the impact on participants of my questions and actions. While this is important in its own right, the fact of my being a health professional, and what this might mean to the generation of interpretation and text, is also of interest, in particular, the way I could generate and influence a particular line of inquiry, or pick up on a particular statement, idea, action or issue. I could have presented many more illustrations and combinations of data and, perhaps, many more directions regarding what was inferred or suggested by the data at various points in the study. In the multiple re-writes and re-configurations of the chapters that make up this study I could have re-worked ideas over and over again in an effort to gain some sort of literary connection with the way that my interpretations unfolded. At every point during the journey there were a range of methodological issues to emerge from my interaction with the data and, for reasons that I hope I have made clear in each of the chapters that make up this research journey, I tell of how I actually did this.

Nevertheless, the ultimate intention of this research journey was to interpret the health and cultural issues to emerge from events occurring simultaneously in the Balkans and in the lives of Serbian Australians. I hope to have explicated the various connections between the many issues arising from being a Serbian Australian in relation to a world catastrophic event. I hope that *all* readers of this research journey come to realise that the participants who opened up their homes, their families, their cultural and religious celebrations - their very selves to me, did so at the same time as there were perilous consequences for their health and wellbeing. In the end, this is how war in the heart of Europe during the 1990s has been deeply felt, researched and interpreted in Australia.

Bibliography

Adams, P. (1996), 'Product we view as news', *The Weekend Australian*, December, 14-15, p. 54.

Ahmed, A. (1993), 'Bosnia: the latest crusade', *The Arab Review*, vol. 1, pp. 7-11.

Ahmed, A. (1995), '"Ethnic Cleansing": a metaphor for our time?', *Ethnic and Racial Studies*, vol, 18, pp. 1-25.

Alexander, J. C. (1995), 'General theory in the postpositivist mode: the epistemological dilemma and the search for present reason', in J. C. Alexander (ed.), *Fin de Siede Social Theory*, Verso, London, pp. 90-127.

Anti Serbian propaganda in Australian newspapers, *Srpski Glas*, July, 17, 1991, p. 2.

Arthur, D., Dowling, J. and Sharkey, R. (1992), *Mental Health Nursing: Strategies for Working with the Difficult Client*, W. B. Saunders, Sydney.

Ascherson, N. (1991), 'Serbs and Croats united in brotherly hate', *The Independent*, July 14, p. 25.

Ascherson, N. (1992), 'To be healthy and happy is sometimes to be mad', *The Independent*, September 22, p. 25.

Atkins, S. and Murphy, K. (1993), 'Reflection: a review of the literature', *Journal of Advanced Nursing*, vol. 18, pp. 1188-1192.

Australian responses to Croatia's and Slovenia's declaration of independence and sovereignty, *Novo Doba*, July 23, 1991, p. 1.

Australian responses to Croatia's and Slovenia's declaration of independence and sovereignty, *Hrvatski Vjesnik*, November 29, 1991, pp. 1-2.

Australian responses to Croatia's and Slovenia's declaration of independence and sovereignty, *Srpski Glas*, December 3, 1991, pp. 2-3.

Banac, I. (1992), *The National Question in Yugoslavia: Origins, History, Politics*, Cornell University Press, London.

Barker, P. (1997), *Assessment in Psychiatric and Mental Health Nursing: in Search of the Whole Person*, Stanley Thornes (Publishers) Ltd., Cheltenham.

Bell, M. (1996), *In Harm's Way: Reflections of a War-Zone Thug*, Penguin Books, London.

Benner, P. (1984), *From Novice to Expert*, Addison Wesley, San Francisco.

Benner, P. (1991), 'The role of experience, narrative and community in skilled ethical comportment', *Advances in Nursing Science*, vol. 14, pp. 1-21.

Benner, P. (1994a), 'Introduction', in P. Benner (ed.), *Interpretive Phenomenology: Embodiment, Caring, and Ethics in Health and Illness*, Sage, Thousand Oaks, pp. xiii-xxvii.

Benner, P. (1994b), 'The tradition and skill of interpretive phenomenology in studying health, illness and caring practices', in P. Benner (ed.), *Interpretive*

Phenomenology: Embodiment, Caring, and Ethics in Health and Illness, Sage, Thousand Oaks, pp. 99-127.

Benson, E. (1991), 'The legend of the Maiden of Kosovo and nursing in Serbia', *Image*, vol. 23, pp. 57-59.

Bollas, C. (1992), *Being a Character: Psychoanalysis and Self-Experience*, Routledge, London.

Bonney, B. and Wilson, H. (1983), *Australia's Commercial Media*, Macmillan, Melbourne.

Borger, J. (1995), 'British troops face threat from Islamic fighters', *Guardian Weekly*, vol. 163, p. 1.

Borger, J. (1996), 'Serb dig up their dead', *Guardian Weekly*, vol. 154, p. 4.

Borrell, J. (1991), 'A cocktail of violence', *Herald Sun*, October 12, p. 15.

Bosnia-Herzegovina: Rana u dusi (A wound to the soul), *Amnesty International Report* January 1993, Amnesty International Index No. EUR 63/03/93, Amnesty International, Geneva, p. 1.

Bosnia-Herzegovina: Rape and sexual abuse by the armed forces, (1993), *Amnesty International Report*, January 1993, Amnesty International Index No. EUR 63/01/93, Amnesty International, Geneva, pp. 1-9.

Bulich, S. (1985), *The Relationship Between Serbian Orthodox Liturgy and Positive Mental Health*, University of Pittsburgh Press, Pittsburgh.

Caroline, H. (1993), 'Explorations of close friendship: a concept analysis', *Archives of Psychiatric Nursing*, vol. 7, pp. 236-243.

Charmaz, K. and Mitchell, R. (1996), 'The myth of silent authorship: self, substance and style in ethnographic writing', *Symbolic Interaction,* vol. 19, pp. 285-302.

Christensen, J. (1996), 'Editorial 2: reflections on doing and writing interpretive research', *Contemporary Nurse*, vol. 5, pp. 48-53.

Clandinin, D. and Connelly, F. (1994), 'Personal experience methods', in N. Denzin and Y. Lincoln (eds), *Handbook of Qualitative Research*, Sage, Newbury Park, pp. 413-427.

Clifford, J. (1983), 'On ethnographic authority', *Representations*, vol. 1, pp. 118-46.

Clifford, J. (1986), 'Introduction: partial truths', in J. Clifford and G. Marcus (eds), *Writing Culture: The Poetics and Politics of Ethnography*, University of California Press, Berkeley, pp. 1-26.

Cohen, D. (1991), 'Real life: my wife, my friend, my enemies', *The Independent*, October 13, p. 22.

Cohen, L. (1993), *Broken Bonds: The Disintegration of Yugoslavia*, Westview Press, Boulder.

Conflict in Croatia affects Western Australia, *Nova Doba*, September 17, 1991, p.8.

Connor, W. (1993), 'Beyond reason: the nature of ethnonational bond', *Ethnic and Racial Studies*, vol. 16, pp. 373-389.

Correnti, D. (1992), 'Intuition and nursing practice implications for nurse educators: a review of the literature', *Journal of Continuing Education in Nursing*, vol. 23, pp. 91-94.

Cosic, D. (1993), 'Solutions the Serbs could never swallow', *The Independent*, April 22, p. 17.

Cowles, K.V. and Rodgers, B.L. (1991), 'The concept of grief: a foundation for nursing research', *Research in Nursing and Health*, vol. 14, pp. 119-127.

Danforth, L. (1995), *The Macedonian Conflict: Ethnic Nationalism in a Transnational World*, Princeton University Press, Princeton.

Davies, J. (1993), 'The historical method in psychiatric research', *Australian and New Zealand Journal of Psychiatry*, vol. 27, pp. 620-629.

Denzin, N. (1994), 'The Art and Politics of Interpretation', in Denzin, N.K. and Lincoln, Y.S. (eds), *The Handbook of Qualitative Research*, Sage, Newbury Park, pp. 500-515.

Denzin, N. and Lincoln, Y. (eds), (1994), *Handbook of Qualitative Research*, Sage, Newbury Park.

Department of Health, Housing and Community Services (1993), *Removing Cultural and Language Barriers to Health*, National Health Strategy Issues Paper No. 6, Australian Government Publishing Service, Canberra.

Djilas, A. (1991), *The Contested Country: Yugoslav Unity and Communist Revolution, 1919-1953*, Harvard University Press, Cambridge.

Doder, D. (1994), 'Serb soldiers led by a born fighter', *The Age*, Monday February 21, p. 6.

Dogan, M. (1993), 'Comparing the decline of nationalisms, in Western Europe: the generational dynamic', *International Journal of Social Science*, vol. 65, pp. 177-197.

Donaldson, L. and Coverley, D. (1992), 'Australians on both sides of frontline', *The Australian*, Wednesday January 22, p. 8.

Dowmunt, T. (1993), 'Introduction' in Dowmunt, T. (ed.), *Channels of Resistance: Global Television and Local Empowerment*, BFI Publishing, London, pp. 1-16.

Doyle, L. (1992a), 'Muslims slaughter their own people', *Independent*, August 22, p. 1.

Doyle, L. (1992b), 'Use troops to stop atrocities', *Independent*, September 1, p 1.

Dragadze, T. (1996), 'Self-determination and the politics of exclusion', *Ethnic and Racial Studies*, vol. 19, pp. 341-351.

Eagar, C. (1993), 'Bosnia: Muslims' bloody battle for a place to call home', *The Observer*, October 3, p. 16.

Fabris, T. (1991), 'ASIO in move to prevent race war', *Brisbane Sun*, August 5, p. 7.

Featherstone, M. (ed.) (1993), *Global Culture: Nationalism, Globalism and Modernity*, Sage, New York.

Fire raid on Serb church, *Telegraph Mirror*, January 31, 1992, p 8.

Fischer, M. (1986), 'Ethnicity and the post modern arts of memory', in J. Clifford and G. Marcus (eds), *Writing Culture: The Poetics and Politics of Ethnography*, University of California Press, Berkeley, pp. 194-233.

Fisk, R. (1992), 'Arab passions fired by Bosnia', *Independent*, August 31, p. 1.

Fontana, A. and Frey, J. (1994), 'Interviewing: the art and science', in Denzin, N.K. and Lincoln, Y.S. (eds), *The Handbook of Qualitative Research*, Sage, Newbury Park, pp. 361-376.

Fox, H. (1993), 'An international tribunal for war crimes: will the UN succeed where Nuremburg failed?', *The World Today*, vol. 49, pp. 194-197.

Friedrich-Cofer, L. and Huston, A. (1986), 'Television violence and aggression: the debate continues', *Psychological Bulletin*, vol. 100, pp. 364-371.

Fuller, J. (1996), 'Community expectations of ethnic health workers: implications for best practice', *Australian Journal of Primary Health Interchange*, vol. 2, pp. 61-73.

Fundamentalist Islam Moves Into the Heart of Europe, *Serbian National Federation of Australia Media Review, No. 4,* Early May, 1993.

Gadamer, H-G. (1975), *Truth and Method*, Sheed and Ward, London.

Gadamer, H-G. (1994), 'Introduction', in Grondin, J. *Introduction to Philosophical Hermeneutics*, Yale University Press, London, pp. ix-xii.

Gadamer, H-G. (1996), *The Enigma of Health,* Polity Press, London.

Gibbs, A. (1990), 'Aspects of communication with people who have attempted suicide', *Journal of Advanced Nursing*, vol. 15, pp. 1245-1249.

Giddens, A. (1991), *Modernity and Self Identity: Self and Society in the Late Modern Age,* Polity Press, Cambridge.

Giddens, A. (1996), *In Defence of Sociology: Essays, Interpretations and Rejoinders,* Polity Press, Cambridge.

Glaser, B. and Strauss, A.L. (1967), *The Discovery of Grounded Theory: Strategies for Qualitative Research*, Aldine Press, Chicago.

Glenny, M. (1992), *The Fall of Yugoslavia*, London, Penguin Books.

Glenny, M. (1994), 'Chaos in new world order', *The Australian*, January 7, p. 9.

Glisic, I. (1994), 'Let's stop behaving as if Serbs are to blame', *The Sydney Morning Herald*, July 11, p. 9.

Goffman, E. (1987), *The Presentation of Self in Everyday Life,* London, Penguin.

Goffman, E. (1989), 'On fieldwork', *Journal of Contemporary Ethnography,* vol. 18, pp. 123-132.

Gortner, S. (1992), 'Toward a cross national nursing research', *Journal of Advanced Nursing*, vol. 17, pp. 403-404.

Goytisolo, J. (1993), 'Torture town', *New Statesman and Society*, December 17/31, pp. 46-49.

Green, A. (1996), *Federal Election Guide: 1996*, Australian Broadcasting Corporation, Sydney.

Grondin, J. (1994), *Introduction to Philosophical Hermeneutics*, Yale University Press, London.

Guba, E.G. and Lincoln, Y.S. (1989), *Fourth Generation Evaluation*, Sage, Newbury Park.

Haber, J., McMahon, A.L., Price-Hoskins, P. and Sideleau, B. (1992), *Comprehensive Psychiatric Nursing*, Mosby, St. Louis.

Habermas, J. (1992), *Postmetaphysical Thinking*, Massachusetts Institute of Technology, Cambridge.

Habermas, J. (1994), *The Theory of Communicative Action Volume 1*, Heinerman, London.

Hagerty, B., Lynch-Sauer, J., Patusky, K., Bouwsema, M. and Collier, P. (1992), 'Sense of belonging: a vital mental health concept', *Archives of Psychiatric Nursing*, vol. 6, pp. 172-177.

Hagerty, B., Williams, R., Coyne, J. and Early, M. (1996), 'Sense of belonging and indicators of social and psychological functioning', *Archives of Psychiatric Nursing*, vol. 10, pp. 235-244.

Hamm, B. (1992), 'Europe-a challenge to the social sciences', *International Social Science Journal*, vol. 64, pp. 3-22.

Hammersley, M. and Atkinson, P. (1990), *Ethnography: Principles in Practice*, Tavistock, London.

Handke, P. (1997), *A Journey to the Rivers: Justice for Serbia*, Viking, New York.

Hartley, J. (1992), *Understanding News*, Methuen, London.

Healey, P. (1996), 'Situated rationality and hermeneutic understanding: a Gadamerian approach to rationality', *International Philosophical Quarterly*, vol. 36, pp. 155-171.

Herman, J. (1992), *Trauma and Recovery*, Basic Books, New York.

Herrnstein Smith, B. (1995), 'The truth/value of judgements', in, R.F. Goodman and W.R. Fisher (eds), *Rethinking Knowledge: Reflections Across the Disciplines*, State University of New York Press, Albany, pp. 23-39.

Hicks, C. (1996), 'Nurse researcher: a study of a contradiction in terms?', *Journal of Advanced Nursing*, vol. 24, pp. 357-363.

Hill, J. (1996), 'Hate's long reach', *The Phoenix Gazette*, August 16, p. 9.

Hill, P. (1993), 'National minorities in Europe', *Journal of Intercultural Studies*, vol. 14, pp. 32-48.

Hill, R. (1993), 'Don't mention the war', *The Bulletin*, vol. 115, pp. 36-38.

Hill-Baily, P. (1997), 'Finding your way around qualitative methods in nursing research', *Journal of Advanced Nursing*, vol. 25, pp. 18-22.

Hutch, M. (1995), 'Nursing and the next millennium', *Nursing Science Quarterly*, vol. 8, pp. 38-44.

Ignatieff, M. (1994), *Blood and Belonging: Journeys Into the New Nationalism*, London, Vintage.

Ilic, R. (1995), 'Covekoljublje' (Love of Mankind) 'The response of the Serbian Orthodox Church in Australia to the Conflict in the Former Yugoslavia', Paper presented to the conference, *The Forgotten Victims: Serbian Casualties and Victims of the Conflict in the Former Yugoslavia*, Macquarie University, New South Wales, 25 March.

Illusion and reality: shaping the media coverage of the Balkan conflict, *Serbian National Federation of Australia Media Review No. 8*, October 1993.

Internationalisation of Croat-Serbian problem and Croatian emigrants, *Hrvatski Vjesnik*, March 8, 1991, p 21.

Janesick, V.J. (1994), 'The dance of qualitative research design: metaphor, methodolatry, and meaning', in N.K. Denzin and Y. Lincoln (eds), *Handbook of Qualitative Research*, Newbury Park, Sage, pp. 209-219.

Johannsen, A. (1992), 'Applied anthropology and post-modernist ethnography', *Human Organisation,* vol. 51, pp. 71-81.

Kanitsaki, O. (1993), 'Acute health care and Australia's ethnic people', *Contemporary Nurse*, vol. 2, pp. 122-127.

Kaplan, R. (1993), *Balkan Ghosts: A Journey Through History*, Papermac, New York.

Karp, D. (1996), *Speaking of Sadness: Depression, Disconnection and the Meanings of Illness*, Oxford University Press, New York.

Kazich, T. (ed.) (1989), *Serbs in Australia: History and Development of the Free Serbian Orthodox Church Diocese for Australia and New Zealand*, Monastery Press, Canberra.

Keating, P.J. (1995), Speech at the Luncheon in Honour of Franjo Tudjman, President of Croatia, Parliament House, Canberra, Australia, Tuesday 20 June.

Kirk, S. (1991), 'Fans banned from Sydney soccer match', *Sydney Morning Herald*, July 3, p. 10.

Knightley, P. (1993), 'Women in the war zone', *The Independent Monthly*, October, pp. 10-16.

Koch, T. (1996), 'Implementation of a hermeneutic in nursing: philosophy, rigour and representation', *Journal of Advanced Nursing*, vol. 24, pp. 174-184.

Kolnar-Panov, D. (1996), 'Video and the diasporic imagination of selfhood: a case study of the Croatians in Australia', *Cultural Studies*, vol. 10, pp. 827-314.

Kovacevic, S. (1992), 'Moral of the war against Croatia: a forensic picture', *Croatian Medical Journal (War Supplement)*, vol. 33, pp. 25-28.

Leininger, M. (1989), *Qualitative Research Methods in Nursing*, Grune and Stratton, New York.

Leininger, M. (1991), 'Ethnonursing: a research method with enablers to study the theory of culture care', in M. Leininger (ed.), *Culture Care Diversity and Universality: A Theory of Nursing*, National League for Nursing Press, New York, pp. 73-117.

Leonard, V. W. (1994), 'A Heideggarian phenomenological perspective on the concept of person', in P. Benner (ed.), *Interpretive Phenomenology: Embodiment, Caring, and Ethics in Health and Illness,* Sage, Thousand Oaks, pp. 43-63.

Lincoln, Y. (1992), 'Sympathetic connections between qualitative methods and health research', *Qualitative Health Research*, vol. 2, pp. 375-391.

Little, G. (1993), *Friendship: Being Ourselves With Others*, Text Publishing, Melbourne.

Loyd, A. (1993), 'Town in fear as gunmen kill and rape', *The Australian*, November 4, p. 8.

Magas, B. (1993), *The destruction of Yugoslavia: Tracing the Break-Up 1980-92,* Verso, London.

Marcikic, M., Kraus, Z. and Marusic, M. (1992), 'Civilian massacre in Dalj', *Croatian Medical Journal (War Supplement)*, vol. 33, pp. 43-48.

Marcus, G. (1986), 'Contemporary problems of ethnography in the modern world system', in J. Clifford and G. Marcus (eds), *Writing Culture: The Poetics and Politics of Ethnography*, University of California Press, Berkeley, pp. 165-193.

Marcus, G. (1994), 'What comes (just) after 'post'? The case of ethnography', in N. K. Denzin and Y. S. Lincoln (eds), *Handbook of Qualitative Research*, Sage, Newbury Park, pp. 563-574.

Marcus, G. (1995), 'The redesign of ethnography after the critique of its rhetoric', in R.F. Goodman and W.R. Fisher (eds), *Rethinking Knowledge: Reflections Across the Disciplines*, State University of New York Press, Albany, pp. 103-122.

Martyres, G. (1995), 'On silence: a language for emotional experience', *Australian and New Zealand Journal of Psychiatry*, vol. 29, pp. 118-123.

Marusic, M. (1992), 'Editorial', *Croatian Medical Journal (War Supplement),* vol. 33, pp. 1-2.

Masanauskas, J. (1991a), 'Serbs in SBS protest', *Age*, October 17, p. 6.

Masanauskas, J. (1991b), 'Serbs protest outside Labour MP's office', *Age*, November 1, p. 15.

Mattingley, C. (1993), *No Guns for Asmir*, Penguin Books, Melbourne.

Meares, R. (1991), 'Families at war split by old feuds', *The Independent*, August 2, p. 12.

Meleis, A. (1992), 'Directions for nursing theory development in the 21st. century', *Nursing Science Quarterly*, vol. 5, pp. 112-117.

Meleis, A. (1995), 'Foreword', in B. Neuman (ed.), *The Neuman Systems Model*, Appleton and Lange, Norwalk, pp. xix-xx.

Mendelson, J. (1979), 'The Habermas-Gadamer debate', *New German Critique,* vol. 18, pp. 44-73.

Miljkovich, E. (1995), 'Serbian Victims in the Current Conflict in the Former Yugoslavia', unpublished paper presented to the conference, *The Forgotten Victims: Serbian Casualties and Victims of the Conflict in the Former Yugoslavia*, Macquarie University, New South Wales, 25 March.

Minas, I.H. and Klimidis, S. (1994), 'Cultural issues in Posttraumatic Stress Disorder', in R. Watts and D. J. de Horne (eds), *Coping With Trauma: The Victim and the Helper*, Australian Academic Press, Brisbane, pp. 137-154.

Misgeld, D. (1979), 'On Gadamer's Hermeneutics', *Philosophy and Social Science,* vol. 9, pp. 221-239.

Mosley, P. (1992), 'Soccer', in W. Vamplew, K. Moore, J. O'Hara, R. Cashman and L. Jobling (eds), *The Oxford Companion to Australian Sport*, Oxford University Press, Melbourne.

National Health Strategy (1993), *Issues Paper Number 6: Removing Cultural and Language Barriers to Health*, Commonwealth Department of Health Housing and Community Services, Canberra.

Nicholson, G. (1991), 'Answers to critical theory', in *Continental Philosophy IV: Gadamer and Hermeneutics*, H. Silverman (ed.), Routledge, New York, pp. 151-162.

O'Brien, B. and Pearson, A. (1993), 'Unwritten knowledge in nursing: consider the spoken as well as the written word', *Scholarly Inquiry for Nursing Practice: An International Journal*, vol. 7, pp. 111-124.

Oiler, C. (1981), 'The phenomenological approach in nursing research', *Nursing Research*, vol. 31, pp. 178-181.

Padgett, D. (1989), *Settlers and Sojourners: A Study of Serbian Adaptation in Milwaukee, Wisconsin*, AMS Press, Inc, New York.

Paris, E. (1961), *Genocide in Satellite Croatia, 1941-1945,* American Institute for Balkan Affairs, Illinois.

Parker, J. (1996), 'Space, time and radical imagination: nursing in the here and now', *Journal of Advanced Nursing*, vol. 24, pp. 1103-1104.

Pascoe, E. (1996), 'The value to nursing research of Gadamer's hermeneutic philosophy', *Journal of Advanced Nursing,* vol. 24, pp. 1309-1314.

Patton, M. (1990), *Qualitative Evaluation and Research Methods*, Sage, London.

Petrovich, W.M. (1915), *Serbia: Her People, History and Aspirations*, George G. Harrap & Company, London.

Plager, K. A. (1994),'Hermeneutic phenomenology: a methodology for family health and health promotion study in nursing', in P. Benner (ed.), *Interpretive Phenomenology: Embodiment, Caring, and Ethics in Health and Illness,* Sage, Thousand Oaks, pp. 65-83.

Poggenpoel, M. (1995), 'The role and functions of the psychiatric-mental health nurse in the care and comfort of individuals, families, and communities subjected to violence', *Holistic Nursing Practice*, vol. 9, pp. 91-97.

Poggioli, S. (1993), 'Scouts without compasses: war in the Balkans is forcing correspondents to rewrite their guidelines', *Nieman Reports*, vol. 67, pp. 16-19.

Polier, N. and Roseberry, W. (1989), 'Tristes tropes: post-modern anthropologists encounter the other and discover themselves', *Economy and Society,* vol. 18, pp. 245-264.

Psychological War Against the Serbian People, *Serbian National Federation of Australia Media Review, No. 3,* April 1993.

Radan, P. (1992), 'A defence of the Serbs', *Quadrant*, vol. 36, pp. 3-4.

Radan, P. (1993), 'Secessionist Self Determination: The Case of Slovenia and Croatia', Paper Presented to the Conference *National Self determination Today: Problems and Prospects*, Centre for Slavonic and East European Studies, Macquarie University, Sydney, November 6-7.

Radmanovic, M. (1990), 'Serbian migrants in Australia: A century passes', Paper Presented to the Conference *Serbian Migrations 1690-1990*, Serbian Studies Foundation, Macquarie University, Sydney Australia, August.

Radojevic, P. and Bolta, B. (1992), *Letter to Australian Prime Minister Paul Keating*, June 3rd.

Reeder, F. (1987), 'Hermeneutics', in B. Saster (ed.), *Paths to Knowledge: Innovative Research Methods for Nursing,* National League for Nursing, New York, pp. 193-237.

Richardson, L. (1994), 'Writing: a method of inquiry', in N.K. Denzin and Y.S. Lincoln (eds), *Handbook of Qualitative Research*, Sage, Newbury Park, pp. 516-529.

Ricoeur, P. (1981), *Hermeneutics and the Human Sciences,* J. B. Thompson (ed.), Cambridge University Press, Cambridge.

Rise of the Fourth Reich: Germany's Role in the Destruction of Yugoslavia, *Serbian National Federation of Australia Media Review, No. 6,* mid-June 1993.

Ritter, S. (1989), *Bethlem Royal and Maudsley Hospital Manual of Psychiatric Nursing Principles and Procedures*, Chapman Hall, London.

Robertson, R. (1990), 'Mapping the global condition Globalisation as the central concept', in Featherstone, M. (ed.), *Global Culture: Nationalism, Globalisation and Modernity*, Sage, London, pp. 15-30.

Robertson, R. (1992), *Globalisation: Social Theory and Global Culture*, Sage, London.

Robertson, R. (1995), 'Glocalisation: time-space and homogeneity-heterogeneity', in M. Featherstone, S. Lash and R. Robertson (eds), *Global Modernities,* Sage, London, pp. 25-44.

Robertson, R. and Chirico, J. (1985), 'Humanity, globalisation, and worldwide religious resurgence: a theoretical exploration', *Sociological Analysis*, vol. 46, pp. 219-242.

Rorty, R. (1979), *Philosophy and the Mirror of Nature,* Princeton University Press, Princeton.

Rosaldo, R. (1993), *Culture and Truth: The Remaking of Social Analysis*, Routledge, London.

Rosenman, S. and Handelsman, I. (1992), 'When victim encounters alien victim in grisly circumstances: a study in hatred and scorn', *Journal of Psychohistory*, vol. 19, pp. 421-461.

Rothschild, J. (1992), 'Friction and Factionalism in the Yugoslav Struggle for Stability', *The Fletcher Forum of World Affairs*, vol. 16, pp. 153-159.

Serbs claim bias, *Herald Sun*, October 6, 1991, p. 13.

Simpson, J. (1993), 'The value of news', *The Spectator*, September 18, pp. 18-20.

Skrbis, Z. (1995), *Ethno-nationalism, Immigration and Globalism, with Particular Reference to Second Generation Croatian Slovenians in Australia*, Doctoral Dissertation, Faculty of Social Science, The Flinders University of South Australia, Adelaide.

Smith, A.D. (1981), 'War and ethnicity: the role of warfare in the formation, self images and cohesion of ethnic communities', *Ethnic and Racial Studies*, vol. 4, pp. 375-397.

Smith, A.D. (1990), 'The supersession of nationalism?', *International Journal of Comparative Sociology*, vol. 31, pp. 1-31.

Smith, A.D. (1992), 'National identity and the idea of European unity', *International Affairs*, vol. 68, pp. 55-76.

Smith, A.D. (1995), *Nations and Nationalism in a Global Era*, Polity Press, London.

Smith, A. D. (1996a), 'Nations and their pasts', *Nations and Nationalism*, vol. 2, pp. 358-365.

Smith, A. D. (1996b), 'Memory and modernity: reflections on Ernest Gellner's theory of nationalism', *Nations and Nationalism*, vol. 2, pp. 371-388.

Spradley, J.P. (1979), *Participant Observation*, Harcourt Brace Jovanovic, New York.

Spradley, J.P. (1980), *The Ethnographic Interview*, Harcourt, Brace, Jovanovic, New York.

Statement of the Holy Synod of Bishops of the Serbian Orthodox Church, Belgrade, 19 May 1995, *South Slav Journal*, vol. 16, pp. 72-3.

Stoddart, B. (1992), 'Ethnic influences', in W. Vamplew, K. Moore, J. O'Hara, R. Cashman and I. Jobling (eds), *The Oxford Companion to Australian Sport*, Oxford University Press, Melbourne.

Stone, A. (1992), 'Yugoslavia's war tears at U.S. communities', *USA Today*, June 16, p. 8.

Strong, G. (1991), 'Hidden casualties of distant war', *Sunday Age*, October 27, p. 6.

Taylor, P. (1992), *War and the Media: Propaganda and Persuasion in the Gulf War*, Manchester University Press, Manchester.

Tensions high, but ethnic groups stay cool: Croats and Serbs in SA determined to keep the lid on their 'hot-heads', *Adelaide News*, September 25, 1991, p. 7.

The Serbs Suffer Too, *The Economist*, 31 October, 1992, p. 50.

The Unseen War: Croatian Land Grab in Central Bosnia, *Serbian National Federation of Australia Media Review, No. 5,* mid-May, 1993.

Thompson, H. (1985), *Hell's Angels*, Ballantine, New York.

Thompson, M. (1992), *A Paper House: The Ending of Yugoslavia*, Pantheon Books, New York.

Totaro, P. (1991), 'Our local Balkan war', *The Bulletin*, December 10, pp. 30-4.

Traynor, I. (1994), 'Pope offers a message of unity', *Guardian Weekly*, vol. 151, No. 12, p. 1.

Traynor, I. (1995), 'Refugees go home to roost', *Guardian Weekly*, vol. 153, p. 4.

Trlin, A. and Tolich, M. (1995), 'Croatian or Dalmatian: Yugoslavia's demise and the issue of identity', in Greif, S. (ed.), *Immigration and National Identity in New Zealand*, Dunmore Press, Palmerston North, pp. 217-252.

Turner, G. (1993), 'Media texts and messages', in Turner, G. and Cunningham, S. (eds), *The Media in Australia: Industries, Texts, Audiences*, Allen and Unwin, Sydney, pp. 203-366.

Ustashi hooligans beat Serbian children in Dandenong, *Novosti*, March 18, 1992, p. 2.

Vitkin, M. (1995), 'The fusion of horizons on knowledge and alterity', *Philosophy and Social Criticism,* vol. 21, pp. 57-76.

van Manen, M. (1990), *Researching Lived Experience: Human Science for an Action Sensitive Pedagogy,* State University of New York Press, New York.

Voices of Reason: Issues in the Debate on Former Yugoslavia, *Serbian National Federation of Australia Media Review, No. 7,* early-September 1993.

Vulliamy, E. (1994), *Seasons in Hell: Understanding Bosnia's War,* Simon and Schuster, London.

Walsh, K. (1996), 'Philosophical hermeneutics and the project of Hans Georg Gadamer: implications for nursing research', *Nursing Inquiry,* vol. 3, pp. 231-237.

Warnke, G. (1987), *Gadamer: Hermeneutics, Tradition and Reason,* Polity Press, Cambridge.

Williams, A. (1990), *Reflections on the Making of an Ethnographic Text,* Studies in Sexual Politics, Sociology Department, University of Manchester, Manchester.

Zametica, J (1993), 'Squeezed off the map', *The Guardian,* May 11, p. 9.

Index

Participants 2, 4, 11–20, 24, 26–44, 45–
    47, 49–51, 53, 56–61, 65–67, 69,
    72, 79–81, 82–106, 108–124, 128–
    132, 136–163, 164–171, 174, 175
Participant observation 18, 19, 24, 27–
    34, 36–40, 44, 46, 47, 49, 51, 53,
    54, 57, 67, 85, 116, 136, 173
  At the cemetery 17, 37, 95–98
  At the scene of property damage and
    death threats 14, 17, 21–28, 33, 43
  In people's homes 4, 5, 11,14, 16, 34,
    40, 54, 57, 63, 95–99
Patton, M. 43
Perpetrators 2, 8, 11
Poggenpoel, M. 119
Poggioli, S. 116
Police 48, 64, 65, 80, 89, 112, 128, 143,
    159, 171
Polier, N. 27
Pope John Paul II 81
Powerless, feelings of 6, 109–111, 122,
    123, 141, 143, 165
Price-Hoskins, P. 87
Property damage 1, 21–27, 30, 33, 45,
    60, 81, 100, 106, 112, 113, 115,
    126, 134, 144–146, 157, 159, 171

Radan, P. 1
Radmanovic, M. 19
Radojevic, P. 113, 133, 150
Rape and sexual abuse 1, 2, 19, 119,
    120, 127
Reflective Journal 22–26, 32, 42, 43, 59,
    65, 95, 99
Refugees 2, 6, 60, 67, 80, 87, 101, 124,
    141, 143, 144, 148, 150, 155–160,
    164, 165, 170
  Doing something to help them 101,
    124, 141, 143, 144, 153–156, 158,
    162, 170
  Humanitarian aid for 60, 131, 141,
    144, 153–155, 162, 170
Revenge 12, 23, 102, 142
Richardson, L. 43
Ritter, S. 29
Robertson, R. 10, 11, 28, 69, 112, 122,
    134, 165
Rorty, R. 51

Rosaldo, R. 28
Roseberry, W. 27
Rosenman, S. 1
Rothschild, J. 1

Sarajevo 1, 19, 47, 49, 51, 67, 73, 76,
    87, 105, 114, 115, 120, 140, 151
  Bread queue bombing in 19, 140
  Jokes about 105,
  Market bombing 45–48
Self disclosure during the research
    process 29, 148
Serbia 2, 11–13, 17, 19, 53, 62, 74, 77,
    86, 88, 93, 94, 100, 108, 110, 131,
    140, 167
  As the motherland 69, 89, 103, 110,
    117, 119
Serbian 1–20, 21–53, 54–81, 82–106,
    107, 109–133, 136–163, 164–175
  Community 23, 57, 63, 67, 85, 90, 98,
    106, 107, 112, 125, 133, 136–165,
    169
  Identity 9, 12, 13, 16–18, 47–49, 55,
    62, 66, 68, 70, 79, 84–108, 110,
    111, 113, 117, 129, 132, 136–163,
    164–166, 168, 169
  Language 22, 24, 25, 31, 34, 35, 37,
    38, 69, 74, 87, 97, 99, 166
  Unity 17, 84, 89, 91, 97, 98,
  Serbians helping Serbians 18, 134,
    137, 150–153, 158, 159
Serbian Americans 58
Serbian Australians 1–20, 21–44, 45–
    53, 54–75, 82–106, 107–133, 134–
    163
Serbian National Federation of Australia
    32, 33, 59–62, 75, 101, 103, 115,
    132, 140
Serbian National Federation of Australia
    Media Review 103, 117
Serbian Orthodox Church 5, 22, 26, 32,
    37, 45, 55, 80, 81, 83–85, 94, 103,
    107, 112, 113, 115, 142–144, 152,
    154, 155, 158–160, 172
  Holy Synod 44
Serbian Orthodox Priests 8, 31, 75, 85,
    95, 142, 144